Geoffrey Hoare's copy, given to L. Carley
by Dr. Jim Hoyland, 2010

See page 311.

D0536528

An Elgar Companion

AN ELGAR COMPANION

Edited by
Christopher Redwood

To my dear friend Geoffrey Hoare,
with all good wishes,

Christopher W Redwood.

27th March 1983.

SEQUOIA PUBLISHING
in association with
MOORLAND PUBLISHING CO LTD
9-11 Station Street
Ashbourne, Derbyshire

British Library Cataloguing
in Publication Data

Redwood, Christopher
    An Elgar companion
    1. Elgar, Edward   2. Composers -
    England
    I. Title
    780'.092'4   ML410.E41

ISBN 0 86190 024 3

Printed in the UK by
Dotesios (Printers) Ltd, Bradford-on-Avon
for Moorland Publishing Co Ltd,
9-11 Station Street, Ashbourne,
Derbyshire, DE6 1DE, England

Contents

		page
Editor's Preface		9

PART I: THE EARLY YEARS

1	*The Black Knight* (review)	11
2	*King Olaf* (review)	14
2	*Caractacus* (review) by E.A. Baughan	19
4	Young Elgar at the Festival by Gerald Northrop Moore	26
5	Edward Elgar by F.G. Edwards (the first full-length interview)	35

PART II: THE 'ENIGMA'

1	The Enigma — I by Richard C. Powell	50
2	The Enigma — II by A.H. Fox Strangways	56
3	The Enigma — III by Prof J.A. Westrup	60
4	The Enigma — IV by Dr Roger Fiske	76
5	The Enigma — V by Prof Ian Parrott	82

PART III: THE 'GERONTIUS' DEBACLE

1	Review from *The Musical Standard* by E.A. Baughan	91
2	A Memory from the Choir by William Bennett	96
3	A Memory from the Auditorium by Mrs Richard Powell	100
4	Hans Richter and *Gerontius* by Gareth H. Lewis	105

PART IV: ELGAR AT HOME

1	Elgar at 'Forli' by R.J. Buckley	111
2	Elgar at 'Craeg Lea' by Rudolf de Cordova	115
3	Elgar at 'Plas Gwyn' by Gerald Cumberland	125
4	Elgar at 'Severn House' — I (unsigned)	137
5	Elgar at 'Severn House' — II by Percy Scholes	140

PART V: MEMORIES OF THOSE WHO KNEW HIM

1	Memories of a Pupil by Mary Beatrice Alder	147
2	Elgar as I Knew Him by Sir Richard Terry	150
3	Elgar: Some Aspects of the Man in his Music by Ernest Newman	154
4	Sir Edward Elgar by Sir Compton Mackenzie	158
5	Elgar — As I Knew Him by Sir Malcolm Sargent	162
6	Memories of my Father by Carice Elgar Blake	165
7	Some Personal Memories of Elgar by Alan Webb	168

PART VI: ELGAR AND OTHER COMPOSERS

1	Elgar and Handel by W.J. Turner	175
2	Elgar, Parry and Stanford by Vincent Waite	178
3	Elgar and Delius by Christopher Redwood	189
4	Elgar and Mahler by Neville Cardus	200
5	Elgar and Strauss by George Sampson	203

PART VII: ELGAR AND THE THEATRE

1	*The Spanish Lady*	209
2	*The Starlight Express* by A.E. Keeton	230

PART VIII: ELGAR'S ART EXAMINED

1	*The Apostles* and Elgar's Future by E.A. Baughan	236
2	Edward Elgar by George Bernard Shaw	245
3	The Violin Concerto by W.H. Reed	251
4	The Two Elgars by Frank Howes	258
5	What have we Learnt from Elgar? by Ralph Vaughan Williams	263
6	Elgar and the Public by C.W. Orr	270
7	Elgar: 'The First of the New' by Hans Keller	275
8	Some Thoughts on Elgar by Donald Mitchell	279
9	Elgar as Conductor by Stephen Lloyd	291

Index	307

Illustrations

opposite page

1	Elgar's Birthplace at Broadheath	32
2	Four figures from the Elgar saga	33
3	The cottage at Birchwood	64
4	The cottage at Birchwood	65
5	Elgar with Hans Richter	96
6	Richter's letter regarding the *Enigma Variations*	97
7	Elgar finishing *The Dream of Gerontius*	128
8	Elgar at 'Craeg Lea'; Elgar about 1905	129
9	Elgar, Carice and Alice	160
10	An unfinished fugue	161
11	Elgar and Carice	192
12	Elgar with Parry and Stanford	193
13	Yehudi Menuhin with Elgar	224
14	George Bernard Shaw with Elgar	225
15	Elgar with W.H. Reed	256
16	Elgar conducting	257

Acknowledgements to Illustrations

I am extremely grateful to the Trustees of the Elgar Birthplace for allowing me to reproduce the following illustrations: 1, 3, 4, 5, 11, 12, 14 and 15; to Dr Terence Rees for number 6; and to Raymond Monk Esq. for numbers 2, 9, 13, and 16.

Editor's Preface

The interest shown in *A Delius Companion* (1976) led one to think in terms of a similar compilation of essays devoted to another composer. The natural choice was Elgar, and the present volume is the result. In this case it seemed a good idea to group the contributions into sections according to content, and it is to be hoped that this scheme will commend itself to the reader. As before, very few of the writings were commissioned specially for the book; however, many of the journals in which they first appeared have long-since disappeared. Not only are they extremely hard to trace, but when located are frequently found to be extremely wearing on the eyes — as my printer and type-setter have discovered to their cost!

I wish to express my thanks to the original publishers for their ready co-operation in granting permission to reproduce copyright material. In the cases where it has not proved possible to trace copyright holders I apologise for not seeking their permission and crave their forbearance — assuming that they do exist. I would like to thank a number of members of the Elgar Society for their willing help, especially Stephen Lloyd, Raymond Monk, Professor Ian Parrott and Jerrold Northrop Moore. My gratitude is also due to Ronald Taylor (Editor of *The Elgar Society Journal*) for permission to reproduce three of his articles; to Jack and Vivien Mackenzie of the Elgar Birthplace (not only for making material available, but also for cups of tea and lifts to Worcester!); to E. Wulstan Atkins of the Elgar Foundation for permission to quote from Elgar's letters and to the Delius Trust for permission to quote from those in their possession. I am also indebted to Lionel Carley, Gareth Lewis, Terence Rees, Robert Threlfall and Vincent Waite for their help in various ways, and particularly to my wife and family for their patience and encouragement.

PART I: THE EARLY YEARS

The Black Knight

After the success of the Overture Froissart, *his first large-scale work, at the 1890 Three Choirs Festival in Worcester, Elgar paused before embarking on another major composition. When he did commence one, the subject he chose was* The Black Knight, *and the work was ready for performance by 1893. It was given its première that April by the Worcester Festival Choral Society, and the* Worcester Daily Times *greeted it enthusiastically with an account which carried the headline* A LOCAL COMPOSER'S TRIUMPH.

The second concert of the season of the Worcester Festival Choral Society took place last evening at the Public Hall. In every particular the concert was a success. Its signal triumph was the proud achievement of Mr. Edward Elgar, aforetime leader of the band. The first performance of Mr. Elgar's new cantata, *The Black Knight*, made the concert specially attractive. The first appearance of Mr. H. Holloway, the hon. organist of the society, as a soloist, and the announcement of an excellent programme of choral and instrumental music, including a selection from *Lohengrin*, drew together an audience filling the hall. The orchestra was composed of 60 instrumentalists, and the chorus of 100 voices, ample guarantees of the strength and efficiency.

The band, under the efficient conductorship of Mr. Hugh Blair, opened with Auber's March *Exhibition*. It begins with a soft low melody for the brass — commenced with some little uncertainty — broadening into vigorous work. This was given with effective force and even a little noisiness. The chorus followed with Gibbons' *The Silver Swan*. The madrigal has some pretty features which were creditably interpreted, but like the band the chorus were not at their best in their initial trial. A Capriccio in B minor from Mendelssohn was selected by Mr. H. Holloway for a solo. It is by no means a showy piece, but yet its beautiful melody gave the pianist some opportunity of display. Mr. Holloway, a brilliant executant, played the solo with perfection. The delicate orchestral accompaniment brightened its effect; and the audience were delighted to pay Mr. Holloway the tribute of his talent in a warm recall.

The Black Knight was the next item on the programme, the modest composer appearing to conduct. It is the greatest effort of composition Mr. Elgar has made. He has done himself eminent credit with instrumental suites and other trifles, but he has not previously ventured upon so large a work as a cantata. Under his direction the band and chorus sympathetically rendered *The Black Knight*. Perhaps the orchestra were a trifle too strong for the chorus here and there, but, that notwithstanding, the performance was a positive triumph for the composer, and his masterly production was applauded with an enthusiasm which broke into positive cheers. The following is the argument of the poem:- At the ancient castle of Hofburg, during the Pentecostal Festivities, the King's son vanquishes all who venture to encounter him in the tilt-yard. An unknown Knight, clad in black armour, who will not give his name, appears, however, and overcomes him in the lists; the arrival of this mysterious warrior is attended with awful signs in earth and air, — the heavens are veiled with mist and the foundations of the castle tremble. In the evening, as the dances are about to commence, an awful shadow enters, and asking the hand of the King's daughter, dances a weird and fearsome measure with her; folded in the chilling embrace the flowers fade and fall from her breast and hair. Oppressed with direful forebodings, the King and his guests come to the banquet, but is alarmed at observing his two children fading under the baneful presence of the sable guest. Before long his worst fears are realized and his misery complete when, after drinking a draught from the hands of the grim visitor, they lay their heads on their father's breast and die. The wretched father prays that he may be taken also, but the Black Knight only replies, 'Roses in the spring I gather.'

The book of words of the concert supplied a reliable analysis of the cantata. In the treatment the poetic legend has received at the hands of the composer, attention was called to several significant themes employed in the course of it. The principal of these is the broad and invigorating melody with which the work opens which may be termed the Pentecostal theme. This is expressive of the joyful emotions called up by the festivities of the season. It is also suggestive, by its freshness, of the growing springtime, and with this latter meaning it is used again at the conclusion of the work. Following this is noted the quasi-contrapuntal treatment of the words 'In the play of Spears,' in which the incisive vocal subject combats a vigorous orchestral counterpoint, producing an effect highly suggestive and picturesque. In the next scene, in which the Black Knight encounters and vanquishes the King's till now victorious son, a melodic figure is first employed, which may be taken as representative of the baneful power of the stranger, at the words, 'At the first blow Fell the youth from saddle bow.' It occurs again in Scene III, after the graceful dance theme when the grim partner of the King's daughter withers with his blighting grasp the flowers in her breast and hair, and again in the banquet scene, after the Black Knight gives the refreshing but fatal draught to the children. In Scene III, particular notice is drawn by the weird and enthralling melodic web which is spun over the movement describing the measure 'weird and dark' danced by the sable guest and the maiden and also of the re-employment at the end of the work of the original Springtide theme, reminding the thoughtful listener that death is but the prelude to an eternal spring, and that though flowers may be taken while yet in the bud, it is only that they may burst into blossom where they can never fade. The cantata is divided into four scenes, with further subdivisions. The composition shows a good usage of power, and was shown last night to be capable of masterly effects. The instrumentation in the scenes of the contest is powerfully weird, and as illustrating the varying styles of the author a fine contrast may be drawn between this and the voluptuous harmonies of the banquet. There is a great beauty in the orchestration throughout.

The second half of the programme was much changed to bring it within the limits of time. Schumann's Symphony in D minor occupied too long a time. The four movements were vigorously played. The chorus sang *Matona, lovely maiden*. So sweet a madrigal needs a little atonement for its appearance at two consecutive concerts, but the parenthetical 'by request' was its own excuse. The chorus sang the madrigal with very delicate expression. Schumann's *Gipsy life*, for chorus and orchestra which was made familiar to the public ear by the old musical society under the leadership of Mr. Caldicott, had to be sacrificed, as also the glee *Allen a Dale*. Two of four sketches by Rubinstein shared the same fate. The band played the two remaining selections from Rubinstein's *Feramors*. They were bright specimens of the ballet order, and were given in an acceptable style. The chorus sang Cowen's chorus, *At dawn of day*, at the close. For reasons unexplained the finale to Act 1 of Wagner's *Lohengrin*, which had been a subject of much expectation, was not included in the programme.

Worcester Daily Times, 19th April 1893

King Olaf

A further three years elapsed before any further notable success occurred, but the year 1896 saw the first performances of Lux Christi *and* King Olaf. *The latter was given at Hanley as part of the North Staffordshire Festival, and* The Daily Telegraph *gave it generous coverage in a piece ascribed to 'Our Special Correspondent', but known to be the paper's chief music critic, Joseph Bennett.*

This morning the one novelty of the Festival — and, I am bold to say, the novelty of the Festival year — was produced with indisputable success. I refer, of course, to Mr. Elgar's *Scenes from the Saga of King Olaf*. This, though a perfectly exact title, is a cumbrous one, and I shall henceforth speak of the work as *King Olaf* simply. I declare my intention in a hurry, because already some reader exclaims 'Mr. Elgar again! We heard of him only a few weeks ago at Worcester. Is this to be an Elgar season?' No doubt, and on the whole deservedly so, if there be any just pretension in the work of an earnest and able musician, who comes to the front by the sheer force of merit, without organised puffery or the aid of any clique. I say this with especial emphasis, because I do not on every point of musical faith and practice see eye to eye with the Malvern musician. He adopts methods which I cannot recognise as of ideal value. But behind all his work lies the power of living talent, the charm of an individuality in art, and the pathos of one who, in utter simplicity, pours forth that which he feels constrained to say, and leaves the issue to fate. Than this I know no more interesting combination. It goes far to disarm the hostility of criticism or, at any rate, to blunt its darts by sheer force of human sympathy.

Mr. Elgar has taken his *Scenes* from Longfellow, but he himself is responsible for the machinery by which they are first connected and then presented. The connection is effected with some ingenuity if only because it avoids plagiarism. Many are the threads upon which story-tellers have strung their narratives, but, as far as I know, it was reserved for Mr. Elgar to imagine an assembly of bards under the presidency of one of their number, who calls for such tales as seem to him good and is obeyed. In carrying out this plan the poetry of Longfellow needed a supplement for which the composer in the exercise of wise discretion called in Mr H.A. Acworth, C.I.E., who, though he could not succeed in making a homogeneous story, went as far as possible in that direction, and generally well discharged a task by no means easy. The result is that besides an introduction and epilogue we have a series of eight scenes through which the connecting link of personality is the figure of the Scandinavian hero. Passing from the prologue, which simply tells of the Saga, the 'Heims Kringla,' we hear the challenge of Thor addressed to the Galilean, 'Gauntlet or Gospel, here I defy thee.' Olaf, the Christian champion, returning to his kingdom, hears the defiance and accepts it. The lists are ready and the first onset is made by the king, who seeks the conversion of the warriors, by whom he is welcomed on landing. Their leader, Ironbeard, is not to be won over, and when Olaf lifts his axe against the image of Thor, the Pagan intervenes only to be himself slain. The incident, as the proverbial schoolboy knows, has a general parallel in English history, and here also the people accept the immunity of the sacrilegious monarch as a proof that his god is the true one. If I may say so without irreverence, Olaf thus scores first in the struggle upon which he has entered. But he is not to go from conquest to conquest. Trouble begins, and, as usual, there is a woman in it, several women, in point of fact. First of all Gudrun, daughter of the slain chief Ironbeard, appears upon the scene. Olaf marries her to redeem himself from the penalty of blood-guiltiness, and on their bridal night he awakes to find her standing over him, dagger in hand. The couple separate next morning, and we hear no more of Gudrun. In the next scene Olaf is keeping high revel when a one-eyed stranger enters to claim hospitality. He is Odin himself, the garrulous Wotan of Wagnerian fame, and of course he begins to discourse at large of 'heroes and their deeds'. 'Then slept the King' — no wonder! But there was much wonder next morning when it was found that the one-eyed wanderer had mysteriously disappeared. He was only a ghost after all, and, quoth Olaf, 'Sure is the triumph of our Faith'. But there is no personal triumph for the king. He goes a-wooing Sigrid, 'the haughty Queen of Svithiod', who likes him well enough, but hates his religion. Olaf, to say the least, behaves rudely to the lady. 'Thou hast not beauty,' he exclaims, 'thou hast not youth. Shall I buy thy hand at the cost of truth?' Then, flinging his gauntlet recklessly, he strikes the Queen on the cheek, and goes his way. Sigrid, with some reason, swears to be revenged, and bides her time. Yet deeper into the waters of trouble wades the King. There comes to his court, Thyri, the errant wife of King Burislaf, and her this Christian champion marries. Thyri is but an agent of Doom. 'Win back my dower,' she pleads and he consents. By this time insulted, Sigrid has married Svend the Dane, brother of Thyri, and finds it easy enough to influence her husband in the direction of a long-sworn revenge. Olaf puts to sea with his fleet; Svend does the same. There is a battle, and the Norway king falls. The epilogue tells us that the Galilean will conquer, but not by the weapons of Olaf.

> Cross against corslet,
> Love against hatred,
> Peace-cry for war-cry,
> Patience is powerful.

The picturesque and dramatic elements in this story so assert themselves even in the baldest summary that there is no need to point them out, nor can it be necessary to show what difficulties they present to the musician. Mr. Elgar was bold when he essayed this task of his own choosing. Let us now see whether the result justifies his temerity.

A mere glance through *King Olaf* proves that Mr. Elgar is much more at liberty in it than in the sacred work he composed for the recent Festival at Worcester. The limitations of religious music, as is now obvious, fettered him. In the secular work he is entirely at large, giving an impression that we see the man following his own instinct and method, and working out results as it pleases him. That is a great point gained. To begin with, not more often in art than in social life does the real man appear in each case. There are conventionalities embodied in public opinion, which issues edicts as from another Sinai, threatening penalties against transgressors. It must not be supposed, however, that Mr. Elgar has struck out new paths. He has merely allowed us to see the methods which his sympathies and judgment endorse, and has followed these with the utmost frankness and simplicity. This may be said in particular with regard to this representative theme, that most conspicuous feature in the structure of modern music as applied to personages and events. Let me now repeat what I have said many times before, namely, that the representative theme, sparingly used for a particular and well-defined purpose, is capable of doing good service, but that when profusely employed as the cardinal feature of a musical design it limits the composer, makes him the slave of his own mechanism, and places

his work in subjection to laws far more irksome and unworthy
than those of the old *contrapuntists*, who after all had learning on
their side. But, while holding this opinion, I do not fail to
recognise that the representative theme and its related usages
have become established, and that the best must be made of it till
another change takes place. In one sense Mr. Elgar has made the
best of it by inventing themes which are distinctive and
characteristic, by so using them that the analogue of the
scriptural wayfaring man cannot easily err therein. His *leitmotiven*
are many. Every personage has one. There are subjects which
stand for creeds and qualities, for this and that, till, as in Wagner,
the music is given up to the enforcement of an applied
significance, and it is all done so cleverly, with such an easy
command of resources, and with such a happy skill in dovetailing
the *motiven*, that no gaps and consequent jerks disturb the flow of
the music. And let it stand that Mr. Elgar has a right to use the
method adopted, the right which comes from ability, and which
only ability can confer.

So far I have dealt only with a matter of procedure lying within
the lines of, so to speak, musical architecture. Now it is necessary
to go beyond and above. It was said of Mr. Elgar's Worcester
Cantata, not without reason, that the composer sacrificed vocal
melody to the exigencies of orchestral effect. The remark does not
apply to *King Olaf*, or, if at all, only in a very limited sense. It now
appears that Mr. Elgar knows how to write effectively, both for
vocal solo and chorus, and that, as a matter of fact, he shows a
peculiar sensitiveness to the effects which can be produced by
such means. This is, perhaps, the most important revelation
made by the new work, because found in connection with a rare
gift of writing for the orchestra. We have plenty of musicians who
can score cleverly; indeed, no musical ability is more common,
thanks to examples set in abundance by modern masters. But it is
one thing to fill in a score, and another to conceive ideas that lend
themselves to the highest orchestral effects. Mr. Elgar, as now
convincingly shown, can do both, and combine with that power
the not less important one of bringing orchestra and voices into
masterly association. Examples might be quoted from many
pages of *King Olaf*, but more especially from the epilogue, in
which the composer rises to a great height of imaginative power
and technical mastery. The work ends quietly, with subdued
expression, altogether ignoring the prevailing idea of working up
to an exciting climax. But impressiveness has no essential
connection with noise, and nothing becomes *King Olaf* better

than the calm setting forth of a moral drawn from a story of strife and turmoil. I have given prominence to the final section, but really it is hard to draw a line between it and other parts of the work, in which appear the same easy mastery of well-judged effects and the same directness of appeal to perception of what is fitting to the scene or sentiment. Mr. Elgar's harmony is free. As may be supposed, he uses every resource in a romantic but not extravagant spirit, and in this case varies the fashionable declamation of the day with genuine vocal melody, aiming thus at a compromise which is all the happier, when achieved, because of its rarity. Dramatic feeling is strong in *King Olaf.* Situations occur again and again to which this is essential, and in every case the need is promptly and successfully met. It would serve little purpose to mention examples in the case of a work not many hours old, but amateurs may be advised to look at the scene with Ironbeard and his men, in which Olaf offers deadly insult to Sigrid, and at the setting forth of the catastrophe. These seem to point out Mr. Elgar as a composer who would probably make a figure on the lyric stage. To sum up a necessarily hurried judgment, *King Olaf* is a work of high importance, one which should turn expectant eyes upon its composer as a musician within whose reach, apparently, lies no common distinction. The performance of *King Olaf* was in all respects most creditable, having regard to the difficulties of the work and the short time allowed for general rehearsal. Chorus and orchestra acquitted themselves, under these circumstances, with real distinction, while the solos were in the perfectly safe hands of Madame Henson, Mr Edward Lloyd and Mr Ffrangcon-Davies, with whose singing only aggravated unreasonableness could find fault. Almost every number was applauded fervently, and, at the close, composer, soloists, band and choir were privileged to divide amongst them the honours of an enthusiastic demonstration.

A selection of miscellaneous pieces followed the new work, and the Festival ended this evening with Dvorak's *Spectre's Bride* and the Choral Symphony.

The Daily Telegraph,
31st October 1896

Caractacus
by E.A. Baughan

Caractacus was first performed under the baton of the composer at the Leeds Festival on 5th October 1898, and is generally regarded as having been one of the first works to bring his name before a wider audience than that of his native Worcestershire. A few days after the event Elgar wrote to his friend Troyte Griffiths that he was sending him a copy of The Musical Standard *'which is the first to give me the place I've fought for'. The* Musical Standard, *a weekly magazine which sold for one penny, was edited at that time by E.A. Baughan, who gave two notices of* Caractacus. *The first was a mere paragraph after he had attended the orchestral rehearsal in London, and a more detailed criticism followed a week later. Both reviews are reprinted here.*

On Thursday morning Mr. Elgar had the satisfaction of finishing the rehearsal of the last number of his *Caractacus*, and of running through a few earlier passages of the work. It is to be hoped that he will be given as much time as possible at Leeds for further rehearsing of his work both of the orchestra and chorus and of the orchestra alone. I have studied the vocal score and have listened attentively to the rehearsals of the orchestra and principals and I have no hesitation in saying that *Caractacus* is not only the most important of the novelties but, viewed quite apart from the Leeds Festival works, is a composition which definitely determines Mr. Elgar's position as the first of modern British composers. Such praise may seem exaggerated in view of the excellent work done by Stanford, Parry and others during their career, but there is just that real musical creation in *Caractacus* that is lacking so often in the work of the more pretentiously academic of our native composers. Again, if ever a national opera were established in England, Mr. Elgar is the one man to whom I should look to give us something worthy of our nation. It is a pity, I think, that *Caractacus* is not to be conducted by a professional conductor at Leeds, for Mr. Elgar is not a good conductor at all, and during the rehearsals it has been evident that he cannot make the men under his command understand to the full precisely the effect he desires to obtain; but the festival fashion puts a premium on the suicide of

composers, and Mr. Elgar will be the latest victim of that fashion.
Incidentally I may be permitted to note that this new cantata has
introduced to us an exceptionally fine dramatic baritone in the
person of Mr. Charles Knowles, of whom I have never heard
before. He is destined, I should think, to take a high position in his
profession, and especially if circumstances should lead him to the
opera-stage.

With the magnificent singing of those Yorkshire voices still
ringing in my ears it is difficult to sit down and criticize Mr.
Elgar's new cantata in cold blood. I am seized with an infinite
regret that I cannot stay in this ugly, dirty, and ill-lit city for the
rest of the festival instead of speeding back to London. This
exordium must be excused, since it is my first visit to Leeds and I
have never before heard the famous Yorkshire singers, except
when a small contingent visited London to take part in Mottl's
performance of the *Choral Symphony*. The certainty of attack,
sonority and purity of tone, the subtle feeling for light and shade
of expression, where can these things be equalled in choral
singing? This is a feature of our musical life of which we may well
be proud. The foreigner visiting us is always astounded, and the
latest to express his astonishment and admiration has been Mons.
Fauré, who has said that to conduct the Leeds chorus is like
playing on a delicately sensitive instrument, so quickly does it
speak to the conductor's touch.

To come to *Caractacus* itself. I must frankly and unhesitatingly
admit that its performance at Leeds has not heightened the
opinion I had already formed of it from a perusal of the score and
from attending the London band rehearsals. One then evidently
made too many allowances for the effect the choruses would
make, and for the uninterrupted performance at the festival. The
libretto of the work has been so planned that Mr. Elgar should
have an opportunity of showing his talent in pastoral, warlike,
patriotic, passionate and mystical music in turn. It may be well
here to quote the argument of the book, as it explains, to a great
extent, the contrast of treatment which makes *Caractacus*
anything but a dull work:-

> The Britons throughout the South, East and centre of England
> having been subdued by the Romans, Caractacus is driven with his
> remaining forces towards the Welsh frontier, and establishes a great

camp on the Malvern Hills, on the summit now known as the British Camp, or Herefordshire Beacon. Wandering in the forest below the hills, Eigen, the daughter of Caractacus, and her betrothed lover, Orbin, are met by a Druid maiden, who enjoins them to warn the King not to advance into the open country against the Romans. This warning they convey to Caractacus. On the ensuing night the omens are taken at a solemn assembly of the Druids. They are read by Orbin, who belongs to the half-priestly order of minstrels, and are declared to be unfavourable. The Arch-Druid deceives the King as to their character, and Caractacus resolves to advance against the Romans. Orbin endeavours to protest, but is cursed and driven forth by the Druids. On the following morning Orbin meets Eigen in a glade of the forest, where youths and maidens are with her gathering flowers for a sacrifice, and bids her farewell, telling her of the deceit practised on the King by the Druids, and of his own expulsion. He adds that he himself is flying from the Druids and intends to join the British forces. In the next scene Eigen and her maidens witness the return of Caractacus with the remnants of his army to the camp on the Malvern Hills after their total rout by the Romans. Caractacus and his family, including Orbin, are soon after betrayed into the hands of the enemy. The last scene represents Caractacus with Orbin and Eigen before the tribunal of Claudius, the Emperor of Rome. Claudius is at first disposed to condemn them to death, but is so struck by the intrepidity of Caractacus that he pardons them and assigns them an honourable residence in Rome. The general lines of history — or, failing history, of tradition — have been followed. The British Camp on the Malvern Hills is locally attributed to Caractacus. It is doubtless a British work, and is of such an extent as infers occupation by very large numbers. The scene of Caractacus's last disastrous battle is much disputed; but it was almost certainly on the line of the Severn (Habren), and may probably have been at Caer Caradoc, in Shropshire. The unusual circumstance of mistletoe growing on the oak may be still observed in the woods below the Herefordshire Beacon. Caractacus's appearance before Claudius in Rome, his bold defence, and the pardon of himself and his daughter are historical. Orbin is an imaginary character.

The verse of the libretto is no worse than usual, and its metres, for the most part, are suitable for musical treatment, and with that one may dismiss Mr. H.A. Acworth, the writer of the book. The fault of its construction is probably due to the composer, for its essential fault is that it requires action to fill up its gaps, and in composing his cantata as if it were an opera Mr. Elgar has seriously limited his work as an example of musical art. There is no question here of bald theoretical objection. If one wants merely to theorize, what excuse can be proffered for such a hybrid form of art at all? But even as it exists there are some kind of rules which may be applied to the cantata, which would make it less obnoxious to one's artistic appreciations. The line which divides it from opera is not, perhaps, very distinct, but it exists nevertheless. Action should be suggested by narrative, and at no time should the music sacrifice its absolute cohesiveness of form in order to step aside and follow the intricacies of an action which does not take place before our eyes. Here, again, I must not be accused of being a theorist or a doctrinaire. To break up musical expression, to destroy its flow by introducing meaningless pauses, absolutely weakens it. Even in opera, where we note with some satisfaction that these breaks have a close connection with the action proceeding on the stage it is doubtful if they really do enhance the effect of the music-drama as a whole; in the cantata where we do not see the action supposed to be taking place, there can be no question that the effect is scrappy and superficial. That great master of music-drama, Wagner, knew this so well that though we do have the action to fit to his music, and can gain some pleasure from the appreciation of the fitness of the expressive medium to the exigencies of drama, yet we are given page after page which can stand alone as absolute music, merely because he almost invariably turned to the interpretation of the emotional content of a scene rather than attempted to describe its physical aspects; so that even such pieces as the *Walkürenritt* or Siegfried's *Trauermarsch*, in themselves so appropriate to the action taking place on the stage, have nevertheless a complete artistic existence of their own.

Mr. Elgar, on the other hand, is ever attempting to paint in tones, or to enhance by the energy of his rhythm and by the palette of the orchestra some of the physical aspects of the situations. We are given the scene in which Caractacus and his fellow captives are marched in triumph through the streets of Rome. The chorus takes upon itself the duty of describing the scene, and the orchestra should have given us a musical expression not of the march through the streets, in which case one pictures a mob of Imperial Roman soldiers headed by a brass band, but of the despair and noble resignation of Caractacus, his love for his country, and, better still, of the composer's ideas of these emotions. It cannot be too often insisted that to make music a mere medium for painting facts or actions is seriously to limit its scope; the abstract has always been the core of great art, and the Berliozs and Richard Strausses, in spite of their extremely clever special pleading, have but emphasized this truth.

With these views of music it is perhaps inconsistent to say that

Mr. Elgar would probably write a better music drama than a cantata, since I hold that even an opera to be considered as art must be able to take its stand as absolute music in a large sense. But to step down from theory once more it is decidedly true that the tone-painting of physical action is more acceptable on the stage than in the concert-room for the simple reason that the accompanying drama makes it intelligible and in his *Caractacus* Mr. Elgar shows over and over again that he has what may be called the operatic instinct in distinction to the music-dramatic instinct. But here is a consideration which forced itself on my mind as I left the Leeds Town Hall on Wednesday night. Has the composer of *Caractacus* the insight in reality, or does he give you the impression of dramatic power simply because he has a complete mastery of the technique of his art and has a certain nervous physical energy that makes for action and movement? A man's mind may have a tendency to these things and yet he may be no dramatist, and if it were not so every sportsman, every devout lover of cricket or football, would be a potential dramatist. In some of the essentials of drama I am afraid I must say that, in my opinion, Mr. Elgar is decidedly lacking. For instance, he has not yet learnt how to differentiate the musical utterances and the general character of the music used in general illustration of his dramatic-personæ, so that his Caractacus and his Druid, his Eigen and his Orbin all speak in the same idiom. And then he quite fails to invent themes that fully express the character of the ideas of his drama. When we want a certain boldness and breadth, a simple majesty and sincere grandeur, as in the musical expression of Caractacus, we are given a theme which has a certain attractiveness but is much too sentimental and nearly commonplace. At times there is even a tendency to a melodious loquaciousness that distantly reminds one of the Mendelssohn ideals of the first half of this century. And yet sometimes the composer can write in a style that entirely commands our respect, and makes us feel that he has not yet given us all that is in him. One of the best things in the cantata, though it will probably be passed over by writers who imagine that attention must be concentrated on the more important numbers, is the speech in which Caractacus bids the Roman emperor to do his worst, 'Heap torment upon torment.' In this we have a really fine dramatic style, in which not for one moment does the taint of an inappropriate melody stultify the composer's intentions. This, with its following chorus, is Elgar at his best. To show how unequal he can be in this respect we had just previously had the lament of Caractacus over his defeat. Possibly, Mr. Elgar had purposely written the music so that it should emphasize the spent feebleness of the warrior after his long day's fight. That would be artistically sound enough, but in no way does such an intention excuse the cut-and-dried character of the melody.

If Mr. Elgar has failed somewhat in rising to the thematic heights demanded by his subject, it may be thought that in the lighter parts of his work, especially in the landscape idylls for which the librettist has given him many opportunities, he would be more successful. But, apart from a certain prettiness, I found them decidedly disappointing. In the love-duet between Orbin and Eigen, however, he reaches a certain tenderness and charm that are delightful in the completeness that arises from the accord of aim and achievement, and in a short chorus descriptive of the embarkation of the British captives in the Roman galleys he perhaps reaches his highest point of inspiration.

The difficulty in criticizing Mr. Elgar's music is that the score is such a good example of clever modern work, in which mere cleverness is never allowed to obtrude itself, that to praise it as it deserves from that aspect would be to give a totally wrong impression of the manner in which it affected one. But having enlarged sufficiently on the failures of the cantata, it is a pleasure to turn to the excellent workmanship of *Caractacus*. After having heard the work at the London band rehearsals I wrote last week that it is one of the most considerable of modern British compositions, and Wednesday night's performance has not made me alter that opinion. The elaborate and appropriate use of representative themes has never been approached by any living native composer; the symphonic accompaniment is varied and elastic; the harmony if out of the way according to the purist has always the merit of sounding natural and unforced; the part-writing is well carried out; and the whole texture of the music flows on from note to note with an easy mastery which proclaims Elgar a composer of decided gifts. You may say of him with truth that he writes *music;* that his mastery of technique comes not from a laborious effort but from his real talent as a composer. Only *Caractacus* does not convince me that he has genius, nor that his talent will be best employed on subjects that may be within his technical powers to express but are as outside his temperament as this of *Caractacus*. And yet I would particularly like to guard myself against the charge of being hypercritical; and therefore without any desire of blunting the edge of the remarks already made, I will conclude this necessarily hasty notice with the statement that, look where we may in the field of modern musical art, we shall scarcely find a composition which shows such decided talent as Mr. Elgar's *Caractacus*. Other works there may be which in general tone aim at a more austere and perhaps higher plane of musical art, but none that I know has the natural ease and genius-like cleverness of Mr. Elgar's score, which, in spite of its musicianship, is never obtrusively pretentious, and has never the air of making cleverness an end in itself. The composer of *Caractacus* has a technical equipment, which, if a few crudities were eliminated, such as the too lavish use of the drums and cymbals to give point to a climax (possibly due to the composer's idea that the Leeds Choir would otherwise swamp his orchestra in the more martial moments of his score), should most assuredly lead him to the high places beside the shrine of art, could we be but certain that in future he will curb a tendency towards too facile melodiousness, and that the rather essential feminity and commonplaceness of some of his themes will give place to a strength and directness of thematic invention that shall destroy the too apparent disparity between his musical thought and his power of working it out. The fault of *Caractacus* precisely lies in that disparity. It only remains to speak of the performance of the work on Wednesday evening. The wonderful Leeds chorus did its work so that the composer only paid it a merited compliment in applauding it when he was recalled to the platform. But the orchestra was not satisfactory; it was rough, and inclined to be too loud at times, and, again, too subdued; also the emphasis might often have been more dramatic. These faults were doubtless due to the inexperience of the composer as conductor. The music is, for the most part, well written for the voice and Miss Medora Henson, Mr. Lloyd and Mr. Andrew Black all sang with much fire and effect. A special word must be said for the excellent work done by Mr. Charles Knowles, a baritone who has a fine voice and an exceptionally just idea of musical declamation. Another local singer who took part in the performance was Mr. John Browning, but I am sorry that I cannot say anything favourable of his singing.

The Musical Standard,
1st and 8th October 1898

Young Elgar at the Festival
by Jerrold Northrop Moore

A hundred years ago, at the Worcester Festival of 1878, Edward Elgar first played in a Three Choirs orchestra. In those days the Festival orchestra was recruited locally, and it was a great moment when the 21-year-old musician took his place beside his father in the second violins for the greatest musical event of his city. His experience as a listener at the Worcester Festival went back to 1866, when he was nine. His membership in the Festival orchestra would go forward to 1893. In 1896 he made his mark as a Festival composer and retired from the orchestra. But until he went to the Festival at Hereford in 1897, when he was 40, Elgar seems to have taken part only in the Festivals at Worcester. This is the story of those thirty years.

In 1866 Edward Elgar was child in a large family living over their father's music shop at 10 High Street, close to the Cathedral. The mother was a Catholic convert, and she brought up all the children as Catholics. Elgar senior, despite his organistship of the Catholic church, remained an obstinate Free-thinker. But a large part of his music-selling business depended on the Cathedral, and his was not the only music shop in Worcester. So the Elgar family's contacts with the Cathedral were kept constant. Edward recalled visits to the Cathedral from the time he was four. A little later, the Cathedral would yield the material he needed to teach himself music:

> I drew my first ideas of music from the Catedral, from books borrowed from the music library, when I was eight, nine or ten. They were barbarously printed in eight different clefs, all of which I learnt before I was 12 . . . I was allowed by Mr. Done [the Cathedral organist] to borrow them, and they were administered to me by friends who were lay-clerks.

Edward Elgar was a middle child in his family. But the death of the Elgars' first-born, Harry, in 1864, made Edward the eldest son. After Edward came Frederick Joseph, whom the family fondly called 'Jo'. Their eldest sister Lucy was to write of him: 'He was called the "Beethoven" of the family, having a very remark-

able aptitude for music from the time he could sit up in his chair'.
But their friend Hubert Leicester (who would grow up to be one
of the great men of Worcester) recalled: 'Jo, though very
intelligent, was curiously undeveloped in many ways'. Two old
sepia photographs show Edward standing close beside Jo, with a
protective hand on the smaller boy's shoulder. Then Jo also fell ill
and died with all his musical promise in the first days of
September 1866. Nearly seventy years later Edward fell into a
reminiscing mood as he wandered with a group of friends and
colleagues through Worcester Cathedral:

> Pausing before a skull, underneath which are two fearsome wings, he
> told us how, as a little boy, the gruesome sight fascinated him, and he
> still remembered the thrill of fear with which he regarded it.

Jo Elgar's burial beside Harry in Astwood Cemetery took
place on the Saturday before the Worcester Festival. Elgar senior
was playing in the Festival orchestra, and he hoped the music-
making might distract Edward's thoughts. He was right. Hubert
Leicester would recall it:

> H. says he can remember E. running down the street from 10 High
> Street to the Cathedral with a large score under his arm... His father
> had obtained for him admission to a rehearsal. He had never heard a
> big band until then, and when he came back it was such a revelation
> to him that he said:

> > 'Oh, my. I had no idea what a band was like. Then I began to think
> > how much more could be made out of it than they were making... If I
> > had that orchestra under my own control and given a free hand I
> > could make it play whatever I liked'.

The work being rehearsed was Beethoven's Mass in C. But
even listening to this choral work, the child's attention had been
seized by the orchestra. Early in 1869 he would acquire an
Orchestral Primer by Beethoven's pupil Anton Reicha.

1869 was the next Worcester Festival year. When the 12-year-
old Edward saw his father working over the orchestral parts of
Handel's *Messiah*, he saw a chance to put his new knowledge to
use:

> ... I composed a little tune of which I was very proud. I thought the
> public should hear it, but my opportunities of publishing it were
> decidedly few. I saw my opportunity when my father was engaged in
> preparing the Handel parts for the forthcoming festival. Very
> laboriously I introduced my little tune into the music. The thing was
> an astonishing success, and I heard that some people had never

enjoyed Handel so much before! When my father learned of it, however, he was furious!

Yet, at the Festival rehearsal, Edward's interest in his little triumph was overborne by the sheer thrill of listening again to the large orchestra. A friend of later years would write:

> One of [Elgar's] recollections was of going into the Cathedral [at the age of twelve] and hearing the orchestra rehearse 'O thou that tellest'. The opening greatly impressed him, and he thereupon resolved to learn the violin.

> He hurried home and begged his father to lend him a violin from the stock of the shop, when he at once retired to an attic and straightaway endeavoured to pick out the beginning of 'O thou that tellest'. The first two notes, A and D, were on the open strings, but then came difficulties. However, the boy was not to be beaten, and at the end of a fortnight he had mastered the violin part of 'O thou that tellest'.

Thus it was the Festival that showed Edward Elgar his instrument — the instrument he was to play in the Worcester orchestra for 15 years. Yet two further Festivals took place before the young man found his place amongst its performers. In 1872 the youth of 15, having finished his schooling, had been put to work in a local solicitor's office by his parents, who hoped for something better than the music trade for their son: there seems to be no record of his attendance at any Festival event that year. Soon the solicitor's office was abandoned at Edward's insistence, and he was allowed to enter the career in music which he demanded.

He would have been ready to join the Festival orchestra in 1875, but in that year there was no orchestral Festival at all. Lord Dudley had given the new Hill organ and subscribed heavily to the Cathedral restoration on condition that the edifice was not used for events at which an entrance fee could be charged. The result was the so-called 'Mock Festival', consisting of three days' choral services and organ music. A single memory of that time would come back as he sat among friends in the Cathedral many years later:

> On someone mentioning the acoustics of the building, Elgar told of the impression he had received from the improvising of S. S. Wesley, who had built up a wonderful climax of sound before, in Elgar's words, crashing into the subject of the 'Wedge' Fugue.

It would have been almost his last chance to hear the great organist of Gloucester, who died in April 1876.

By 1878 other councils prevailed at Worcester, and there was once more to be an orchestral Festival in the Cathedral. Among the performers engaged was the 21-year-old Edward Elgar. He was now a fully fledged musician, supporting himself by lessons and local engagements to play, serving in his father's shop when he had to, composing small pieces when he could.

One work in the Festival programme that year was Mozart's G minor Symphony. Through the summer before the 1878 Festival, young Elgar studied this model:

> I . . . ruled a score for the same instruments and with the same number of bars as Mozart's G minor Symphony, and in that framework I wrote a symphony, following as far as possible the same outline in the themes and the same modulation. I did this on my own initiative, as I was groping in the dark after light, but looking back after thirty years I don't know any discipline from which I learned so much.

When the Festival came in September, this model-symphony was still unfinished.

The performers were placed in front of the choir screen. Edward took his place beside his father in the second violins. The programmes included *Messiah, Elijah* and the *Hymn of Praise,* Part I of *The Creation,* Mozart's *Requiem,* and Spohr's *Last Judgment.* There were also several modern English works. But with these the young second violinist found fault:

> We had been accustomed to perform compositions by Sir Frederick Ouseley, Dr. Philip Armes and others of the organists and professors of music who furnished meritorious works for festivals, but they lacked that feeling for orchestral effect and elasticity in instrumentation so obvious in the works of French, Italian, and German composers.

Again the Three Choirs Festival was teaching Edward Elgar about the orchestra. But one other impression of the 1878 Festival would linger for more than half a century:

> Sir Edward said he remembered when he was playing second violin in the orchestra and some of Stainer's charming music was being performed. He remembered Stainer walking up and down, in a nervous sort of way, until the composition was over. That was in the South aisle. Stainer had left a very fragrant memory, not only in the Cathedral, but wherever he passed by.

It was an experience, after all, to be so close to a famous musician as he listened to his own work.

Three years later, for the 1881 Festival, young Elgar secured his place at the last desk in the first violins, while old Elgar remained in the seconds. For this Festival an orchestral platform was erected in the west end of the Cathedral, as it is arranged for Festivals to this day: only the seats in the nave ran east and west (which they did until 1954). One of the Festival works of 1881 was *The Widow of Nain* by a local conductor, Alfred James Caldicott. When a harp became available at the last minute, young Elgar promptly demonstrated another side of his orchestral skill by writing out a harp-part for Caldicott's work almost on the instant. But the Festival work which electrified him that year was Alexander Mackenzie's cantata *The Bride,* for it appealed directly to his orchestral imagination:

> The coming of Mackenzie then was a real event. Here was a man fully equipped in every department of musical knowledge, who had been a violinist in orchestras in Germany. It gave orchestral players a real lift and widened the outlook of the old-fashioned professor considerably. *The Bride* was a fine example of choral and orchestral writing [and] had a rousing reception. I had the honour to meet the composer the following morning and actually shook hands with him at Sansome Lodge.

Yet Mackenzie was to be dwarfed three years later when the 1884 Worcester Festival played host to Antonin Dvorak. Elgar played in performances of Dvorak's new Symphony in D major (now numbered 6) and the *Stabat Mater* under the composer, and afterwards wrote to a friend:

> I wish you could hear Dvorak's music. It is simply ravishing, so tuneful and clever and the orchestration is wonderful; no matter how few instruments he uses it never sounds thin. I cannot describe it; it must be heard.

By then Edward Elgar had begun to feel the strength of his own desire to be a composer and not a performer. He had already attempted to write one orchestral overture, and was engaged on another. But neither work would come to fruition. It needed an assurance outside himself to sustain the creative effort of big work. Before the next Worcester Festival, in 1887, he had met the woman. She was Caroline Alice Roberts, the daughter of a late Major-General in the Indian Army, living with her widowed mother in a country house at Redmarley on the southern border of Worcestershire (now in Gloucestershire). But their social spheres were widely different and the engagement was delayed.

The 1887 Worcester Festival would show Elgar a telling contrast. It brought Frederic Cowen, a man only five years

Elgar's senior, yet already the composer of several symphonies and of a new oratorio *Ruth*, which he conducted at the Festival. In later years Cowen was to write: 'I little knew then the genius that was under the guidance of my baton'. Nobody knew it in 1887, for there was nothing to know — nothing beyond a handful of small pieces published and a quantity of music for the Catholic church in manuscript. The accomplishments of the 35-year-old Cowen could only emphasise the distance from any similar goals of the 30-year-old Elgar.

A year later he was engaged to Alice Roberts, and in May 1889 they were married. Almost immediately the atmosphere changed. The old Worcester Cathedral organist William Done — the same man who had lent books from the Cathedral library to the child a quarter-century earlier — was persuaded to agree that young Mr. Elgar should be requested to write an orchestral work for the Worcester Festival of 1890. It showed some courage, for there was no evidence whatever of Edward Elgar's ability to write music of more than four or five minutes' duration. The recent work he had to show Mr. Done was the recently-published *Salut d'amour*, written a year earlier on his engagement to Alice. But the old man replied generously:

College Green, Worcester
Jany. 1st 1890

Dear Mr. Elgar,
Thank you very much for your kind letter, and for your good wishes of the season. I shall be very much pleased to receive the score of your new composition (it will probably come tomorrow) and I shall study it with much pleasure as the work of one whose talent I have always recognised and admired. It will be a pleasure to you to know that the proposal to introduce your orchestral piece at the Festival will meet with no opposition. I must not take the credit of it to myself — as it scarcely required a word of recommendation from me. I will take care to give you a good Orchestra and fair opportunity of rehearsal. Will you kindly tell me whether any extra instruments will be required. I hope not, as the orchestra is so small.
With kindest regards and best wishes,
Believe me
Dear Mr. Elgar
Yours very faithfully
W. Done

Through the winter and spring of 1890 Elgar made several beginnings. It was not until 25th May that he recognised the theme which would carry him to a successful issue: *'Commenced*

Froissart'. The next two months were almost entirely devoted to the new work, but at the end of July the Overture stood finished — a structure of 340 bars on 24 separate instrumental staves, altogether more than 8,000 bars. It was incomparably the biggest work Edward Elgar had ever written, and the best.

He was still playing in the Festival orchestra, but he would take the baton to conduct the first performance at the Wednesday Evening Secular Concert which was then a staple of the Festival week. The Secular Concerts at Worcester were held in the Public Hall (which stood for many years in the Cornmarket until it was destroyed for a car park). The Wednesday Evening Secular Concert in 1890 was to be recalled vividly by a young man of 21 who would later become organist of Worcester Cathedral, conductor of the Festivals, and one of Elgar's closest friends — Ivor Atkins. In 1890 Atkins was assistant to the Hereford Cathedral organist George Robertson Sinclair, and this was his first Three Choirs Festival:

> Never before had I heard such a wonderful combination of a first-rate chorus and orchestra. I was naturally specially interested in Elgar, knowing that he was to produce a new Overture whose very title attracted me, for I had just been reading Froissart's *Chronicles*. Sinclair pointed Elgar out to me. There he was, fiddling among the first violins, with his fine intellectual face, his heavy moustache, his nervous eyes and his beautiful hands.
>
> The Wednesday evening came. I had not dress clothes with me, having come over from Hereford for the day, so crept up the steps leading to the back of the orchestra and peeped from behind those on the platform. The new Overture was placed at the end of the first half of the programme.
>
> The great moment came, and I watched Elgar's shy entry on to the platform. From that moment my eyes did not leave him, and I listened to the Overture, hearing it in the exciting way one hears music when among the players. I heard the surge of the strings, the chatter of the woodwind, the sudden bursts from the horns, the battle call of the trumpets, the awesome beat of the drums and the thrill of cymbal clashes. I was conscious of all these and of the hundred and one other sounds from an orchestra that stir one's blood and send one's heart into one's mouth.
>
> But there was something else I was conscious of — I knew that Elgar was the man for me, I knew that I completely understood his music, and that my heart and soul went with it.

Such a response, from a man half a generation younger, hinted at the appeal Elgar's music might command — if only he could continue to write it.

1 Elgar's birthplace at Broadheath, drawn in 1856. His parents stand in the foreground with sister Lucy, brother Harry leans on a tree, while sister Polly is seen in the porch with her nurse. In front of the coach-house on the left is Uncle Henry Elgar.

2   Four of the figures from the Elgar saga: violinist W. H. Reed,
'variations' Troyte Griffiths and Dorabella,
and Mrs Carice Elgar Blake.

After the 1890 Festival a long time elapsed before Elgar took up another large project with success. When he did, he completed a setting for chorus and orchestra of an old German ballad, *The Black Knight*. It was finished in October 1892 and scored for orchestra through the following winter. *The Black Knight* was given its première in April 1893 by the Worcester Festival Choral Society. But there was no performance at the next Worcester Festival that September. On his own copy of the Festival programme Elgar noted: 'I played first violin for the sake of the fee as I could obtain no recognition as a composer'.

It was the last time he would play in the Festival orchestra. Within the next three years everything was to change. The seeds sown by his wife's constant encouragement began to bear fruit. Both *Froissart* and *The Black Knight* were performed outside Worcester. One result was a commission for the North Stafford-shire Festival in October 1896. But Elgar meanwhile offered to write a large work for the Worcester Festival of 1896. And this also was accepted.

Elgar's Worcester Festival work was a setting of St. John's story of Jesus healing the blind man. The libretto was by Edward Capel-Cure, a son-in-law of the Fittons of Malvern (whose daughter Isabel was shortly to figure in the *Enigma Variations*). Capel-Cure suggested the title *Lux Christi*: that was later subjoined to the less Romish-sounding *The Light of Life*. The story of the blind man's healing seemed to hint at autobiographical significance. This was recognised at the time, but it was also seen that the allegory was not exact. After the 1896 Festival *The Sunday Times* critic wrote:

> Seldom does the dip into the 'local art' lottery yield a prize so conspicuously promising as Mr. Edward Elgar. Here is a musician of whom Worcester has perfect reason to be proud, and the place accorded his short oratorio, *The Light of Life* in Tuesday evening's programme, was eminently justified by the critical verdict of the following day . . . The best number in the work is the chorus 'Light out of darkness', and this is of such excellence that I cannot help looking to Mr. Elgar for a really fine work when he comes across a 'book' which appeals in every sense to his strong artistic temperament.

The Dream of Gerontius was then less than four years away. Neither it nor any later major work would be written for a Three Choirs Festival. Yet Elgar's thirty years' experience of the Festival at Worcester had given him the basis on which he built his mature expression. He was to acknowledge it to his friend

W. H. Reed, who for many years led the London Symphony
Orchestra at Three Choirs Festivals. Reed recalled:

> He was immensely pleased when he heard those passages which he
> had noticed himself when he had first taken part as an orchestral
> player in such works as *Elijah* or *Messiah*. Year after year at the Three
> Choirs Festivals, his head would appear round a pillar in the
> cathedral to catch my eye when the altos and tenors enter, with their
> A and C respectively, in the concluding bars of 'All we like sheep'
> *(adagio)*. He revelled in the sweeping passage for the violins in 'Thou
> shalt break them' . . .

Reed lies buried now in the Cathedral near the spot where Elgar
used to stand listening. Above that spot the 'Gerontius' window
commemorates the achievement of a great composer. It is not far
from an 18th century monument on which a skull surmounts the
wings of death.

Edward Elgar
by F.G. Edwards

Following on the success of such works as King Olaf (*1896*), The
Banner of St George (*1897*), Caractacus (*1899*) *and especially the*
Variations on an Original Theme (*1899*), *Elgar's fame in the country
of his birth increased rapidly. To coincide with the first performance of* The
Dream of Gerontius *at the Birmingham Musical Festival on 3rd
October 1900* The Musical Times *published the longest appreciation of
the composer that had appeared in any national publication up to that time.
Although unsigned, the article is known to have been written by the
magazine's Editor, F.G. Edwards. The same issue contained a specially-
commissioned photograph of Elgar and the part-song* As Torrents in
Summer *from* King Olaf.

In a somer seson · whan soft was the sonne,
I shope me in shroudes · as I a shepe[1] were,
In habite as an heremite · vnholy of workes,
Went wyde in his world · wondres to here.
Ac on a May mornynge · on Maluerne hulles,
Me byfel a ferly[2] · of fairy, me thouzte.
LANGLAND'S *Piers the Plowman.*

While beyond, above them mounted,
And above their woods also,
Malvern hills, for mountains counted
Not unduly, loom a-row —
Keepers of Piers Plowman's visions, through the
    sunshine and the snow.[3]
ELIZABETH BARRETT BROWNING.

The Malvern uplands are to be seen, not described. No
appreciative mind can fail to be impressed with the bold outline,
the imposing abruptness, and the verdant loveliness of these
everlasting hills. Nature has left the impress of her smile on this

---

[1] Shepherd.   [2] A wonder.
[3] The Malvern Hills are the scene of Langland's visions, and thus
present the earliest classic ground of English poetry.

favoured region, and hill and valley combine to produce a landscape of fascinating picturesqueness. It is a steep climb to the hilltop above Malvern Wells, but it more than repays the wayfarer who has eyes to behold and a soul to satisfy. The enjoyment of a quiet stroll along these grassy heights is greatly enhanced by the companionship of one who habitually thinks his thoughts and draws his inspirations from these elevated surroundings. He points out a noble peak once the site of a Roman encampment, and as he tells you that its thereabouts is traditionally associated with Caractacus you instinctively think, 'and thereby hangs a tale' — if not a cantata. Not far off is Wind's Point, the charming retreat of Jenny Lind, where the great singer drew her last breath. In descending from the summit, on the Worcestershire side, an exceedingly pleasant detached house is reached. It stands on the steep hillside, and from the little terrace in front of the house the view is as beautiful as its range is extensive. It begins and ends with two cities so long associated with the Three Choirs Festivals — Worcester on the left, Gloucester on the right. Between these extremes, through which the Severn flows its tranquil course, lies the vale of Evesham, where Muzio Clementi, 'the father of modern pianoforte-playing', had his cottage and where he died. The venerable Abbey of Tewkesbury comes within the range of vision, and, on a clear day, even the historic battlefield of Edge Hill, although forty miles distant. Here, in the midst of these delightful Malvern surroundings — how welcome their tranquillity — is located the home of him who forms the subject of this biographical sketch.

Edward William Elgar was born at Broadheath, four miles from Worcester, 2nd June 1857. His patronymic is of Saxon origin, and may be found as Aelfgar, which being interpreted means 'fairy spear'. He is the eldest surviving son of Mr W.H. Elgar, of Worcester, and of Ann Greening, descended from a fine old yeoman stock of Weston, Herefordshire, and therefore intensely English. In the eventide of their lives Mr and Mrs Elgar have the satisfaction of witnessing the fame of their gifted son. A native of Dover, his father became an assistant in the music-publishing house of Messrs Coventry and Hollier, then in Dean Street, Soho. There he used to hear Dragonetti play the pedal part of Bach's organ fugues on the double bass, and doubtless sold many copies of Dragonetti's special arrangement of the fugues for pianoforte and double bass (or violoncello), originally published by Coventry and which are now in Messrs Novello's catalogue. In 1841, Mr W.H. Elgar settled in Worcester and, with his brother (who was an excellent viola player and organist), started a music selling business of his own. Mr Frank Elgar, the composer's younger brother, is not only an excellent oboe player, but he is a born conductor. He has a complete military band, formed of civilians in Worcester, and instructs an instrumental class of about forty pupils at the Victoria Institute.

Mr Elgar, Senior, was, however, much more of a musician than a business man. He was not only an excellent performer on the violin, but held the post of organist of St George's Roman Catholic Church, Worcester, for the long period of thirty-seven years. At his instigation the Masses of Cherubini in D and Hummel in E flat were first heard at the Three Choirs Festival, in the orchestra of which (at Worcester) he played amongst the violins. Mozart and Beethoven were his 'dearly beloved' composers, and as his son Edward points to a portrait of Mozart on the wall of his study, he remarks: 'That is my man.' Thus the boy entered the world and was nurtured in a rarefied atmosphere of music. Who will say that he has failed to rise to the heights of so rich an inheritance?

Edward received some music lessons (pianoforte) at the inevitable dame school, but, like so many successful musicians, he has been almost entirely self-taught. Until his fifteenth year he received his general education at Littleton House, near Worcester. As a boy he would sit by his father's side Sunday by Sunday in the organ loft of St George's Church and would frequently extemporise the voluntaries and accompany the services. He worked through Rink, and Best's *Organ School* entirely by himself, and read every book he could find on the theory of music. At the age of fifteen he began to learn German, with a view of going to Leipzig for the further study of music; but financial difficulties stood in the way, and thus the budding composer escaped the dogmatism of the schools. He played much of the pianoforte music of Kozeluch, Schobert, and others, and of Emanuel Bach, then not so much known as now, and gained much practical experience in reducing scores for the pianoforte.

After leaving school young Elgar entered a solicitor's office, but he remained at the desk for twelve months only, as his ambitions were set in the direction of other deeds than those associated with the law. Nevertheless this business experience has been of great value in developing those methodical habits which are so natural to him, but which so many musicians unfortunately lack. He read a great deal at this formulative period of his life. A pile of old books, shot on the floor of the loft of a stable, was a source of omnivorous attraction to the thoughtful youth. In this way he made the acquaintance of Sir Philip Sydney's *Arcadia*, Baker's *Chronicles*, Drayton's *Polyolbion*, etc. He played the bassoon in a wind-instrument quintet of performers — two flutes, oboe, clarinet, and bassoon — and wrote 'lots of music for that combination'. But he by no means neglected his fiddle. He played in the orchestra of the Worcester Philharmonic Society (under the late Mr Done), and in various orchestras in the regions round about Worcester, and made frequent appearances as a solo performer on the violin.

Not the least interesting feature of Elgar's picking-up period was the Worcester Glee Club. This old Society, founded so long ago as 1810, occupied a prominent place in the musical life of the city. Cathedral lay clerks and citizen amateurs week by week joined their forces in a feast of vocal harmony and right good fellowship. An additional accompaniment to these unaccompanied glees (if the suspicion of a bull may be allowed) was furnished by churchwarden pipes solemnly smoked by the senior Apollos. The proceedings always commenced with *Glorious Apollo*, and seven other glees and two songs completed the programme. As a boy young Elgar attended many of the meetings, and later he played the accompaniments at the weekly gatherings, and led the small orchestra at the monthly concerts of vocal and instrumental music. He thus became familiar with the grand old school of English vocal music at a very impressionable period of his life. Concerning these meetings of the Worcester Glee Club, a well-known musician of that city sends us the following recollections:-

> The Worcester Glee Club was founded in 1810, and held its meetings at the Crown Hotel weekly, from October to April, on Tuesday nights. These meetings were famous in their day, and brought together a large number of the citizens. The lay clerks of the Cathedral were the mainstay of the vocal music, and they were reinforced for the 'instrumental nights' once a month by the leading professional and amateur performers in the city. The Elgar family became associated with the club about 1843, in the person of Mr W.H. Elgar, father of Edward. He played second violin. At that time Louis D'Egville was leader, and the band included three or four members of the Hopkins family and Messrs Holloway and Rickus of the Cathedral choir. Corelli was largely drawn upon, Handel's Overture to *Saul* was a favourite, and Haydn's symphonies were often heard. The rich store of our great glee writers furnished the vocal music, and they were very well done in those days. Not many songs were sung, and they were of a healthy, vigorous type.

'Commodore' Hood was chairman, and his speeches on the opening night of the season, liberally interlarded with nautical terms, caused much amusement and are now remembered as being very remarkable. People came from far and near; one old clergyman from Bromyard was a regular attendant, walking in on Tuesday, staying at the hotel all night, and walking back on Wednesday. Commercial men so timed their journeys as to be at Worcester on a Tuesday, and one of the fraternity showed his appreciation of the pleasure he received by presenting to the club a grand pianoforte. The late Dr Done was one of the pianists of those days, and many amusing stories are told of that time. One of the richest was of a visit to a double-bass player, who was found to be so engrossed in a passage of Corelli's that he did not hear the repeated knockings at the door of his room, which, when opened, revealed the artist, in a great state of determination to master the difficulty, keeping time by an improvised metronome which consisted of a half-brick slung by a rope from a hook fixed to one of the beams in the ceiling.

Mr Edward Elgar was drafted in to play first violin when a small boy, Mr Spray being leader, and Mr A.R. Quarterman, pianist. Mr Henry Elgar (who had joined in 1850) rendered very able assistance at the harmonium on 'instrumental' and ordinary nights. Great changes had taken place in the instrumental music — Rossini, Auber, Mozart, Wallace, Balfe, Bishop, Bellini, and others being represented by overtures. The glees, etc, of S.S. Wesley, Walmisley, Beale, G.W. Martin, Goss, and Cummings were added to those of the old composers, and the modern English and German part-songs found a place in the programmes, which also contained a goodly number of high-class songs. For about two years Edward was accompanist. In this his marked ability was at once manifest, though he would always insist that he was not a pianist. His accompaniments were a great delight to singers and audience. Programmes had now been printed some years. In 1879 we find him announced as 'pianist and conductor', and four members of the family appear in the list of the band, which then embraced all the wood-wind. The young conductor and leader, as was to be expected, brought forward music of the modern school, which he arranged for his small means with great skill, and took great pains to rehearse the young players in their, to them, perhaps, difficult parts, no doubt gaining in this way much knowledge which has proved very useful. Many pieces of his own composition for the glee party, band, and solo voices appeared in the programmes, and were always received with favour and created an interest in the future of the young musician, though few at that time discerned the bright light which was to break upon these later days.

Is it not a thousand pities that this time-honoured practice of glee and unaccompanied part-singing should be in danger of suffering neglect? It is an inheritance peculiar to this land of ours that should be cherished and carefully nurtured.

A great event in the young man's life was his visit to London in the autumn of 1877 to take a short course of lessons on the violin from Mr Pollitzer. He stayed in London for twelve days at a cost £7 15s 9d, which amount included £3 12s 6d for his five lessons and his railway fare. Elgar had saved out of his scanty earnings the necessary wherewithal for this lesson-taking expedition, and he enjoyed the supreme satisfaction of relying upon his own resources and making the most of his self-made opportunities during his sojourn in London 'down Pimlico way'.

Mr Pollitzer, in recalling those days, says: 'I always thought him a most earnest musician . . . . Mr Elgar, although leaning towards the modern German school, does not lose either his love or respect for the composers of the past.'

In the year 1879 Edward Elgar, aged twenty-two, became bandmaster at the County Lunatic Asylum, which post he held for a period of five years. 'No wonder that Elgar's music is so mad,' some unthinking individual may be ready to exclaim; therefore it may be just as well to state that the young bandmaster's duties were associated with the attendants, and not with the poor unfortunate patients in the wards. One whole day every week Elgar spent at the Asylum, where he not only conducted the band, formed of the attendants, but coached the individual players in their respective instruments. The band consisted of

Flute	Euphonium	Violins (1 and 2)
Clarinet	Bombardon	Pianoforte (with
Cornets (1 and 2)	Double-bass	occasional additions)

For this curious combination of players upon instruments Elgar wrote some sets of quadrilles, polkas, etc, for which he received from the Board the regulation payment of five shillings per set! He also arranged accompaniments for Christy Minstrel songs, at the remuneration of eighteenpence per burnt-cork ditty. 'How lowering to his taste,' someone may be inclined to remark. Not so, good reader. This practical experience proved to be of the greatest value to the young musician and the future composer of *The Dream of Gerontius*. He acquired a *practical* knowledge of the capabilities of these different instruments — not only by hearing them, but in those hours of 'coaching', when flute, clarinet, and so on, talked to him, so to speak, in their own language. He thereby got to know intimately the tone colour, the ins and outs of these and many other instruments. Thus when he conceives a certain phrase he instinctively feels the double association of the melody and the instrument that is to play it — not a tune that might be given to this or that member of the orchestral family, but the colourable conception of the theme and its absolute fitness for a particular instrument. There is a great deal more in the cultivation of this tone-colour in music than most people realise. But to return to — or take our places for — the Elgarian quadrilles. It may not be without interest to give an eight-bar specimen of one of these dance tunes (unpublished, of course) composed for the Lunatic Asylum band which the composer has kindly reduced to pianoforte score specially for this article —

QUADRILLES FOR AN ECCENTRIC ORCHESTRA.

Mr Elgar was professor of the violin at the Worcester College for the Blind Sons of Gentlemen. His most distinguished pupil there was Mr William Wolstenholme, the well-known composer, to whom Elgar showed great kindness. He wrote down the whole of young Wolstenholme's 'exercise' from his dictation. But this was not all. When young Wolstenholme was about to go up to Oxford to be examined for his Bachelor in Music degree, the Principal of the College said to Elgar: 'I don't know how Willie will get on at Oxford; he is so nervous with a strange amanuensis. Could you not manage to go up with him?' Always ready to lend a helping hand to anyone, Elgar at once said 'Yes', and spent three days at Oxford, rendering valuable help to his clever sightless pupil.

Up to the year 1889, Mr Elgar continued to practise his profession in his native city and its neighbourhood by teaching and playing in the orchestra. He made his first appearance at a Three Choirs Festival in 1878 (at Worcester), when he played as a humble second fiddler in the orchestra. Some of his recollections of orchestral makeshifts at the Worcester concerts of his early days are very amusing. For instance, a performance of *Elijah* with the accompaniment of strings, one clarinet, one trombone, and one harmonium. The opening phrase of Macfarren's overture to

St John the Baptist, assigned by the composer to the trumpet (Shophar), played on the organ, with the registration of diapasons and mixtures! At the urgent request of Mr Henry Elgar the passage was allowed to be played on the alto trombone. Again, the absence of any bass in purely wood-wind passages owing to there being no second bassoon player. No one, except Elgar, seemed to miss it, and no one in authority thought of supplying the missing bass on any other instrument.

A much better state of things prevailed in Birmingham, where Mr Elgar was a valued member of Mr Stockley's orchestra. It was Mr Stockley who first introduced our composer to a larger public than that of Worcester. The occasion was one of the veteran conductor's orchestral concerts, given on 13th December 1883, in the programme of which there figured *Intermezzo* (Elgar). Even the title of this early achievement furnished a certain amount of 'copy' for one of the critics, just as the *Variations* did for certain of the London scribes sixteen years later. This is what the gentleman of the press said:-

> Judging from results, the director will not regret giving a helping hand to rising talent. The *Intermezzo* written by a permanent member of Mr Stockley's orchestra, Mr Elgar, justifies his assumption of a place in the programme. He dubs his piece *Mauresque;* but why Mauresque? If we eliminate some of the unimportant effects supposed to give local colour, the term goes by the board. After all, however, 'What's in a name?' and waiving this prevalent but not always justifiable musical nomenclature, we hasten to give Mr Elgar every credit for a musicianly work. A unanimous recall served to discover quite a young composer to the audience; and, as Mr Elgar is not deficient in scholarship, has plenty of fancy, and orchestrates with facility, we may hope he will not 'rest and be thankful', but go on in a path for which he possesses singular qualifications.

One is sometimes tempted to ask: 'What's in a criticism?'

In connection with the performance above referred to, Mr W.C. Stockley writes us under date 12th September 1900:-

> Mr Elgar played in my orchestra for some little time as a first violin. But my first real knowledge of him came from Dr Herbert Wareing, who told me that Elgar was a clever writer, and suggested that I should play one of his compositions at one of my concerts. At my request Wareing brought me a Romance (I think it was), and I at once recognised its merit and offered to play it. This I did, and his modesty on the occasion is certainly worth notice, for on my asking him if he would like to conduct, he declined, and, further, insisted upon playing in his place in the orchestra. The consequence was that

he had to appear, fiddle in hand, to acknowledge the genuine and hearty applause of the audience. Soon after he did me the honour of dedicating an orchestral piece to me, entitled *Sevillaña*, which I also did at one of my concerts. The occasion I have referred to was, *I think*, the first introduction, on a large scale, of any of Elgar's compositions, and thus you may think it worth mentioning.

Returning to the Worcester period, it must be recorded that in the year 1882 Mr Elgar paid a visit to Leipzig, where he sojourned for three weeks, listening to all the music that was available in that musical centre. In the same year (1882) he became conductor of the Worcester Amateur Instrumental Society, and wrote notes for the analytical porgrammes of the interesting concerts given by that Society. In 1885 he succeeded his father as organist of St George's Roman Catholic Church, Worcester. Anyone going into the organ loft of that church may find large manuscript volumes containing many sketches and small compositions written by the composer of *King Olaf*. He resigned this organistship in 1889, and has not since held an appointment. All this time of weary waiting to be 'discovered', Mr Elgar was composing, composing, composing. He wrote several Masses and other church music and heaps of chamber music, all of which, it is perhaps hardly necessary to say, remains in manuscript.

On 8 May 1889, Mr Elgar married the only daughter of the late Major-General Sir Henry Gee Roberts, K.C.B., a very distinguished Indian officer, and who received the thanks of Parliament for his brilliant military services. On her mother's side, Mrs Edward Elgar is descended from the celebrated Robert Raikes, the founder of Sunday Schools.

After his marriage he decided to reside in London, though he still retained a connection with his native heath by a weekly visit to Malvern to fulfil teaching engagements. He also led the orchestra in important concerts at Worcester. For these perform-ances he always charged a fee, which, however, he remitted on the understanding that the amount (three guineas) should be expended on making the band more complete. But no one in London would look at his compositions. Three chances presented themselves, each of which would have been a good 'open door' to the young man from the faithful city; but the great metropolis proved unfaithful to him and the wind of fate closed those doors with a bang, almost before the handles had been turned. He left London in 1891 and for the last nine years has resided at Malvern, where on the production of *King Olaf* in 1896, at the Hanley

Festival, appreciation and fame at length came to him. He now devotes himself entirely to composition, amidst ideal surroundings for a composer of poetic temperament who loves the open-air life and all the delights of hills, and fields, and flowers.

The following is an attempt at a complete list of Mr Elgar's *published* compositions, with the names of librettists of choral works and the dates of first performances:

CANTATAS

The Black Knight (Der schwarze Ritter), (Op. 25). The poem by Uhland, translated by Longfellow. (Worcester Festival Choral Society, 1893.)
Scenes from the Bavarian Highlands (Op. 27), chorus and orchestra. (Worcester Festival Choral Society, April 1896.)
Scenes from the Saga of King Olaf (Op. 30). Poem by Longfellow, with additions by H.A. Acworth, C.I.E. (North Staffordshire Musical Festival, Hanley, 1896.)
The Banner of St George (Op. 33). The words by Shapcott Wensley. (The Queen's Diamond Jubilee celebrations, 1897.)
Caractacus (Op. 35). Words by H.A. Acworth, C.I.E. (Leeds Musical Festival, 1899.)

SACRED WORKS

The Light of Life (Lux Christi), (Op. 29). The words written and arranged by the Rev E. Capel-Cure. (Worcester Musical Festival, 1896.)
Te Deum and Benedictus in F (Op. 34), for chorus, orchestra, and organ. (Hereford Musical Festival, 1897.)
The Dream of Gerontius (Op. 38). Words by John Henry Newman. (Birmingham Musical Festival, 1900.)
Litanies and other church music.

ORCHESTRA

Froissart, Concert-Overture (Op. 19). (Worcester Musical Festival, 1890.)
Three Pieces (Op. 10). *Mazurka, Sérénade Mauresque,* and *Contrasts (the Gavotte, AD 1700 and 1900).*
Imperial March (Op. 32). (Queen's Diamond Jubilee, 1897.)
Variations on an original theme (Op. 36). (Richter Concert, London, 19th June 1899.)

VOCAL MUSIC

Spanish Serenade (Op. 23) for chorus and orchestra.
Sea Pictures (Op. 37), words by various poets, for contralto solo voice and orchestra (sung by Miss Clara Butt at the Norwich Musical Festival, 1899).
Three-part songs (Op. 26) for female voices; part-songs (unaccompanied), songs, etc.

INSTRUMENTAL (VARIOUS)

Pieces for violin and pianoforte; pianoforte solos; a Sonata for the organ (composed for the visit of the American musicians to Worcester Cathedral in July, 1895), and a book of organ voluntaries.

Amongst a large number of manuscript compositions are symphonies, quartets, trios, etc.

As we have already mentioned, Mr Elgar now devotes himself entirely to composition, with, however, one exception — that is, the conductorship of the Worcestershire Philharmonic Society. This organisation, founded in 1898, is in an extremely flourishing condition with its 300 subscribing members. All the rehearsals and concerts take place in the day-time. Every work is given absolutely complete in regard to detail. 'If a composition required forty harps, forty harps would be supplied, even if they had only to play three notes,' emphatically observes the enthusiastic and thorough-going conductor. It is no wonder that the motto of the Society is 'Wach' auf!' It is only just to a valued colleague to mention that Mr Elgar receives the greatest assistance from his excellent accompanist and sub-conductor, Mr G. Street Chignell, of Worcester.

It is now time to refer to the personality of the subject of this biographical sketch, though this is not an easy matter through the medium of cold type. In the first place, Mr Elgar is another instance of success following upon self-help of which so many examples have been furnished in this series of biographical sketches during the last three years. With the exception of those violin lessons from Mr Pollitzer, Mr Elgar is entirely self-taught. He has spared no pains, energy, or trouble in the acquirement of the necessary equipment for his life-work. For instance, in his youthful days he would leave his home at Worcester at six o'clock in the morning, and travel all the way to London, a distance of 250 miles, in order to listen to a Crystal Palace Saturday concert, returning at 10.30pm.

'I have never had a lesson in orchestration in my life,' says Mr Elgar. All his achievements in this direction are the result of practical experience, keen observation, and constant study of scores. There are some people who think that he could only have acquired this wonderful knowledge of orchestral artisticness — the word 'effects' is too commonplace in such a connection — from some ponderous theoretical tome. Here is a letter that he has recently received:

> SIR, — I am anxious to study orchestration. As you appear to have mastered the art, kindly tell me from which book you learnt it. — Yours truly,
>
> *** * ***

Another is from a correspondent who frankly confesses entire ignorance of the 'Euphenium', and whose communication implies that the air should occasionally be given to the drums! But the would-be orchestratist must speak for herself:

> I am sending my humble attempt. I *copied* the *names of the instruments* from a score that was *lent me last summer. What the Euphenium* IS, *or how to write for drums I have* NO IDEA. It would be a great help if you would write over the piano score in pencil when to give the air to other instruments. I have *no conception of how what I have written would sound.* If I could borrow *some more scores* of waltzes, I feel it would help me very much. Do the cornets and violas have the tum tum accomp. always? *That must be dull for them to play.* I have not sent the *coda* as it will be the same as the first movement, with a few bars to finish with. I forgot to pack up Mr Prout's book on instrumentation so I daresay the double notes to *second violins may be all wrong, and a great deal else besides.* It is very good of you to take so much trouble.

> P.S. — You see I have condensed every two bars into one in the first movement since I showed it you.

The use of the *Leitmotiv* is a well-known characteristic of Mr Elgar's method in composition. In this connection he has been charged with copying Wagner. 'But', he observes, 'I became acquainted with the representative-theme long before I had ever heard a note of Wagner, or seen one of his scores. My first acquaintance with the *Leitmotiv* was derived (in my boyhood) from Mendelssohn's *Elijah,* and the system elaborated from that, as my early unpublished things show.'

The personality of a man often shows itself in his letters. Here are a few extracts from sundry communications to the present writer which may be offered as samples of an epistolary style that is decidedly fresh and unconventional in its mode of expression:

> . . . As to myself the following are F A X about me. Just completed a set of Symphonic Variations (theme original) for orchestra — thirteen in number (but I call the *finale* the fourteenth, because of the ill-luck attaching to the number). I have in the Variations sketched portraits of my friends — a new idea, I think — that is, in each variation I have looked at the theme *through* the personality (as it were) of another Johnny. I don't know if 'tis too intimate an idea for print, it's distinctly amusing . . . .

Other compositions are nebulous at present.

Also the bulbs are coming up at the Cottage and the draw-well is being pumpified — but that won't interest you.

In connection with these much discussed Variations, Mr Elgar tells us that the heading *Enigma* is justified by the fact that it is possible to add another phrase, which is quite familiar, above the original theme that he has written. What that theme is no one knows except the composer. Thereby hangs the *Enigma*.

> . . . I've just finished a *Partrigal** (S.A.T.B.) to order and feel weak.
>> Always yours,
>>> EDWARD ELGAR.

* I make you a present of this word. It is what is known to the cataloguist as a 'Madrigalian Part-Song'.

> . . . I SAY: I went over to Sheffield to conduct a Festival rehearsal. Do you know that the chorus is absolutely the finest in the world! Not so large as Leeds, but for fire, intelligence, dramatic force, they are electrical. *Do* go to the Festival. For the first time in my life I've heard *my* choral effects (*Olaf*) and very terrifying they are.
>> LAUS DEO!
>>> (and COWARDUS).

Like many earnest and even serious-minded men, Mr Elgar has a pretty wit in his walk (or walks) and conversation. A clever musical instance of this is furnished in the following Tschaïkow-skian version of *God save the Queen*, which, notwithstanding its *à la Russe* superstructure of five-four time, furnishes a sort of sixes and sevens touch to the rhythm of our National Anthem:

One of the treasures in the study is the baton used by Mr Elgar on all festival occasions, and on which he has inscribed the titles of works conducted therewith and the dates of all their various performances. Upon his attention being directed to the remark-able indentations of the upper end of the stick, Mr Elgar says: 'Oh! Parry did all those. He used this baton at a performance of his *Judith* at Worcester in 1891. I played first fiddle then and put my stick on his desk. I wanted to make it immortal. He did not break it!'

The composer of *King Olaf* is a great lover of books. He not only reads and digests them, but carefully marks what seem to him to be striking points as specially worthy of attention. Some prized first editions are in his library. Pictures of every school, and literature, especially of the last century, have a strong fascination for him, also old furniture, of which he has many interesting specimens. In addition to his house at Malvern he has a tiny cottage in the woods, far away from the hum of human life, trains, and even tramps. Here, five miles from a railway station, he makes sketches and orchestrates amidst surroundings that are as beautiful as they are tranquil and brain-refreshing. We give a view of this solitary domicile where dress suits are unsuitable.

A former hobby of our composer was scientific kite flying. His great idea was to invent a kite which would enable him to vary its surface resistance according to the force of the wind that was blowing. He made many experiments, but as the Americans are similarly at work on a colossal scale, he has given up the pastime of kite flying. He used to have a string of kites, of various shapes and sizes, one under the other. So strong in mid air was their resistance to their captive rope that, on one occasion, he and a friend, pulling with all their might, could not bring high-flyer down to earth without invoking the aid of a strong navvy. Golf — how he loves it — and bicycling have superseded kite flying as outdoor recreations.

Before bidding adieu to one of the foremost of British composers of the present day, it is only natural that some information should be sought from him on the subject of his latest work, *The Dream of Gerontius,* which is so soon to be produced at the Birmingham Festival. 'This is the beginning of it', he says, as he hands us a little copy of Newman's famous poem.

The book was a wedding present to me (in 1889) from the late Father Knight, of Worcester, at whose church I was organist. Before giving it to me he copied into its pages every mark inserted by General Gordon into his (Gordon's) copy, so that I have the advantage of knowing those portions of the poem that had specially attracted the attention of the great hero. It seems absurd to say that I have written the work to order for Birmingham. The poem has been soaking in my mind for at least eight years. All that time I have been gradually assimilating the thoughts of the author into my own musical promptings.

It is in this spirit that Edward Elgar conscientiously follows the bent of his genius. A man of high ideals, the possessor of a fine artistic temperament, and an intensely poetical musician, he is known and respected for his kind-heartedness, his modesty, his sincerity, and his steadfastness of purpose. He has already achieved great things in the realm of art and has come into the front rank of English composers.

The Musical Times,
1st October 1900

PART II: THE ENIGMA

The Enigma — 1
by Richard C. Powell

Mr Richard Powell entered the Elgar saga through his marriage to Dora Penny (Dorabella *of the* Variations). *In this article, written shortly after Lady Elgar's death in 1920, he propounded publicly for the first time what has remained one of the most plausible of purely musical theories to explain the Enigma.*

In the year 1920 I became obsessed by the puzzle presented in Elgar's *Enigma Variations*. A good deal of thought resulted in the writing of an argument which I discussed with some of my friends in the musical profession. It was suggested to me at the time that the argument should be published, but my conviction that the matter would be distasteful to Elgar forbade it. The argument has been unaffected by the passing of thirteen years and is printed below without alteration.

As the name (Enigma) implies, the original theme of the Elgar *Variations for Orchestra,* published in 1899, contains a puzzle the solution of which has never been made public. It is very probable now (August 1920), since the death of Lady Elgar, that only the composer knows the solution.[1] It is common knowledge that the *Variations* are musical pictures of certain of Sir Edward Elgar's friends and the work is dedicated to 'My friends pictured within.' Although Elgar has never explained the mystery of the original theme, he has made certain statements regarding it which have been generally understood to mean that the theme is a sort of counterpoint on another air that could be superimposed upon it and would fit in with it, and it is easy to understand that anyone having knowledge of this air would 'mentally' hear it when the theme was played.

This is the conclusion that has been drawn from the statement of the composer that another tune 'goes with' the theme. In his book, *Elgar,* Mr. Ernest Newman, dealing with the *Variations,* has written as follows: 'The meaning of the word "Enigma" in

---

[1] I have reason to think that Lady Elgar was the composer's only confidante.

connection with the score is that, according to the composer, "another and larger" theme which is never heard "goes with" the theme we hear and with each variation of it; but what this other enigmatic theme is, nobody knows.'[2]

So far as I am aware Elgar has never given the smallest indication as to what sort of tune the tune 'that goes' is, whether a subject from some classical work, a traditional melody, or some air to be found in church music, but one of two things is clearly certain: either the tune in question is almost unknown, or else he chose a fairly (or very) familiar tune and wrote his theme in such a fashion that it is most unlikely to suggest to anyone the true explanation.

It seems quite safe to use this argument as a great number of people must have tried, in the last twenty-one years, to unearth the solution of the mystery and, as far as I can learn, no one has succeeded.

Granting this point, it is clear that one must either look for a tune that one probably does not know, or for a more or less familiar air that will not, at first sight, appear to fit any too well. With this difficulty to face it appears to me that the best method to pursue in attempting to solve the problem is to ignore for the moment the text of the music and try to construct a hypothesis, considering only the general form of the work and the known circumstances under which it was composed. Attacking the problem from this angle two facts stand out: (1) it was written about the composer's friends; (2) it was written for the composer's friends.

It is worth while to note that the persons portrayed and commemorated in this fashion were not celebrities; they were friends, close friends, and in one case more than that. Another reflection suggests itself; it is almost impossible to believe that Elgar, when thinking out the scheme of this very peculiar, if not unique, work, would select for his unheard melody a tune drawn from the classics or the church, for it must be remembered that most of the friends commemorated were only amateur musicians and one was not even musical. Furthermore, most of them were not of his religion.

The conclusion is thrust upon one that the tune must be a tune which everybody knows, the more so in that the spiritual

---

[2] The assertion that the unheard theme 'goes with' all the Variations seems, on the face of it, absurd, the treatment of the theme in the different variations being so diverse.

connection and impulse would be very weak if the tune were unknown to the subjects of the work. If, then, the tune is one which everybody, even the unmusical, is sure to know, it must be a traditional song: no other kind of tune could possibly meet this requirement.

Following this line of constructive reasoning, the tune to look for is a very well-known traditional song having peculiar associations with the idea of friendship.

There is one song in English, and I think only one, which exactly fulfils these conditions; namely, *Auld Lang Syne*. I think it is safe to say that everyone who is capable of knowing a tune at all must know that, and its associations with friendship are unique.

Take then, the tune of *Auld Lang Syne* and see how it fits in with the theme of the *Variations*. In accordance with the argument previously put forward this tune, being very well known, must not be expected to fit well at first sight; nor does it, being in the major, whereas the theme of the *Variations* begins in the minor, to mention only one difficulty. But it will be found that this is one of the rather uncommon tunes the first half of which can be turned into the tonic minor without any trouble and with the minimum of melodic alteration.

Auld Lang Syne begins on the fourth beat of the bar and the theme on the first, so it is necessary to leave the first note of *Auld Lang Syne* hung up in the air, so to speak, synchronising the first beat of the second bar with the first beat of the first bar in the theme. Then it will be found that two bars of *Auld Lang Syne* are equivalent to one bar of the theme and that the first section will come to an end on the third beat of the fourth bar of the theme.

Leaving that point for the moment and turning to the text of the theme it will be seen that at the end of the sixth bar a double bar is written which appears to be quite pointless on the printed page; but it is not uncommon for a double bar to be written between the first section and the refrain of such a tune as *Auld Lang Syne:* this is suggestive. After the double bar in the theme the key changes from G minor to G major, returning after four bars to a slightly altered repetition of the first section. The four-bar major section of the theme will be found to fit in the most remarkable way with the eight-bar refrain of *Auld Lang Syne,* both harmonically and — which cannot be described — sympathetically. After this the repeated first section of the theme and the first section of *Auld Lang Syne* run concurrently, again in the minor, for three bars and three beats, at which point *Auld Lang Syne* ends.

Now, if this is carefully gone into it will be found that there is only one thing really wrong and that is that the first section of the theme and its subsequent repetition are too long. This objection cannot be disposed of, as far as I can see at present, except on the ground that the composer found it impossible to hide *Auld Lang Syne* as much as he wished if he made all three sections of his theme the right length, and so he adopted the plan of extending the first section and its repetition.[3] Whether this is the true explanation or not, if the composer had kept his theme to the correct length the mystery would not have remained unsolved till now; the mere rhythm would surely have given it away almost at once. This last assertion assumes, of course, that the result arrived at is correct, but if incorrect it would be applicable in some degree to any other well-known tune.

That there is a considerable weight of evidence to support the conclusion reached is undeniable, how much it is only possible to demonstrate with the additional aid of a piano and a voice. There are also certain minor indications tending in the same direction of which I have not made use; but, even with these added, it is impossible to arrive at absolute certainty failing a statement by Elgar himself, or by some person who has shared his knowledge.

I think it very likely that we shall never have this certainty. When Elgar wrote the work he probably thought that someone would guess the truth almost at once and he would not have cared if it had then become public property; but after the lapse of twenty years which have seen the death of several of the friends, one can understand that he might shrink from recalling buried memories.

Elgar's *The Music Makers* should be studied in relation to the whole of the foregoing argument. In this work the composer made numerous quotations from his own compositions and their appositeness from his point of view may be presumed. Fragments of the enigma theme appear more than once and a knowledge of the composer's psychology and personal history are necessary for an understanding of the use which he has here made of them.

It has been suggested that the idea of an unheard melody 'going with' the theme of the Variations was in the nature of a leg-pull on the part of the composer. Without going into details I may say that the strongest evidence exists in disproof of this suggestion. There is no doubt whatever that the Enigma did exist; the question is now, does it exist any longer?

---

[3] It seems possible to me that the composer may regard these extensions as pieces of 'symphony.'

To the above article the editor of Music and Letters, *A.H. Fox Strangways added the following paragraphs:*

The author of this article has been careful to base his argument solely on what he actually knows. Taking that argument as it stands, it is permissible to point to a passage in the Finale, **65**.5 to **66**.4 (repeated at **74**) which may be considered to be circumstantial evidence.

1. Whatever the buried tune were, it could hardly help being at least hinted at in the Finale, in which most of the salient themes of the *Variations* appear. This eight-bar tune is not one of those themes: there is nothing at all like it on any preceding page, and the novelty of the section is perhaps announced by the double-bar.

2. In this section the metre (- ᴜ - -) is the same as in *Auld Lang Syne,* the time (common) is the same, and the key (G) is the same as it was in the Andante. The tempo of the buried tune is practically the same, for by the metronome the four bars of Andante would play fifteen seconds and the eight bars of Allegro twelve seconds, which the *poco più tranquillo* would increase to about fifteen seconds; that is, a tune whose bars are half-bars of Andante is at the same pace as one in which they are whole bars of Allegro.

3. This **65**-tune corresponds closely in its general lie with the eight bars which form the second half of *Auld Lang Syne:* both rise to the submediant at the halfway-house, in both the melodic phrase synchronises with the bar, and in both the bars are grouped as 2+2+4. Also, *Auld Lang Syne* has at the end of each bar an upward fling, and this **65**-tune has at the end of each bar a downward droop.

Supposing a composer wished to set an ingenious puzzle, these are some of the methods he might adopt.

Music & Letters,
July 1934

The Enigma — II
by A.H. Fox Strangways

A.H. Fox Strangways was the editor of Music & Letters when Richard Powell published his proposed solution to the Enigma and, as will have been observed, he added certain observations of his own in support of the theory. In the following issue he perhaps found it necessary to redress the balance by writing, as it were, a letter to himself casting doubt on the ideas that had been put forward.

I enjoyed Mr R.C. Powell's article on the *Enigma* and your editorial comment thereon, and have followed some of the correspondence to which they gave rise.

We are concerned more with the tune itself, *Auld Lang Syne*, than with the process by which it was discovered. The mention of it has raised three objections:

(a) that a tune so trite and with such superficial or perfunctory associations is unworthy of Elgar's work;

(b) that A.L.S. can hardly be called a 'larger' tune, and that it does not 'go with' all the variations; and

(c) that it does not go properly even with the original statement of the theme.

Let us examine these.

(a) If A.L.S. *is* the hidden tune, its triteness may possibly be a reason why Elgar did not actually insert it, but left it in the first instance as a puzzle for his friends. As to the associations, they *are* a drawback, but the tune is sound and pentatonic enough; and because a tune, like a word, is often used in a paltry sense it does not follow that we should not use it occasionally in its right sense. The fear that we shall never again be able to hear the *Enigma* without thinking of A.L.S. seems to me as groundless as a fear that we shall always hear 'Yehudi Menuhin' at a particular moment in the Violin Concerto or 'Alassio' in a particular phrase of *In the South*. I tried deliberately to hear A.L.S. in the *Enigma* at Leeds in October, and found that the flow and ingenuity of the whole thing swept me past it.

(b) What Elgar may have meant by 'a larger tune' we can only

guess, since we do not know what tune he had in mind. All we
know is that he was setting a puzzle, because he said so, and that
implies that it was some generally accepted tune; and a tune
generally accepted might well be described as 'larger' than the
theme of a particular composition. His composition is to us now so
distinguished that we may feel inclined to reverse the comparison;
but Elgar's modesty was not in a position to do that at the
beginning of the century when he used the word.

I cannot make out that he actually said that the tune goes with
all the variations; but if he did say it, what he may have meant by
'goes with' may perhaps be argued from two instances. In the
'Romanza' he quotes Mendelssohn, and the only traces of his
own theme in that whole variation are the viola sixths which
accompany the clarinet and the unison at **58**; but they are enough
to entitle it to be called a variation. Again, in 'Nimrod' (who used
to discourse to him on the slow movements of Beethoven's
sonatas) Elgar has told us that the opening bars are made to
suggest the *Pathétique*, a thing which few would have thought of
unaided. His quotations are therefore elusive. His music is full, in
fact, as his life was, of the treasuring up and chortling over little
oddities and appropriatenesses of word, action, or event: this
playful allusiveness was to him the salt of life. We shall hardly be
wrong if we take this to be what he meant by one thing 'going
with' another.

(c) The matter has, however, been narrowed down mainly to
the question whether A.L.S. fits the explicit theme of the *Enigma*.
We may brush aside the objection that it has to be turned into the
minor in order to fit, since there is a perfectly good musical reason
for the *theme* being in the minor, viz., to balance the preponder-
ance of major variations. Meanwhile, if A.L.S. is the implicit
tune, the minor, or some similar device, is required to hold a *tune*
so commonplace at a respective distance, as Stanford also found
with this same tune in *The Critic*. And we need not waste time in
explaining that when a song is put into full dress it usually has a
few bars to introduce it or, as here, to dismiss it.

The clashes, small or great, which are involved do not seem
much more daring than in the second Rasoumoffsky (Russian
theme). We must however attend to bars 4 and 9, which are
described as being not what Elgar would write. The point of the
criticism of bar 4 has escaped me: it seems to me very much what
he *would* write, and not unlike what he *did* write in *The Apostles* (at
'Save me, I perish,' **103,** and 'I have sinned,' **169**) to go no further.
Bar 9 undoubtedly does not fit, though it is more euphonious than

those suggest who quote only the inner parts, since the holding notes of flute and hautboy tell more than the moving parts of the strings. But the composer could have made it fit with a turn of the wrist if he had wanted to: it is not difficult, in fact, to see the small change in the note-values which would do it — as, also, why he did not make such a change. What he did write at the corresponding place is seen in Variation I (at **3**.3), but that, being in contrary motion, is different. More conclusive, however, are certain 'consecutives' which have been pointed out as between A.L.S. and the theme, which are not in his manner. When he wants consecutives he takes them as in bar 6 — the identical pair, as it happens, that Stanford wrote in 'When I listen to thy voice' — but it is inconceivable that anyone should write incidental consecutive octaves between treble and bass, such as would have been involved where the major section begins.

All this only supports Mr. Powell's postulate, that the 'familiar air' must be one which will not, at first sight, appear to fit any too well.' Lest any should think, however, that this is merely an extenuating plea offered by one who has a weak case, some evidence is forthcoming which no one will dispute. A friend, a Mr Hussey, wrote in 1929 to ask Elgar if A.L.S. *was* the implicit tune. A postcard came back which he allows me to quote: 'No Auld Lang Syne won't do. E.E.'

Now 'won't do' is quite as cryptic as 'goes with' and 'larger'. Did he mean 'won't answer my conundrum', or 'won't fit my theme', or simply, 'I am not going to say yes or no to your question'? I think he meant all three; for obviously A.L.S. does not fit even the theme exactly, and as he had kept his secret for so many years he was obviously not going to blab it now. As to A.L.S. being the solution of his puzzle, it is possible to think that the truthful answer might have been either yes or no: in the following way, among many ways in which the thing might have happened.

Suppose that he heard this tune at some gathering and with it heard in his head, as anyone might, some sort of counterpoint; that this counterpoint interested him and he worked it out, and played the result to his wife one night; that when she asked what it was, he said 'Nothing' (because at that moment it was nothing), 'but something might be made of it' (because he was already partly foreseeing the use he would make of it); and that when he came to be immersed in his work he thought no more of the original tune, only of his own invention — in his own words, 'I could go on with those themes (not, that theme) for half a day.'

Suppose all that, or some similar incidents, would it not be equally true if he asserted at one time that 'there is a larger theme which goes with mine,' and denied at another that any particular tune was that theme?

The gravamen of the whole matter is that the suggestion of such a tune as this in some way belittles Elgar — that by such a treatment of it he shows himself less of an artist than we know him to be. But is that so? Take this little story. He was staying at a country house where a German ambassador and his wife also were staying, and on Sunday none of the three went to church with the rest, because they were of another religion. The Germans walked in the garden, and when they came to the maze, Elgar heard him persuading her to go in — 'es ist ja ganz leicht!' He also saw, from a neighbouring rise, the ambassador take fragments of paper out of his pocket and drop them at corners. He entered after them and dropped other paper at other corners. When his design had succeeded and the ambassadress, a little footsore, was now beginning to tell her husband what she thought of him, Elgar emerged and blandly asked if he could be of any help. The husband, with rage in his eye and suspicion in his heart, thanked him; and the incident closed.

And put with that a little story of another artist, Vivier, who also died in sole possession of *his* secret (of blowing four simultaneous notes on the horn). Sitting one day in a diligence he suddenly began to feel in every pocket for some document of importance, as his face showed it to be. Finding at last in a hip-pocket a bit of paper he read it intently, started, threw it down, and rushed out. A passenger picked it up and found — a blank sheet.

A man does not cease to be an artist because he can enjoy fun that has nothing to do with his art. But when he can combine the two it is possible that he may enhance both; and we may then even think him more, not less, of an artist.

I must apologise for the length of this letter; but as someone asked me to induce my friend, the Editor of this magazine to 'kill all this nonsense about the *Enigma*,' I thought I had better be explicit.

Music & Letters,
January 1935

The Enigma III
by Professor Sir Jack Westrup

The title of this paper is intentionally ambiguous. It is meant to be taken in its most obvious sense as a reference to Elgar's Variations. But it also implies a discussion of the composer's personality. The two topics are inevitably linked, and one throws light on the other. I cannot promise a brilliant illumination, and it is better to say straight away that I offer no startling revelations. But I hope it may be possible to suggest trains of thought which others can work on. In a sense this is an interim report. I have been thinking about this subject now for several years, and I expect to go on thinking about it for a good many years to come. There might be an argument for suspending judgment until my own mind is clearer. But as I still cannot see daylight at the end of the tunnel I thought it would be worth while to set down what ideas I have on paper and subject them to the scrutiny of a critical audience.

It is a good idea to start with facts, particularly as these are often misrepresented. The work which we are going to discuss is entitled *Variations on an Original Theme for Orchestra*. The first page gives us the first six bars of the theme, followed by a double bar. Above this is printed the single word 'Enigma'. This heading somehow came to give its name to the whole work. Everyone nowadays speaks of the 'Engima Variations'. But this is not the title which Elgar gave them, nor does he refer to them by this name in his correspondence. At what point the heading 'Enigma' was introduced is not clear. From the autograph[1] it looks as if it was added after the score was completed. The original sketch[2] bears the inscription 'Theme'.

What does 'Enigma' mean? The composer answered this question — or rather refused to answer it — in the programme notes which he wrote for the first performance:

The Engima I will not explain — its 'dark saying' must be left

---

[1] Facsimile of p. 2 in *My Friends Pictured Within*, London, n.d.
[2] Facsimile in Percy M. Young, *Elgar O.M.*, London, 1955, facing p. 113.

unguessed, and I warn you that the apparent connection between
the Variations and the Theme is often of the slightest texture;
further, through and over the whole set another and larger theme
'goes', but is not played . . . So the principal Theme never appears,
even as in some late dramas — e.g., Maeterlinck's 'L'Intruse' and
'Les Sept Princesses' — the chief character is never on the stage.[3]

On the other hand he was rather more explicit when he came to
write about *The Music Makers* in 1912:

> I have used the opening bars of the theme (Enigma) of the
> Variations because it expressed when written (in 1898) my sense of
> the loneliness of the artist as described in the first six lines of the Ode
> and to me it still embodies that sense; at the end of the score of the
> Variations I wrote 'Bramo assai, poco spero, nulla chieggio' (Tasso):
> — this was true in 1898, and might be written with equal truth at the
> end of this work in 1912.[4]

How much the theme meant to him is clear from the fact that it
makes its appearance in the orchestral introduction of *The Music
Makers,* where it helps to establish a mood of unrest curiously
remote from the poet's text. When he goes on to set the opening
lines he allows himself three quotations: 'Dreamers of dreams'
suggests *The Dream of Gerontius;* 'lone sea-breakers' the first of the
Sea Pictures. The 'Enigma' theme is used to illustrate 'sitting by
desolate streams'. Elgar's note explains its relevance to a feeling
of desolation; but what has it got to do with streams? I shall return
to this question later. For the moment I merely want to
emphasize the profoundly elegiac character of the theme. Elgar
marked the penultimate bar 'mesto' and he used the same term
above a quotation of the opening bar in a letter to Miss Dora
Penny.[5] Furthermore the quotation in this letter serves as his
signature. The lonely artist, 'sitting by desolate streams', is
himself.

This simple identification is made still clearer in a letter which
Elgar wrote to Ernest Newman, in which he discusses the first
symphony[6]:

> As to the 'intention': I have no tangible poetic or other basis: I feel
> that unless a man sets out to depict or illustrate some definite thing,

[3]   Mrs. Richard Powell, *Edward Elgar: Memories of a Variation*, 3rd ed.,
London, 1949, p. 121. The dots after 'is not played' are in the original
text.
[4]   The original draft of this note is in British Museum Add. MS 47908,
fo. 87.
[5]   10 October 1901. Facsimile in Powell, *op. cit.*, between pp. 38-9.
[6]   4 November 1908.

all music — absolute music I think it is called — must be (even if he does not know it himself) a reflex or picture, or elucidation of his own life, or, at the least, the music is necessarily coloured by the life. The listener may like to know this much and identify his own life's experiences.

We know also from Canon Temple Gairdner's correspondence with Elgar[7] how intensely personal is the second symphony and what nonsense it is to describe it as a picture of the Edwardian age (whatever that may be). All this may seem the merest platitude; but it is not universally accepted. Mr. Richard Powell strongly disagrees with my interpretation of the theme. He writes to me[8]:

> I am afraid I cannot agree that the Theme of the Variations is full of deep melancholy. I have been familiar for the past 50 years with what my wife has to say about the circumstances in which the work was composed. This has never varied and flatly contradicts your idea. Elgar, like many others, artistic and otherwise, was apt to swing from high spirits to depression, but my wife has always said that high spirits prevailed when the Variations were written.

In an earlier letter[9] Mrs Powell herself adds this postscript:

> When I arrived at Malvern the day I first heard Elgar play any of the Variations music on the piano, there was a great deal of fun and laughter, and the music appeared to be on the way to becoming a family joke. I knew so many of the people whom Elgar had so amusingly portrayed, and the caricature element caused the whole afternoon to be a riot of humour.

It would be impertinent to cast any doubt on Mrs Powell's recollections. I am quite sure that she has accurately described what she witnessed. At the same time there seems to me to be some confusion of thought here. In the first place, not all the variations are caricatures by any means. No one could use this term to describe the portraits of Lady Elgar (Var. I) or Miss Isabel Fitton (Var. VI) or Jaeger (Var. IX) or Basil Nevinson (Var. XII), nor do I suppose that Mrs Powell meant to do so. She speaks of 'the caricature element' and is obviously referring to those variations which were intended to be humorous. But by emphasizing this element of humour she tends to give the impression that the whole work is a joke. It is true that Elgar exclaimed 'Japes!' (a favourite word) when he invited her to come and hear him play the

---

[7] Referred to in *W.H.T.G. to his Friends,* 1930.
[8] 14 January 1960.
[9] 9 January 1960.

variations, and that he told Jaeger that the result of his essay in portraiture was 'amusing to those behind the scenes'.[10] But all this does not disprove the plain evidence of the music. Secondly, even if all the variations were riotously funny, there would be no reason for supposing that the theme was intended to be. And thirdly, we have Elgar's own description of what the theme meant to him.

At this point I should like to go back to his programme notes for the first performance. 'The Enigma', he wrote, 'I will not explain — its "dark saying" must be left unguessed'. This is a very puzzling statement, and is made more puzzling by the fact that he never did explain it. It was quite natural, of course, that he should propound a musical riddle. He was always interested in cryptograms, acrostics and crossword puzzles. Furthermore, he was a great admirer of Schumann, and had borrowed from the *Abegg* Variations and *Carnival* the idea of writing a piece on the letters of a name — the *Allegretto on G.E.D.G.E.*, dedicated to the Misses Gedge (*c.* 1888). It is quite possible that we have here some kind of musical cipher or anagram, which defeats any attempt at solution because we have no clue. But what is meant by the Enigma's 'dark saying'? Does this refer simply to the mood which Elgar associated with it and which he revealed in his notes on *The Music Makers;* or is there some further association, perhaps with some private experience which he preferred to keep entirely to himself? I cannot answer this question, but shall return to it again at the end of the paper.

Our puzzle does not end here. The theme itself is peculiar — 'a very odd tune', Mrs Powell thought it when she first heard it in 1898.[11] The mood is akin to the opening bars of *King Olaf;* there are also affinities with the Prelude to *Gerontius.* But the rhythmical structure of the tune is unlike Elgar's normal practice. One can, of course, find parallels elsewhere in single phrases; but I cannot think of any complete melody organized in this curious fashion. And when we turn to the original sketch — or at any rate the earliest sketch that survives — there is still more material for mystification. I am not referring to the fact that the middle section (in the major) was originally planned to last eight bars instead of four. That is merely a normal matter in which the composer exercised his judgment; and most people would agree that his judgment was sound. The two things which are peculiar

---

[10] Letter to Jaeger, 25 October 1898: Young, *op. cit.,* p. 282.
[11] *Op. cit.,* p. 12.

in the sketch are a pencil note at the top of the page and the indications for performance (also in pencil) written over the first two bars. (The theme itself is written in ink, with a certain amount of harmonic filling up in pencil, and differs from the final version only in one or two minor details.)

Elgar's handwriting is not always easy to read, and there are one or two words in his letters which have defeated the most persistent scrutiny. However, the inscription at the top of the page is reasonably clear; it appears to read: 'For fuga'. This could be interpreted in two ways. Either the theme itself was conceived as a fugue subject, which seems unlikely in view of the fact that each bar begins with a rest (excluding the middle section in the major): or else the theme was originally the countersubject to a fugue, either by Elgar himself or by some other composer. No such subject by Elgar seems to have come to light, and if we are to look for a subject by some other composer the search is likely to be almost endless. There is, of course, a third possibility. The words 'For fuga' may have been scribbled at the top of the page before the theme was written down and may have been intended for something quite different. This on the whole seems less likely; but even if we reject this possibility, there is a good deal of material for speculation.

The markings over the first two bars are even more peculiar. Over the second beat of the first bar (the two quavers B flat and G) is written 'pizz.' and over the third and fourth beats (the crotchets C and A) 'arco'. In the second bar 'pizz.' comes over the crotchets on the second and third beats, and 'arco' over the two quavers on the fourth beat. This alternation is strange enough in itself, but is made even stranger by the fact that the theme is in ink, with the bowing marks exactly as in the final version, and shows no signs of having been written on top of a pencilled original. If we disregard the bowing and consider the alternation of 'pizzicato' and 'arco' as a form of interpretation which was at some time in Elgar's mind, we have a curious suggestion of ballet music — almost a faint echo of the dance of the sugar-plum fairy in *Casse-Noisette*. And this suggestion brings to mind a conversation recorded by Troyte Griffith[12], in which Elgar said that the Variations would have been performed long ago as a ballet if they had been written by a Russian. He said 'he visualised the scene as a banqueting hall', which is incidentally the setting of the last section of *The Black Knight*. The fact that he liked Dorabella to dance to her

---

[12] Young, *op. cit.*, p. 278.

3 The cottage at Birchwood.

4 The cottage at Birchwood.

variation[13] is also relevant.

There are some further puzzles in the variations themselves. The first is concerned with Variation XIII, which bears the sub-title 'Romanza', obviously added after the score was completed. The person commemorated here is represented by three stars. Elgar's note on this variation, written for a set of pianola rolls[14], is as follows:

> The asterisks take the place of the name of a lady who was, at the time of the composition, on a sea voyage. The drums suggest the distant throb of the engines of a liner, over which the clarinet quotes a phrase from Mendelssohn's 'Calm Sea and Prosperous Voyage'.

It is generally accepted that the lady in question was Lady Mary Lygon, later Lady Trefusis. This identification has been challenged, but in a copy of the piano duet version belonging to Sir Ivor Atkins Elgar himself wrote the names of all his friends above their respective variations, and this one is headed 'Lady Lygon'. This would seem to clinch the matter. But the asterisks still require explanation. The explanation generally given is that Lady Lygon was on her way to Australia with her brother and that a letter asking for permission to use her initials failed to reach her before she left. But according to Percy Young's biography[15] Elgar finished orchestrating the Variations on 21 February 1899, and 'on that day Lady Mary Lygon and Winifred Norbury came to tea'. If this is correct, Lady Lygon was not at sea when the work was written, and there could have been no reason why she should not have been asked there and then if she had any objection to her initials being used. It is difficult to see what objection she could have had: it may merely be that Elgar did not ask her and took the opportunity to satisfy his passion for mystification. When Mrs Powell guessed the identity of E.D.U. in the finale, he told her it was a secret, though later on, when he wrote his notes, he made it quite clear the E.D.U. was the composer.

Similarly with the violin concerto. In a letter to Nicholas Kilburn[16] Elgar translated the Spanish inscription: 'Here, or more emphatically *in here* is enshrined or simply enclosed — buried is perhaps too definite — *the soul of...*?' and added: 'The

---

[13] Powell, *op. cit.*, p. 15.
[14] Reprinted in *My Friends Pictured Within*.
[15] *Op. cit.*, p. 87.
[16] 5 November 1910: Percy M. Young, *Letters of Edward Elgar*, London, 1956, p. 201.

final 'de' leaves it indefinite as to sex or rather gender. Now guess.'
The words 'or rather gender' suggest that the inscription does not
necessarily refer to a person; and in fact the suggestion has been
made that the soul enshrined in the concerto is that of the violin.
But Lady Elgar told Mrs. Powell that the five dots stood for the
name of Julia Worthington, and asked her never to reveal the
secret.[17] Here again there seems no reason why there should have
been any secrecy. Mrs. Worthington was a close friend of the
Elgars, but there was no mystery about the friendship. One can
only suppose that Elgar felt the relationship to be too intimate for
publication. It is worth noting that in his notes on the Variations
he does not identify all the characters by name. Among those
whose identity is not revealed are Troyte Griffith, Winifred
Norbury and Mrs Powell (Dorabella).

The other variation which calls for comment is No. XI. Here is
Elgar's note:

> George Robertson Sinclair, Mus.D., late organist of Hereford
> Cathedral. The variation, however, has nothing to do with organs or
> cathedrals, or, except remotely, with G.R.S. The first few bars were
> suggested by his great bulldog Dan (a well-known character) falling
> down the steep bank into the river Wye (bar I); his paddling up
> stream to find a landing place (bars 2 and 3); and his rejoicing
> bark on landing (2nd half of bar 5). G.R.S. said, 'Set that to
> music'. I did; here it is.

The comment is often made on this description that Elgar was
deliberately making fun of people who had quite naturally
assumed that the passage for bassoons and double basses
represented Sinclair playing the pedals. (Sir Percy Hull tells me
that Sinclair's pedalling was remarkable for its precision and
accuracy.) But the matter is not quite so simple as that. Elgar told
Jaeger that he had tried to imagine each of his friends writing his
(or her) own variation, 'if they were asses enough to compose'.[18]
Furthermore, the Variations are 'dedicated to my friends
pictured within'.

It is well known that Sinclair and his dog Dan were
inseparable. Dan even attended chorus rehearsals and growled
when people sang out of tune[19]. A caricature published in *The
Musical Times* in 1900 shows the conductor with Dan's head and
the dog with Sinclair's. But it would be going rather far to suggest

---

[17] Powell, *op. cit.*, p. 86.
[18] Young, *Elgar, O.M., p. 282.*
[19] Powell, *op. cit.*, p. 80.

that Sinclair and Dan formed a composite entity, or that if
Sinclair had written his own variation it would have been all
about Dan. 'Love me, love my dog' is all very well, but if you are
writing a work dedicated to your friends you would not normally
substitute the dog for the friend. It is true that Elgar later said that
the variations were not all portraits: 'Some represent only a
mood, while others recall an incident known only to two persons'.
This is in some degree true of the 'Nimrod' variation. Everyone
who knew Jaeger says that he was a much more lively character
than one would guess from this solemn Adagio; and his letters
confirm this impression. On the other hand his variation does
clearly represent something in him which endeared him to Elgar,
quite apart from the allusion to Beethoven which I shall discuss
later; and that is obviously why his music turns up again in *The
Music Makers* at the words

> But on one man's soul it hath broken,
> A light that doth not depart.

It is essential to distinguish between the initial impulse and the
finished piece. Elgar took a great interest in Dan and wrote
fragments of music to illustrate his moods in Sinclair's visitors'
book.[20] The interesting thing about these fragments is that some
of them were later incorporated in published works. A passage
representing Dan musing on the muzzling order (19-20 April
1898) found its way into *The Dream of Gerontius*. Another,
describing Dan triumphant after a fight (8-10 July 1899) turns up
again as the opening of *In the South*. A third — 'Dan wistful outside
the cathedral' (11-13 July 1902) — is a familiar and very striking
passage in *The Spirit of England*. It is worth noting that in each of
these cases the composition in which the fragment is used is later
— in the last case considerably later. It is, of course, well known
that many of Elgar's works embody material written much
earlier; for example, a discarded setting of the words 'And that a
higher gift than grace' in *Gerontius* was later used for the words 'To
the old of the new world's worth' in *The Music Makers*. It might be
argued that he used fragments of works already sketched in order
to illustrate the moods of Dan. But it is difficult to imagine that he
would have chosen from *Gerontius* a passage with such solemn
associations to represent a dog musing on the muzzling order.

Two points emerge from this discussion — one general, the
other particular. The first is that no one can ever tell what is going

---

[20] Printed in Young, *op. cit.*, pp. 398-401.

to start a train of thought in a composer's mind or how he will use
the ideas that come to him from some everyday experience. I can
remember many years ago walking along the cliffs on the East
Coast on a rough evening, and how there came to my mind
immediately a splendid orchestral tutti that would have made a
good opening for a symphonic poem on the sea. The symphonic
poem was never written, but years later the same passage was
used quite successfully as the opening of a wedding march, and
nobody would have guessed its origin without being told. This is a
very humble illustration; but on a more exalted level we can see
the same thing happening with Elgar's *In the South*. Anyone who
did not know would imagine that this buoyant opening was
inspired by the brilliant sunshine of Italy. And the case is made
even more complicated by a letter which Elgar wrote to Adela
Schuster after the death of her brother Frank in 1928[21]:

> I want something radiant, bright & uplifting for dear Frankie's
> memorial stone & I cannot find it. Forgive me that I have failed. I
> have said in music, as well as I was permitted, what I felt long ago, —
> in F's own overture 'In the South' & again in the final section of the
> second symphony — both in the key he loved most I believe (E flat) —
> warm & joyous with a grave & radiating serenity: this was my feeling
> when the overture was dedicated to him 24 years ago & is only
> intensified now.

So the dog Dan and the sun of Italy and affection for a friend all
contributed to *In the South*. The second symphony also owes
something to Venice; and the gnarled trees at Brinkwells have
their echo in the violin sonata and the string quintet.[22] Elgar was
obviously susceptible to visual impressions — and sometimes to
impressions that were more than visual. Writing to Ernest
Newman about the second symphony[23], he says:

> There's one *passage* . . . which might be a love scene in a garden at
> night when the ghost of some memories comes *through* it; — it makes
> me shiver.

But there is nothing supernatural about the incident recorded by
Sir Ivor Atkins in his vocal score of *Gerontius*. He tells us that the
setting of the words 'In all his works most wonderful' was written
after Elgar had helped a shepherd to get his sheep in from the
snow.

---

[21] Young, *Letters of Edward Elgar*, p. 300.
[22] W.H. Reed, *Elgar as I knew him*, London, 1936, pp. 63-4.
[23] 29 January 1911.

Rivers always meant much to Elgar. 'Play it like something we hear down by the river', he once said to the London Symphony Orchestra when he was rehearsing the second movement of the first symphony.[24] In particular he loved the Teme and at one time wanted his ashes to be scattered in the water. His thoughts went back to the river when he was lying in the nursing home at the end of his life. 'I lie here hour after hour thinking of our beloved Teme', he wrote to Florence Norbury[25], 'surely the most beautiful river that ever was and it belongs to you too — I love it more than any other — some day we will have a day together there'. Was it perhaps by the Teme that he had had a picnic with his sister Lucy in 1886? 'High jinks', he wrote to his friend Dr C.W. Buck; 'a squestered spot by the river 9 miles out.'[26] Mrs Elgar Blake has told me[27] that 'the Teme seemed to haunt him in his last illness . . . He talked incessantly about [it].' Is it surprising that the words 'sitting by desolate streams' in *The Music Makers* should have suggested the quotation of one of his most personal themes?

The second point to be noticed is that Elgar put his compositions together from isolated scraps. We have the evidence of several of his friends on this matter: a preliminary run through in private generally meant loose sheets all round the room. His autograph sketches, now in the British Museum, confirm the picture. It is difficult for anyone looking at them now to imagine how such an apparently disorderly mass of material came to be welded into works which seem to have a compelling unity. But this was Elgar's method. His imagination was fertile. Anything that might be useful was jotted down, and then when the time came there was a process of assembling and rejecting the raw material. Few of us could produce a work like *Gerontius* by this method; but with Elgar it worked wonders, over and over again. It is only when it failed that we notice the seams.

To return to Sinclair and his dog. If the moods of Dan could produce material for *Gerontius* and *The Spirit of England,* there is clearly no reason why a representation of Dan in the river should not provide the material for a portrait of a cathedral organist. For all Elgar's disclaimer, I cannot help feeling that he was quite aware of the fact that the quavers in the bass suggested organ

---

[24] Reed, *op. cit.,* pp. 140-1.
[25] 15 October 1933: Young, *Letters,* p. 320.
[26] 18 July 1886: *ibid.,* p. 25.
[27] 23 March 1960.

pedals. The origin of the music is one thing, its application
another. Furthermore, the rushing semiquavers which portray
Dan falling into the water would serve equally well to describe his
master, who by all accounts was a man of great energy. Anyone
who doubts this should read Elgar's account of a bicycle ride with
Sinclair, as told to W.H. Reed.[28] One gets the same impression
from the vigorous passages for brass in this variation, which
suggest an organist rejoicing in his solo reeds. But one puzzling
thought still remains. If Elgar obeyed Sinclair's injunction to set
Dan's adventures in the Wye to music, how was it that he did so by
means of a variation on the 'Enigma' theme? I leave this question
unanswered for the moment. We shall consider its implications
later.

And now for the greatest mystery of all, which has exercised a
good many minds to no purpose and has led to some curious
conjectures. In his programme note, after mentioning the
Enigma's 'dark saying' and pointing out the slender connection
between the theme and some of the variations, he goes on:

> Further, through and over the whole set another and larger theme
> 'goes', but is not played.

This rather obscure statement has been variously interpreted.
Taken quite simply, it seems to say: 'I have written variations on a
theme, which you have heard at the beginning. But there is also
another theme associated with the variations, and this is never
heard'. We are not told in what way this unheard theme is larger
than the Enigma, nor is it clear what is meant by the words
'through and over'. What is certain is that 'theme' means a tune.
This is clear from the context. First we have a reference to the
slender connection between the theme and some of the
variations, then immediately after we are told about 'another
and larger theme'.

Everyone who knew Elgar at the time is quite emphatic that he
meant a tune. Hence the suggestion that the larger theme is
friendship — reinforced by a quotation from the *Religio Medici*
which includes the word 'Enigma'[29] — can hardly have any
foundation. But though the larger theme is a tune, there is no
evidence that Elgar meant to imply that it is in any sense a
counterpoint to the variations. The natural interpretation of his
language would be to suppose that the variations have a double

---

[28] Reed, *op. cit.*, pp. 36-8.
[29] Diana M. McVeagh, *Edward Elgar*, London, 1955, p. 26.

association, first with the Enigma theme, and secondly with the larger theme which is not heard. This might be held to explain why in some of the variations the connection with the Enigma theme is slight or, in some cases, virtually non-existent. It might very well be that these variations have a much closer connection with the unheard theme.

I have called Elgar's statement 'rather obscure', but the obscurity lies only in its lack of any clue to the larger theme or to the nature of the association. It certainly does not afford any grounds for supposing that his theme is a counterpoint to the Enigma theme; yet this is precisely what nearly everyone seems to have assumed. It is significant that when Elgar passed on to Ernest Newman[30] a solution propounded by the American critic Henry Krehbiel, he said:

> By all means get all the fun you can out of the *theme* which does not in the least 'go' with the Var .

The word 'go' is here in inverted commas, as it is in the programme note, and Elgar does not say that the suggested theme does not fit the Enigma theme; he says it does not 'go' with the variations. His reluctance to disclose the secret is well known. Here once again we do not know if there were any real grounds for secrecy or whether he was enjoying a mystification which became so much a habit that he could not bring himself to break it. Mr Wulstan Atkins tells me that he more than once asked Elgar what it was but never got an answer. The most he extracted was an admission that Elgar had once stuck numbered bits of paper on the keys of Troyte Griffith's piano, so that if he hit on the keys in the right order he would get the missing tune. But this curious revelation may have been nothing more than a leg-pull; and in any case Troyte does not seem to have been particularly musical, so that even if the story were true he may not have been much wiser after the experiment than he was before. We know that he once asked Elgar if the tune was 'God save the King' — to which the answer was 'No, of course not'.

Of the attempts made to find a counterpoint to the Enigma theme, which I consider to be misguided, the best-known is Mr Richard Powell's suggestion of 'Auld lang syne'.[31] This involves putting half of it in the minor, and leaving part of the Enigma theme without any counterpoint, and results in a number of

---

[30] Letter of 30 March 1920.
[31] *Music & Letters*, XV (1934), pp. 203-8.

progressions which are so clumsy that it is inconceivable that Elgar could have written them. However, Mr Powell is still convinced, as he says in a recent letter to me[32], that this is 'the only solution that meets the known terms of the problem'. His article in *Music & Letters* was followed by a long letter from Fox Strangways, who was not inclined to dismiss the suggestion out of hand but mentioned incidentally that a friend had asked Elgar about 'Auld lang syne' and got the answer: 'No. "Auld lang syne" won't do.' In the second edition of her memories of Elgar, published in 1947, Mrs Powell says that 'since 1934 (when her husband's article appeared) certain things have happened or have come to light which make the case for "Auld lang syne" a very much stronger one than it was then.' She hints at evidence of a private nature which she would not feel justified in publishing. This is merely piling secrecy on secrecy. The appetite is whetted but remains unsatisfied.

In 1953 the Americans entered the field with a competition organized by the *Saturday Review*. The prize-winning suggestions were as follows:

1st   'Una bella serenata' from *Cosi fan tutte*.
2nd   'Agnus Dei' from the *Mass in B minor*.
3rd   Slow movement of Beethoven's *Pathétique sonata*.
4th   'God save the King'.

Other suggestions included 'When I am laid in earth' from *Dido and Aeneas* and 'None shall part us' from *Iolanthe*. Of these the 'Agnus Dei' and 'When I am laid in earth' may be considered to express a mood related to the 'Enigma' theme. 'God save the King' can be ruled out for reasons already mentioned. The pieces from *Cosi fan tutte* and *Iolanthe* seem quite irrelevant: the first is based merely on the fact that Variation X is called 'Dorabella' — Elgar's nickname for Miss Dora Penny (later Mrs Richard Powell). The remaining suggestion is interesting. Elgar himself admitted that the 'Nimrod' variation alluded to Beethoven's slow movement and explained the reason:

> The variation bearing this name is the record of a long summer evening talk, when my friend discoursed eloquently on the slow movements of Beethoven, and said that no one could approach Beethoven at his best in this field, a view with which I cordially concurred.

This seems satisfactory enough, but it is not the whole story.

---

[32] 9 January 1960.

We have to supplement it from a talk which Mrs Powell had with Elgar in 1904.[33] He revealed that he was depressed at the time and had written to Jaeger to say that he was going to 'give it all up and write no more music'. Jaeger replied with a very long letter in which he protested vigorously against this defeatist attitude and suggested coming down for a talk. When he arrived the two went out for a long walk. 'Then he went at it again', said Elgar, 'hammer and tongs, and he preached me a regular sermon and sang Beethoven at me . . . He said that Beethoven had a lot of worries, and did *he* give it all up? No. He wrote more, and still more beautiful music. "And that is what *you* must do".' This account is illuminating, not only for what it tells us about Jaeger but also because it shows that Elgar's notes on the variations are not always as frank as they might be. Once again there is a veil of secrecy.

The American suggestion means that the 'Nimrod' variation was written first: in other words the Enigma theme is a variant of 'Nimrod' and not the other way about. This is not a complete impossibility but it does not strike me as very convincing. It is not inconceivable that something like the 'Nimrod' variation should have been evolved from Beethoven's slow movement, but it is not very likely that its contours would have taken this particular shape, whereas if the Enigma theme came first the melodic curve of 'Nimrod' is easily explicable. Furthermore, if Elgar was cheered and encouraged by his talk with Jaeger, it is unlikely that he would subsequently have written a theme expressing the artist's sense of desolation. The natural order would be: (1) Enigma theme — 'I am depressed'; (2) 'Nimrod' variation — 'My faith is restored'. At the same time we cannot exclude the possibility that *one* of the variations preceded the theme. And this brings us back to a final discussion of the Enigma and its 'dark saying'.

There are several possibilities to be considered. First, as I have already suggested, the theme may be the record of a very personal experience, possibly of an emotional character. That experience may be associated with the River Teme. It may have occurred many years earlier when Elgar was a young man, or it may have happened after he was married. It is even possible that the theme is associated with Elgar's love of animals. In his bachelor days he had a dog called Scap, which he acquired from his friend Dr Buck. He was devoted to his animal, but had to give him up when

---

[33] Powell, *op. cit.*, pp. 110-11.

he married. A week before his wedding at the Brompton Oratory he wrote to Buck[34]:

> My only regret at leaving [Worcester] . . . is about my dear, dear, companion, poor old Scap; he is lying at my feet now as he has ever done these $3\frac{1}{2}$ years: my sister Lucy will take great care of him & he knows her as well as he does me & for a month or two he will be here & at Stoke, but the parting will be bitter on my side: poor fool. He knows nothing of it.

The reason for this separation is simple: Lady Elgar did not like dogs. Mrs Elgar Blake has written to me[35]:

> We never had dogs when I was a child — never indeed until after my mother's death. The excuse always was that it was too difficult as we so often went away and let the house or shut it up. That was perfectly true — but the real thing I believe was that Mother was absolutely undoggy! You had only to see her talk to a dog and you realised she had not a clue! Cats yes, though we never had one for the same reason — but dogs no.

When we recall Elgar's intense interest in Dan and the use he made of the various interpretations of his moods, it is not wholly fantastic to suggest that the Enigma theme may have had its origin as a lament for the loss of a great happiness.

The second possibility is that the theme is the product of a musical experience — that is to say, just as the 'Nimrod' variation started from Beethoven, so the theme may have been suggested by a passage in the work of some other composer. The sort of passage I have in mind is the setting of the words 'Eli, Eli, lama, sabachthani' in Bach's *St Matthew Passion*. It is easy to imagine that the opening of this bit of recitative, with its atmosphere of profound grief, may have accorded with Elgar's mood at the time and that he may have developed the Enigma theme from it. No doubt there are several other possible origins of a similar kind. The third possibility is that the Enigma theme was preceded by one of the variations. I have already given reasons for rejecting the theory that it grew out of the 'Nimrod' variation. But the possibility that it was suggested by Sinclair's variation is much more plausible. As I suggested earlier, if this variation begins with a representation of Dan falling into the Wye, it is difficult to see why that representation should borrow its material from the Enigma theme. The rhythmical shape of the theme is peculiar. In

---

[34] 29 April 1889: Young, *Letters*, p. 41.
[35] 23 March 1960.

the Sinclair variation the notes are presented in a simple, straightforward fashion. Is it impossible that the theme should be simply a reorganization of this sequence of notes, shaped in such a way as to fit into Elgar's mood of despondency at the time?

I have asked a good many questions and answered none of them decisively. The Enigma remains an enigma. And, as Dr. Percy Young says, there is yet another enigma — the enigma of existence. Whatever the merits may be of Elgar's earlier works, no one can pretend that they make any approach to the level of imagination and technical resource displayed in the Variations. Here is something that is quite inexplicable. What change occurred in Elgar's make-up that enabled him, at the age of 42, to produce a masterpiece? There are, of course, affinities with earlier works. 'Dorabella' belongs in a sense to the world of *The Wand of Youth,* and the exuberant finale (which Elgar called No. XIV because thirteen was an unlucky number) is a distant cousin of the final section of *Caractacus:* in fact, there are passages in this section which almost sound like another variation.[36] But the whole level of the new work is so much higher that it might almost, apart from similarities of idiom, be the work of another man. And to make the riddle even more puzzling, Elgar was shortly to complete *Gerontius.* There may be clever analysts — psycho-analysts perhaps — who can solve this greater enigma. I must myself confess defeat.

I cannot end this paper without expressing my warmest thanks to those who have helped me so generously with its preparation — by letting me talk to them, by answering tiresome letters and by letting me see unpublished material: Mr. Wulstan Atkins, Mrs. Elgar Blake, Sir Percy Hull, Mrs. Ernest Newman, Mr. and Mrs. Richard Powell, Sir William Walton and Dr. Percy Young.

Proceedings of the Royal Musical Association
23rd April 1960

---

[36] Figs. **58-61** (vocal score, pp. 193-6).

The Enigma — IV
by Dr. Roger Fiske

Before the war I used to visit an elderly spinster aunt who lived at East Grinstead in Sussex. Her musical interests, never very strong, had been eroded over the years by her interest in the local church, and thus it came about that she introduced me to a fellow-parishioner called Mrs Powell without mentioning her claim to immortality. 'A very great dear', my aunt had said; it was a phrase she had also been known to use of St Paul. About the third time I met Mrs Powell, she discovered that I was studying at the Royal College of Music, and I discovered that she was Elgar's 'Dorabella'. She invited me to tea.

Mrs Powell had not yet published her book, *Edward Elgar, Memories of a Variation,* but her husband, Richard Powell, had recently suggested a solution to the 'enigma' in *Music & Letters* (July 1934). He was a quiet, agreeable man with beautiful Edwardian manners, and though he was usually out-talked by his animated, voluble wife, he held his own with her; I thought them an unusually intelligent and charming couple. I remember Mrs Powell showing me her vocal score of Elgar's *Caractacus;* she had stuck into it photographs of the British Camp on Hereford-shire Beacon, and other parts of the Malvern Hills connected with the cantata; these had been amusingly captioned by Elgar himself.

When I confessed that I had not read Mr Powell's article, he lent me a copy to take away. The article suggested, for the first time, that the enigma, the unheard tune that fitted the theme, was *Auld lang syne.* The puzzle would have point only if it could be appreciated by the friends to whom the Variations were dedicated; most of these were not particularly musical, and therefore the 'hidden' tune must not only be very popular, but traditional rather than classical. *Auld lang syne* fitted the occasion as did no other tune, and Mr Powell showed that it also fitted the theme.

When I returned the article, I said I thought it very convincing. 'Very convincing', said Mrs Powell aggressively, 'but it happens to be completely wrong.' I asked how she knew, and she said that the last time she ever saw Elgar (who had recently died), he himself had told her that the 'hidden' tune was not in fact *Auld lang syne*. Her husband, I remember, said nothing, and that seemed to be that.

In the 1950s I was producing music talks for the BBC, and I twice got Mrs Powell to broadcast about Elgar. After the second programme, those of us who had just been working on it were talking to her about her memories of Elgar, and someone asked her about the famous enigma. Immediately she was unresponsive. When pressed, she said gruffly and awkwardly, 'I prefer not to talk about it'.

I accompanied her to the entrance of Broadcasting House, and offered to get her a taxi to take her to Victoria. She asked me if I would go with her, as there was something she wished to tell me. In the taxi she said that she now *knew* the solution to the enigma, and she asked me to keep to myself what she was about to say. And then, to my stupefaction, this strong-minded old lady started to cry. Richard had been right, it was *Auld lang syne*, and only recently had she been able to face up to the fact that, at their very last meeting, Elgar had lied to her. She had known for years that he had stopped wanting her to solve the puzzle. Looking back on that last conversation, she had come to realize that his tetchy behaviour had been quite out of character. He was a bad liar, and had shown it. That he had lied to her of all people was more than she could bear.

Mrs Powell has been dead for some years, and the confidence can reasonably be broken, especially as it involves no cataclysmic revelation. What one old lady said in a taxi may not be proof, but corroborative evidence is strong, and since that day I have never doubted that Mrs Powell was right. I shall now try to substantiate her case, and while doing so, I shall take note of a paper, 'Elgar's Enigma', that Sir Jack Westrup read to the Royal Music Association in April 1960. Though he rejected *Auld lang syne*, and though he had no solution of his own to offer, much that he said was of interest and relevance.

The all-important fact — and it is a fact even though Sir Jack thinks otherwise — is that the enigma is a hidden tune that fits the Theme in counterpoint. Elgar told a number of people, including Mrs Powell and 'Troyte', that it was a very well-known tune, and as late as 1923 he told 'Troyte' that he was surprised no one had guessed it.[1] Mrs Powell spent hours wrestling with the problem,

---

[1] *Memoirs of a Variation*, 1947 ed, p.119

and at first Elgar encouraged her to keep on trying. 'Jaeger' knew the answer from the start, and in 1899 he told 'Dorabella' to be 'a good girl, and not ask me about that. I do not suppose I could keep it from you if you were to plead with me, but the dear E.E. did make me promise not to tell you'.[2] In the first of all books about Elgar (1904), R.J. Buckley wrote 'The theme is a counterpoint on some well-known melody that is never heard'. It is inconceivable that so many people could be wrong on such a subject. Mrs Powell, one of the least vague people I ever met, *knew* there was a hidden tune that fitted the theme. We can be quite certain that there was.

Yet this very well-known 'hidden tune' has not so far been identified to general satisfaction. There is only one possible explanation. Elgar misjudged the difficulty of his puzzle, and covered his tracks too well. (Anyone who has ever made up a crossword puzzle knows how blindingly obvious a clue can seem to the setter when, to the solver, it seems opaque beyond hope). It follows that we must expect subterfuge, especially perhaps in the composer's public utterances, and we find it in the much-quoted programme note that he wrote for the first performance. 'Through and over the whole set another and larger theme "goes" but is not played.' This seems to imply that the 'hidden' tune fits the variations as well as the theme, and though no tune could possibly do so, the idea has had its adherents. No doubt Elgar was well pleased with the effect of this red herring. But, as Mrs Powell realized by 1946, this 'larger theme' is quite distinct from the 'hidden' tune,[3] and in 1955 Diana McVeagh convincingly suggested that it was Friendship. Indeed the dedication, 'To my Friends pictured within', points to both the 'hidden' tune and the 'larger theme'. In such circumstances, what else could the 'hidden' tune be but *Auld lang syne*, with its nostalgic opening, 'Should auld acquaintance be forgot'?

As Sir Jack Westrup showed, the limited application of the enigma is apparent in the score, for the word does not occur on the title-page, but only above the music of the theme, and this limitation is also hinted at in what Elgar wrote about *The Music Makers*, the cantata in which he used tunes from his earlier works (I have to thank Sir Jack for this quotation).

---

[2] *ibid*, p.28
[3] *ibid*, p.121; also *Edward Elgar* by Diana McVeagh, p.26

I have used the opening bars of the theme (Enigma) of the Variations because it expressed when written my sense of the loneliness of the artist as described in the first six lines of the Ode.

Later in the cantata Elgar quoted this same 'theme (Enigma)' at the words 'sitting by desolate streams'. Sir Jack was puzzled that the theme should have these melancholy associations for the composer, whereas, according to Mrs Powell and her husband, 'High spirits prevailed when the Variations were written'. I do not find any contradiction here. In the broader sense, Elgar was an inveterate composer of descriptive music, and I believe that it was part of his plan to start by depicting his own loneliness as a struggling composer, and then to show how Friendship turned him into a gregarious success. Michael Kennedy has pointed out that the very first phrase on the violins is in the rhythm of the composer's name, Edward Elgar, so it would seem that the theme represents him as well as the finale.

The minor key of the theme not only suggested the melancholy years when nothing went right; it also made possible the enigma. If *Auld lang syne* had fitted a theme in the major, everyone would have guessed it at once. The theme had to be in the minor to make the puzzle sufficiently difficult. I regard this as a predictable subterfuge.

As we have seen, Elgar at first expected his enigma to be solved, but when it became clear that the Variations were to be a lasting success he changed his attitude. Mrs Powell, one of those who noticed the change, decided that the enigma must be silly because he seemed to be growing ashamed of it, and she told me that she spent days going through popular songs of the time trying to make them fit. It may well be that Jaeger advised Elgar to conceal his puzzle in the interests of the music. By 1910 Elgar did not in the least want his enigma solved.

It must be remembered that in the whole of Victoria's reign no English composer had written a lastingly successful orchestral work. Elgar had no grounds for thinking his Variations would be played for more than a year or two. It was one thing to amuse one's friends with a rather frivolous puzzle in ephemeral music, quite another to admit to such a 'jape' in a constantly-performed masterpiece. Elgar came to hate the very mention of the enigma, and it would not be surprising if he sometimes bent the truth in his attempts to hush it up. What seemed a good jape in 1898 seemed a very silly one a few years later.

Richard Powell's solution has not been generally accepted for two reasons, and much the more convincing is Elgar's denial of it.

Mr Powell prefaced his 1934 article by saying that he had originally written it in 1920, but had not published it while the composer was alive because he knew it would have worried him. It seems to follow that about 1920 Mrs Powell asked Elgar if *Auld lang syne* were the answer, and that Elgar replied equivocally and said he hoped the subject would not be pursued. In *Music & Letters* for January 1935 (p.38), its editor, A.H. Fox Strangways, mentions that in the late 20s a Mr Hussey (presumably Dyneley) had written to Elgar suggesting Mr Powell's solution, and got in return a postcard that read 'No, Auld lang syne won't do, E.E.' Mr Fox Strangways, already convinced by Mr Powell's article, regarded this as a piece of carefully-worded subterfuge, and it seems to me to be evidence in favour of what, on the surface, it refutes.

It looks as though Elgar had not yet brought himself to the denial direct, but he soon did. Within a year or two of 1930 Mrs Powell insisted on an unequivocal answer, and she was not alone in getting one. In the first edition of her book, she mentions that she hardly knew W.N., the eighth 'Variation', and had scarcely ever corresponded with her, but in the revised 1947 edition she added the following:

> In a letter to me, Winifred Norbury, wrote: I always consider that I know the hidden tune in the Enigma, but he said I was wrong when I told him.

They had surely just been corresponding about *Auld lang syne,* and there may well have been other sentences on the subject that Mrs Powell preferred not to publish for what, according to Sir Jack, she described as 'personal reasons'. We have seen what these were at the beginning of this article, and they were so strong that she got right through the 1947 edition of her book without once mentioning *Auld lang syne,* even in the additional chapter on 'The Enigma'. Had she been relaxed on the subject, she would have done so. Her mind must already have been riddled with doubt, and indeed shame on her hero's behalf, for her to have suppressed her own husband's theory so totally. She was a sensitive woman as well as a shrewd one, and she knew Elgar and his moods very well indeed. If she came to believe that a man she so revered had been lying to her, then he almost certainly had been.

The other reason for not accepting *Auld lang syne* is, allegedly, **that it does not fit the theme well enough (see ex. on p.81).** I have given *Auld lang syne* as it occurs in Victorian song-books such as Elgar might have known. Where there is a choice of notes, those

with their tails up are from Boosey's *Song of Scotland,* those with their tails down from *Gaudeamus.* The latter fit very slightly better. But bar 9 does not fit very well in either version, and we must suppose that Elgar was more concerned with his sequence than his mystery. The remarkable thing is not how badly the tune fits, but how well. Sir Jack Westrup mentions that in 1953 the American *Saturday Review* offered a prize for the best solution to Elgar's puzzle, and awarded it to someone who suggested 'una bella serenata', the terzetto from near the beginning of *Così fan tutte.* Anyone who thinks *Auld lang syne* fits badly should try the Mozart tune, which I cannot persuade to fit at all. The second prize was won by the Agnus Dei from Bach's B minor Mass, and that doesn't fit nearly as well either. Considering how very hard it is to find anything that will go with Elgar's theme even badly, it is surely past coincidence that *Auld lang syne* should fit as well as it does. Also it accords with the dedication, whereas the Mozart and Bach solutions would be quite pointless, as well as being unknown to nearly all the dedicatees.

There is another important clue, as Fox Strangways pointed out in a postscript to Richard Powell's article. In the finale, at figs **65** and **74,** there is music that seems to have very little indeed to do with Elgar's theme. It is true that some of the contrapuntal figures in the accompaniment have some relevance, but they hardly justify the introduction at this late stage of what sounds like new music. What does justify it is the rhythm, the rhythm of *Auld lang syne*.

When Fox Strangways published Richard Powell's solution, he received a good many letters of protest from people who felt that so distinguished a composer would never have resorted to anything so trivial, and feared for his reputation if the solution were accepted. We need have no such fears today. The puzzle and indeed the concealment of its solution are both characteristic of the composer, and no one in their senses will think the worse of him for indulging his love of mystification. The reason for the concealment no longer applies. The puzzle, surely, is solved.

The Musical Times,
November 1969

The Enigma — V
by Professor Ian Parrott

---

(1) THE DETECTIVE WORK

My attention was first drawn to the Enigma when contemplating the variation G.R.S. — Sinclair, the highly skilled organist who was known to me by his pupil and assistant, Edgar Broadhurst,[1] never to have played a wrong pedal note. Having this special — and I think unique — knowledge (since I was a pupil of Broadhurst) made it particularly hard to swallow the extraordinary notion that the bass figure in bar 2 represented the wild, uncontrolled, Gadarene plunge of a boisterous bulldog down the banks of the Wye. It was similar to being told that the world in which we live was the result of a 'Big Bang'. To me it just isn't as plausible as the notion that the world was created in a meaningful way by God.

I looked at the scoring for two bassoons, *mf*, and doublebass, *p*, *without* 'cello, and was convinced, as were Dunhill,[2] Maine[3] and others, that this represented a graceful tribute to a very good pedaller, not to a doggy paddler. Elgar deliberately confused the issue by writing for the Pianola Rolls, 1913, that

> the first few bars were suggested by his (Sinclair's) great bulldog Dan falling down the steep bank into the river Wye . . . .

My short article dealing with this, 'Variation for a Dog?', appeared in *Music Teacher* as long ago as January 1956, receiving some good-humoured opposition from Mrs Powell (Dorabella). Then, in March 1968, I gave a lecture, subsequently published, for the Elgar Society, called 'The Enigma, A New Slant', going through the various musical ideas for solving the Enigma. This involved noticing many signs of the composer's love of Bach and also his love of the key of G minor. At the end of the 'Enigma'

---

[1] E.C. Broadhurst (1877-1967) was Sinclair's assistant at Hereford Cathedral from 1892.

[2] 'We jumped to the conclusion that this represented the musician's skill on the pedal-board of his instrument, only to be corrected by the composer.' T.F. Dunhill, *Sir Edward Elgar*, Blackie, 1938, p.84.

[3] 'Unquestionably brings organ music to mind'. Basil Maine, *Elgar, His Life and Works*, G. Bell & Sons, 1933, Book 1, p.112.

theme in draft, Elgar has written 'tierce de picardie'. He loved technical terms[4] and they often acted as stimulus if not as jokes. Much of this triggered off the next stage on the purely musical side by my quoting Sir Jack Westrup.[5] The peculiar theme, he said, was probably preceded by one of the variations

> . . . in the Sinclair variation the notes are presented in a simple, straightforward fashion. Is it impossible that the theme should be simply a re-organisation of this sequence of notes?

These notes are remarkably like the opening of Bach's unfinished *Pedal Exercitium* in G minor:

When I came to write my book on Elgar for the *Master Musicians* series in 1971,[6] I developed the idea that composers, by and large, do not write themes in which each bar starts with a rest. It looked therefore as if the Sinclair version of the theme was indeed the theme. And, vice versa, the theme, as it stands, is more like a variation.[7]

So much for the musical side so far.

If anyone reads the original programme note carefully, it will appear that there are *two* parts to the Enigma:

(1) The larger theme that 'goes' but is not played (there is no suggestion of counterpoint, but on the contrary 'the principal theme never appears, even as in some late dramas — e.g. Maeterlinck's *L'Intruse* and *Les Sept Princesses* — the chief character is never on the stage.'

Mr Fiske, in his chapter, claims *as a fact* that the enigma is a hidden tune that fits the Theme in counterpoint. There is no evidence (a) that it is a tune nor (b) that there is any counterpoint. These ideas, you will find, have come only from misinterpretation of the facts.

---

[4] See opposite page 113 in Percy M. Young, *Elgar, O.M.*, Collins, 1955.
[5] Professor J.A. Westrup, *Elgar's Enigma*, R.M.A., 23rd April 1960.
[6] Ian Parrott, *Elgar*, Dent, 1971. (Second Impression, 1977).
[7] Op.cit. (2nd Ed.), p.45.

(2) The 'dark saying' which 'must be left unguessed' and this *may* be the one and only Enigma on its own.

Before I properly exhausted the possibilities of the musical puzzle, I turned back to the philosophy behind this 'dark saying'. It was after giving my talk in Carmarthen at the invitation of the then Bishop of St Davids, the Right Reverend John Richards, in 1969, that he suggested a connection with St Paul.

(2) THE 'DARK' SAYING

I can do no better now than quote from my book for the next part of the unravelling and might mention, in passing, that Sir Jack Westrup, the general editor, was a Classics scholar. He it was who insisted that I should have the Greek as well as the Latin text included.

> Elgar was a Roman Catholic, helped his father as organist and was familiar with the language of the Roman Mass. Were not his friends to see themselves through these variations as in the Vulgate version of I. Cor. xiii. 12: 'Videmus nunc per speculum in aenigmate',* words which come in the Quinquagesima Mass in the Epistle?** The last word is from the Greek αἰνιγμα, which is translated in the Revised Version margin as 'in a riddle'. The passage in the Authorized Version is: 'For now we see through a glass darkly; but then face to face: now I know in part, but then shall I know even as also I am known.' Elgar gave a clue by his use of the word 'dark', in the meaning of obscure, literally or figuratively. The *New English Bible* has: 'Now we see only puzzling reflections in a mirror, but then we shall see face to face. My knowledge now is partial; then it will be whole, like God's knowledge of me.' For further confirmation of how Elgar felt about himself — his reaching maturity as a composer but massive lack of recognition — we may read the verses of the Bible before and after verse 12:
>
> 11. When I was a child, my speech, my outlook, and my thoughts were all childish. When I grew up, I had finished with childish† things.

---

* Βλέπομεν γὰρ ἄρτι δι᾿ἐσόπτρου ἐν αἰνίγματι, τότε δέ πρόσωπον πρὸς πρόσωπον ἄρτι γινώσκω ἐκ μέρους, τότε δὲ ἐπιγνώσομαι καθὼς καὶ ἐπεγνώσθην.

**   Elgar knew his Vulgate (letter of 11th April 1902 to Jaeger) and his liturgy (ditto, 1st March 1903); he quoted Titus I. 12 (ditto, 22nd March 1903).

†   In a letter of 4th July 1901 to Jaeger, Elgar refers to Gerontius's memory (remembrance) of the soul — an utter childish (childlike) peace'.

13. In a word, there are three things that last for ever; faith, hope, and love; but the greatest of them all is love.

If the above solution is correct, Elgar's remark of November 1899 to Dorabella fits into place: 'Haven't you guessed it yet? Try again.' 'Are you quite sure I know it?' 'Quite.' And on another occasion: 'Well I'm surprised. I thought you of all people would guess it.'* This could now be interpreted as meaning that the daughter of a clergyman (Dorabella's father was Rector of St Peter's Collegiate Church, Wolverhampton, from 1895) should know her Bible.

Elgar orchestrated the work during early February (the autograph bears the inscription: 'Ended Feb. 19th 1899'). In a letter of this date to Jaeger he calls it just *Variations*, and on another occasion 'symphonic variations'; the word 'enigma' is not used until May, so it seems. The score was sent to Richter's manager on 21st February† and the great conductor's acceptance of it proved to be a turning-point in Elgar's career.

In 1899 Quinquagesima Sunday fell on February 12th. So the reading of I. Cor. xiii must have been in the composer's mind during the final week's scoring . . . .

And I. Cor xiii is a chapter divided into thirteen verses: an interesting coincidence when one thinks of the thirteen friends 'pictured within' the *Variations*. According to Mrs Elgar Blake,†† her mother's diary for Sunday 12th February 1899 has the entry: 'E. to S. Joseph's.' Elgar, therefore, did go to Mass that day — at the nearest Roman Catholic church in Malvern. So, from Quinquagesima 1899, Elgar and his thirteen friends were to see each other in a new way.

Incidentally, Basil Maine received the same 'appreciative and very kind but evasive' support from Elgar's daughter that I did.[8]

(3) THE LARGER THEME THAT 'GOES'

Since completing the book in 1971, I thought again of the musical side. I had concluded that the great J.S. Bach was a powerful influence and had given many examples of Elgar's enthusiasm. When in 1905, for example, he was expected to equip the music department in the University of Birmingham, the first thing he thought of was the Bach Gesellschaft edition.

---

*   Powell, *op. cit.*, p. 119.

†   Young, *op. cit.*, p. 87; McVeagh, *op. cit.*, p. 27.

††   Letter of 26th April 1969.

[8]   Review of my book in *Eastern Daily Press*, Norwich, 20th August 1971.

The general influence of Bach was undoubtedly there but there was something further which then presented itself: the actual letters B.A.C.H. Now once again I thought of the word 'goes', which had been so completely misread by innumerable would-be solvers of the last seventy years or more. Surely it never implied fitting in tunes to go in counterpoint with the Enigma theme such as *God Save the Queen, Home, Sweet Home, Rule Britannia, Ta-ra-ra-boom-de-ay, Auld Lang Syne*[9] or Chopin's G minor Nocturne. Nor, I think, was it Friendship or the words 'Edward Elgar.[10] A different approach was needed.

As I have said, the impeccable organist, Sinclair, led me on to the even greater or 'larger' composer-organist, J.S. Bach. A 'larger theme which goes but is not played'? Perhaps just the influence of the great composer is the solution, I thought. I will return to this. Before doing so, it might be interesting to speculate on why Elgar deliberately misled everyone on the obvious organist connection, diverting attention to the dog.

When he first gave cryptic names to the movements and also invented the overall name of 'Enigma', Elgar was clearly anxious that people should try to solve all the puzzles. (He had previously tried out a difficult cipher on 'Dorabella'.[11]) Diana McVeagh says,

> Elgar, who, when the work came out, seemed almost to want his secret to be guessed ... in later years replied to questions about it with answers as enigmatical as the enigma.[12]

So it could be argued that solvers, having dealt with the titles of the movements in a fairly summary fashion — in spite of doubts as to the identity of *** later raised by Rosa Burley[13] — were well on the way to solving the main problem. And this was something much more personal and private, which was clearly painful to the composer. He then seems to have thrown out a smoke-screen over his real feelings, making outrageous, whimsical or humorous comments when tackled. We should not forget the retiring, sensitive portrait painted with skill by Michael Kennedy in 1968:

---

[9]   Elgar wrote on a postcard in 1929: 'No. Auld Lang Syne won't do. E.E.'
[10] Michael Hurd, *Elgar,* Faber, 1969, p.61.
[11] See 'Elgar's Cipher Letter to Dorabella' by Eric Sams, *Musical Times,* February 1970. Curiously the word 'dark' seems to appear.
[12] Diana McVeagh, *Edward Elgar: his life and music,* Dent, 1955, p.26.
[13] Rosa Burley & Frank C. Carruthers, *Edward Elgar, the record of a friendship,* Barrie & Jenkins, 1972, pp.125-7.

Somewhere . . . something or someone wounded him so deeply, so irreparably, that he never fully recovered.

This showed itself in the solitude of certain passages in his music, said Kennedy, and it came out also, I think, in his love of riddles, misleadings and what he called 'japes'.

Elgar was always very reticent and unwilling to discuss the inner meaning of anything he had composed . . . he would change the subject abruptly . . . .[14]

Michael Kennedy did me the honour, in *The Daily Telegraph* of 21 March 1977, of describing me as 'Britain's current Enigma-Solver-in-Chief'; and I am pleased to see that in the second edition of his book he has made some reference to my researches.[15]

(4) CONCLUSIONS

In 1973 I followed up the researches by an article in *Music & Letters* called 'Elgar's Two-Fold Enigma: A Religious Sequel'. I looked at several translations of the St. Paul quotation, which were to mean so much to a composer, who in 1899 changed from a provincial nobody into a world-famous composer and who was too shy to shout to the roof-tops his extrasensory awareness of it. One of these was J.B. Phillips in Modern English of 1960:

At present we are men looking at puzzling reflections in a mirror. The time will come when we shall see reality whole and face to face.

This reminds us of Elgar's curious phrase about his friends 'pictured within', which would seem to imply a mirror image compared with the later 'break-through'. William Tyndale's version of 1534 uses the phrase

even in a darke speakynge

and Luther's *Biblia* of 1767 has

Wir sehen jetzt durch einem Spiegel in einem dunckeln Worte.

'Spiegel', from the Latin Speculum, means 'mirror', a much better word than the familiar Authorised Version 'glass'.

My article continued:

---

[14] William H. Reed, *Elgar as I knew him*, Gollancz, 1936 & 1973, p.140.
[15] Michael Kennedy, *Portrait of Elgar*, O.U.P., 1968, second edition 1982, p.95.

. . . In an age of punning Elgar consolidated his wife's name, Caroline Alice, into Carice. This is also 'Caritas'. We have had faith and hope, as in Tasso, but no one can deny that Elgar was thinking of love as "the greatest of these" (I Cor. xiii. 13).* Most people know of the 'amusing' change from Jaeger to 'Nimrod', but again there was something very deep in the relationship between Elgar and this discerning man; and his variation, more than any other, is actually played on religious occasions, because of its obvious suitability. Furthermore, the full title of the Old Testament character was not merely 'Nimrod', but 'Nimrod', the mighty hunter before the Lord'.

For the 'Apostles' (1902) and 'The Kingdom' (1905), Elgar no longer relied on a librettist. He compiled his own text from the New Testament. Theology had been one of his interests from early life: both his father and mother, in their different ways, encouraged a scholarly interest as a Catholic; and he was deeply Christian, bewildered though he soon became by the contradictions of the world. A perverse streak which made him stand out against dogmatism in music theory also acted in other ways. Almost certainly the words of his early school-teacher, Francis Reeve, to himself aged 11 and about 27 other boys, acted as a challenge: "The Apostles were poor men, young men, at the time of their calling; perhaps before the descent of the Holy Ghost not cleverer that some of you here". 'The Apostles', unorthodox both musically and theologically, was already under way when Elgar first met Canon Gorton at Morecambe. Gorton became a useful theological adviser as well as a close friend. After looking at the Revised Version in 1903 for a clearer view of Judas, Elgar lent him his own copy (which he had bought that year) of Whateley's 'On the Apostles' (1998), so the advice was frequently both ways. Elgar accumulated, mainly at this period, no fewer than 58 substantial books on religious matters, the titles including 'The First Century of Christianity' in two volumes, 'The Bible in Modern English' in four. Three books on 'Antichrist' and one on 'Traditional Aspects of Hell' were placed in his library next to various works on 'The Acts' and 'Revelation' together with a large commentary on 'St. Paul's Epistle to the Ephesians'. A more than conscientious job merely to compile his own libretti, one might suppose.

I went on with Elgar's strange interest in G major-minor.

. . . No work integrates the major and minor in a stranger way than 'In Smyrna' for piano, completed during the first two days of October 1905. Contrary to any established pattern (of minor changing to major) it starts in G major and ends in G minor — with some 'Enigma'-like alternation in between.

---

* In a letter to Walford Davies of 13th November 1908 Elgar equates the two words, charity and love, while referring to his Symphony No. 1.

On 15th September Elgar's friend Frank Schuster took him on a Mediterranean cruise. On the way to Athens they crossed the Corinth Canal by train, and on the way home they 'passed slowly through' the Canal by warship. Visits were made to Stamboul (Istanbul) and Smyrna (Izmir). Since they were the guests of the British Navy there was obviously no time to linger anywhere. Elgar did keep a record, however, — an exercise book bought in Corfu — and he did manage in the very short time available in Smyrna to write the new piece and also to purchase a 'Red Letter' New Testament to replace a lost copy which he had been working on for *The Kingdom* and the third oratorio. On 29th September he wrote on arrival: "This was my first touch with Asia . . . Smyrna — one of the seven churches". This cryptic remark shows that St. Paul was not far from his mind. The opening words of Revelation are: "John to the seven churches which are in Asia . . . Ephesus, Smyrna, Pergamos, Thyatina, Sardis, Philadelphia and Laodicea" — all places on Paul's missionary journeys; he travelled from Corinth to Ephesus and, after being there three years, wrote his first epistle to the Corinthians.

Leaving Smyrna in the early hours of 3rd October Elgar arrived back in England on 12th October — "this dreary civilization" — and the next day he "rehearsed *The Apostles!* — and the last music I had heard was the Dervishes in Smyrna". Even with the comparatively recent revelation of a large number of letters to Lady Stuart of Wortley, we may be able now to re-assess the words he wrote on the sketch of the first movement of the violin concerto in February 1910: "Where Love and Faith meet There will be light". Many other minor enigmas can be sorted out now, following both St. Paul and Bach. Other people have added ideas: one, a classics scholar, suggested that a Greek hearing St. Paul using the word 'Enigma' would think of the riddle of the Sphinx;* another said we need not banish Dan, the dog, completely since Elgar, in his deliberately misleading note on G.R.S. in 1913, referred to "his rejoicing bark" — and in Worcestershire this could be taken as 'Bach'. A final interpretation of one of Elgar's conundrums fits into place. Elgar wrote BACH as a single note on crossed staves at the age of 8.** Now we can see more clearly that BACH always 'goes' with the 'Enigma' theme but is not heard, from the first note (B) to the last (H); and two *tenuto* notes in the middle section are A and C. Maurice Jacobson has suggested that I can now clinch this with a re-interpretation of what Elgar wrote to Jaeger in 1900, that he had "looked at the theme through the personality (as it were) of another Johnny." This is now Johannes Sebastian Bach. Jaeger's full name was August Johannes Jaeger.

---

* Musicians then might think of Schumann.
** Percy Young, *Elgar, O.M.*, p. 49.

In *The Music Review* for November 1976 there is a fair amount of correspondence on the subject, much of it from Theodore van Houten, and I am taken to task rather as if I were a dogmatic anti-dog man. This is not so. I have shared much of Elgar's love of dogs and also of horses. I am asking the musical reader merely to study the score and from the internal evidence to note that the variation G.R.S. is clearly about an organist (who has pulled out the tuba stop on the bass theme's final appearance (bars 51 and 52) and who was known to be a keen admirer of Bach). Perhaps I may mention that my piece for organ (first played by Jennifer Bate in 1976) with the self-evident title of *Homage to Two Masters* is now published as the third movement of a *Suite*.

The *Times Literary Supplement* of 30th July 1971, when reviewing the appearance of my *Master Musicians* volume, said that I offered

> a solution which seems more plausible than others;

and the *Music & Letters* reviewer of October 1971 said

> If one is willing to think in another dimension than music (and when discussing Elgar, why not?), his argument becomes quite plausible.

Perhaps 'plausible' is the best word that can be offered for my solution to the Enigma of Elgar if not for the enigma of the Universe.

PART III: THE 'GERONTIUS' DÉBÂCLE

It is well known that the first performance of The Dream of Gerontius, *at the Birmingham Triennial Festival on 3 October 1900 under Dr Hans Richter, was a disaster. Various commentators have advanced various reasons for the débâcle, and this section comprises four views of the event. First comes the following week's review from* The Musical Standard, *again by E.A. Baughan. This is followed by two firsthand accounts: the first by William Bennett, who had been a member of the choir and was looking back thirty years later, and the second by Mrs Richard Powell ('Dorabella' of the* Variations), *who was in the audience and who wrote her piece nearly sixty years after the event. Finally, Gareth Lewis advances his own explanation for the disaster, based on observations of Richter's career as a conductor.*

Review from the *Musical Standard*
by E.A. Baughan

My report of last week took us to the Wednesday night of the festival. Before going farther I would like to say a few words more on the subject of the choir's singing in general and its performance in Mr Edward Elgar's *The Dream of Gerontius* in particular. There have been apologists for the choir, of course, and to a certain extent some of the apologies put forward have weight. There is certainly something to be said for the disadvantage under which the chorus laboured in losing Dr Swinnerton Heap when the rehearsals were half through. Mr Stockley is an experienced choir-trainer, but his ideas necessarily clashed with those of his predecessor. Then it is held by the choristers themselves that Mr Elgar went the wrong way about to make known his criticism. A letter from a chorister, who must be nameless, speaks of the 'gross insult' of which the composer was guilty in telling the choir that it was 'all wrong' and that the Chorus of Demons was sung like a drawing-room ballad — and especially when, my correspondent naïvely remarks, 'we had

shouted ourselves hoarse.' Mr Elgar's protest was possibly ill-
timed and unnecessary; at any rate no good is ever done by
making sweeping criticisms which leave no room for, and do not
suggest, improvements. Doubtless Mr Elgar's protest took the
spirit out of the chorus, and it seems to have so seriously injured
the pride of many that it is quite a question if all did their loyal
best with the composition on Wednesday morning. My correspondent speaks of the immense difficulty of the work, and thinks
that some of the notes are almost impossible to sing. But then as I
believe only some seven choral rehearsals of *The Dream of Gerontius*
took place, it is not possible that a modern work of the calibre of
Mr Elgar's could be adequately sung after so few rehearsals. As to
the composer's irritation I can quite understand it. He has been
working at the Birmingham composition for many years; it
contains the best music he has ever written — in fact the best
music of the modern English school, in spite of the absurd
comparison made by a critic in *The Times* of Elgar with Parry and
Stanford (to Elgar's detriment, of course); and, although difficult
enough, it is not by any means impossible. As a fact the
Birmingham chorus sang the music fairly well so far as accuracy
went — at least one might have excused mere slips and
unsteadiness — but the performance was lamentably poor in
intelligent expression. Intelligence is not, I am sorry to say, a
matter of rehearsal only. A semblance of it can be manufactured
by mere careful preparation, but it is apt then to degenerate into
mere virtuoso tricks of light and shade, such as Mr George Riseley
can obtain from his Bristol chorus. The Birmingham choir was
particularly unintelligent throughout the festival. It laboured to
produce as much noise as possible, just like the least good of the
brass bands of the North. It seemed to be impossible for it to sing
piano for more than a couple of bars without rising quite
unwarrantably to a forte and thence to a fortissimo. Its
crescendos never swelled out gradually; its diminuendos were
hardly marked at all. And very seldom did it give us the right tone
colour. This was particularly noticeable in Coleridge-Taylor's
Hiawatha. The performance was bright and vigorous to a degree
— accurate, too. But point after point of fun and pathos was
missed — especially the pathos. Although I say the chorus sang
unintelligently I do not mean to infer that the enthusiastic ladies
and gentlemen composing it have no sense of the fine shades of
musical meaning. On the contrary I am sure they have, from one
piece of evidence alone — the singing of Brahms's *Requiem* on the
Friday morning. It was not by any means perfect; it was rough;

the quality of voice (perhaps unavoidably at the end of a festival) was occasionally poor, especially among the tenors, who sometimes exhibited quite a German reediness; but the intelligence was there. It may be said that Bach's *St Matthew Passion* should also be bracketed with the *Requiem,* but the kind of intelligence I mean is not demanded by modern performances of Bach with their absence of emotional expression (which Bach experts hold is the right way to sing Bach) — for if you sing your parts accurately you will give a good performance of the work. And the Birmingham singers did sing fairly accurately. But why was the Brahms Requiem so much better performed than the *Elijah* or than even Dvorák's *The Spectre's Bride* on the Thursday evening? I may be wrong, but I believe the reason is to be found in the fact that Dr Richter himself was more in sympathy with the work than with any of the others, with the exception of the orchestral compositions, in the programme. How else is one to account for the expressiveness with which the chorus sang 'How lovely is thy dwelling-place' or 'Here on earth have we no continuing city'? And is it not possible that the rough-shod energy with which the chorus trampled out the fun and pathos of 'The Song of Hiawatha' was a good deal due to Richter's want of sympathy with the score? Of course I do not know that he was really unsympathetic, but his straightforward conducting certainly looked as if he were. And that brings me to an important point to be considered with regard to these festivals in the future. I must ask my reader's patience while I give a few lines to its consideration, and leave for the present the few details that are required to make this notice of the Birmingham Festival complete.

It is perhaps necessary for the *éclat* of a festival that it should be conducted by a musician of eminence; but apart from the attraction of Dr Richter's name on the bill I think the Birmingham Festivals lose by retaining him as the conductor. He is not, except in one or two works, a great choral conductor. His sympathies do not lie that way. One might ask, perhaps, what conductor of modern mind could sympathise with *Elijah, Messiah, Israel in Egypt,* Sir Hubert Parry's mock Bach, and Dvorák's puerilely romantic *The Spectre's Bride?* But Dr Richter, I fancy, does not sympathise deeply with any choral music. He certainly does not conduct it well. That is one point. The other is common to all the festivals. The chorus at Birmingham is trained by one man and no less than fifty-five rehearsals were held of one sort or another. Dr Richter and the composers of the novelties attended at least one of the choral rehearsals at Birmingham. Then the whole force is put under the chief conductor's control for a Friday evening, the whole of a Saturday and part of a Monday. How, in the name of commonsense, are good results to be obtained? The chorus master is not a machine; he has his ideas: the chief conductor is not a machine; he has his ideas. What is the chorus to do? At Birmingham it seemed to wait anxiously on Dr Richter, and the consequence was the performances were nothing more than rehearsals. I should not have been surprised if the conductor had stopped the choir and orchestra and bade them begin again at 'one, two, three, four, five — eight bars from forty-six.' The whole arrangement is absurd. There are two alternatives. First, the choir-trainer should conduct the choral works, and many a chorus-master is quite capable of doing so, the orchestral programme being left to the distinguished conductor, native or foreign. Secondly, the conductor-in-chief, if he is to conduct right through the festival, must be accustomed to choral as well as orchestral conducting, and he himself must direct a fair number of the choral rehearsals either with or without a local orchestra. As a matter of fact I believe Sir Arthur Sullivan did do so at Leeds, and at his own expense. Of course this would cost a deal of money. The net profit of the Birmingham Festival will, I hear, exceed £5,000. That sum goes to the General Hospital. Now, supposing my conductor-in-chief were obliged to give a month of these choral rehearsals previous to the festival, it would not cost (I suppose) more than £1,000 — I put the sum very high. The charity would still benefit to the extent of £4,000. Many people will make a clamour that I should advocate a course of action which would result in lessening the sum handed over to a doubtless deserving charity; but I think music has her claims, too, and she will persistently demand that they be paid in full or the festivals in time will cease to be. The outcry this year has been very general and has not been confined to a few confirmed grumblers. Some gentlemen on the Press, I see, have taken it for granted that the appointment of Dr Sinclair to the choirmaster-ship of the Festival Choral Society will have a marked effect on future festivals. But the Festival Choral Society does not supply all the voices for the festival chorus, and, moreover, Dr Sinclair would never be able to give much time to the training of the festival chorus itself as his own Hereford Festival falls on the same year, and he is not free from it until the middle of September. As he is hardly likely to give up Hereford for the sake of the Birmingham Festival we cannot look to the energetic young conductor as the possible reformer of Birmingham. A change or reform, however, has got to be made if Birmingham desires to keep her position in the musical world.

The Musical Standard,
13th October 1900

A Memory from the Choir
by William Bennett

Many different theories have been advanced for the failure of the chorus in the first performance of *Gerontius* at the Birmingham Festival of 1900, and many condemnatory articles have been written blaming the singers for their lack of interpretative power. One who was a chorister on that memorable occasion feels it time that he should attempt some explanation from the standpoint of the choir. First, let a few examples of the criticisms of the performance be quoted. Sir Richard Terry in his book *On Music's Borders*, published by Fisher Unwin in 1927, wrote:

> Nineteen-hundred saw the production of Elgar's *Gerontius* at the Birmingham Festival, marking a new epoch in choral work. Its disgraceful rendering by the choir showed to what depths of incompetence that self-satisfied and complacent body of once-famous singers had sunk. When the composer was obliged to tell them that they did not understand his music (which was obviously true) their friends raised a howl of indignation at the impertinence of a mere composer in telling a body of such authority as lay-clerks and soulful amateurs that they were not perfect.

The *Musical Times* after the first performance reported (November, 1900):

> The production of *Gerontius* at the Wednesday morning performance was the great event of the Festival and the feature which will be the best remembered. Unfortunately the memories will not all be as pleasant as they should be owing to the shortcomings of the chorus. The defects may have been due to specific accidental causes.
>
> We understand that Hans Richter did not see the full score of *Gerontius* till the evening before he conducted the first orchestral rehearsal at Queen's Hall.
>
> Owing to the lamented death of Dr Swinnerton Heap, which occurred during the progress of the choral rehearsals for the recent Birmingham Festival, Mr Stockley kindly undertook to discharge the duties of choir-master at the recent meeting.

Now to cite Grove's *Dictionary of Music* (1927 edition):

> At its first appearance *Gerontius* seemed to miss fire. Probably

5 Elgar with Hans Richter.

My dear Mr Verl.: Herewith you receive the list of the works, which will be performed in the coming 6 Concerts; the distribution is depending upon circumstances — but this must not be announced. It is not excluded, that one novelty will be added. Please ask Mr Elgar, whether we shall have the very first performance of his interesting work, or the first a. s. C. ? I shall bring the *Scores* of Glazounow, Tschaikowsky, Rimsky-Korsakow, Svendsen and *Siegfried* Wagner; the parts must be bought. As for Mozarts Symphonie, Mr Mappleson must provide the Orchestralparts of the Breitkopf & Härtel *Mozart-Edition*. With best regards yours sincerely

Hans Richter.

6   Richter's letter to his agent arranging to give the first London performance of the *Enigma Variations*.

Richter, in spite of his great Wagnerian experience, understood this subtle combination of voices and orchestra less thoroughly than he had grasped the orchestral style of the *Enigma Variations*. Certainly the Birmingham choir was puzzled by its startlingly new choral idiom.

Fourthly there are Mr Basil Maine's remarks in an article in last December's issue of the *Monthly Musical Record*:

> The failure of the first performance of *Gerontius* is famous. The Birmingham chorus could not rise to the occasion, spite of Richter's conducting and his belief in the greatness of the music.
>
> Some say that his zeal led him to overwork the chorus, but this excuse is hardly good enough. A festival of that kind always involved arduous and concentrated preparation. A more probable reason is that the singers did not understand the music and had not developed a technique sufficient to meet its exacting demands.

First let me answer Sir Richard Terry by saying that if he had been a chorister he would have known that the reason of the failure was not an incompetent choir but an incompetent choir-master — incompetent, that is, by modern standards. Sir Richard speaks of 'lay clerks' in the choir and 'soulful' amateurs. There were no lay clerks in the choir. Such clerks as were there were from counting-houses, not cathedrals. And as for 'soulful amateurs', Birmingham does not breed them. Only twelve choristers out of 350 were 'soulful' enough to refuse the honorarium of £3 or £4 (there were two grades of choristers) granted according to a signed contract to singers who agreed to attend all rehearsals and all performances.

Grove hits the right nail on the head in its statement that 'the choir was puzzled'. It certainly was, but that is not all the story.

Mr Maine is wrong in thinking that Dr Richter overworked the choir through his zeal for the work, but he is right in saying that 'they had not developed a technique sufficient to meet the exacting demands.' But the choir could have developed that technique had the choir-master enjoyed any understanding of the nature of poetry and had he been a musician conversant with modern developments and in sympathy with Elgar's setting of Newman's poem — a poem which neither he (I venture to say) nor more than half a dozen of the 350 choristers had heard of prior to the festival. Not only had they never heard of it before; but even then they did not trouble to find out about it more than could be gathered from the single-voice chorus parts from which they sang.

The choral programme of the week was a very full one. It included the first performance in Birmingham of Bach's *St Matthew Passion*. Yes, the first! For although Stockley had been conductor of the Festival Choral Society, which supplied most of the members for the Triennial Festival, he had in his forty years' conductorship never attempted a work by J.S. Bach, his nearest approach to J.S. Bach being a motet by Johann Christolph Bach (J.S. Bach's uncle), *I wrestle and pray*. Coleridge-Taylor's *Hiawatha* was also down for its first Birmingham Festival performance, and also Parry's 12-part Psalm *De Profundis*. Dvořák's *Spectre's Bride* and Brahms's *Requiem* were also sung in addition to the usual *Messiah* and *Elijah*.

Stockley at the age of seventy or thereabout had resigned from the Festival Choral Society in 1896 and had incidentally been asked to resign the conductorship of the local orchestra by some of his leading supporters. Dr Swinnerton Heap succeeded him as conductor of the Festival Choral Society in 1896 and as choir-master to the festival of 1897. He commenced the choir-training for the 1900 festival, but he was taken ill in March and he died on 11th July 1900. The festival committee, instead of appointing a young musician acquainted with modern choral developments, chose the line of least resistance and brought Stockley forth after four years of retirement, during which I question whether he had heard any choral or orchestral music. No doubt Dr Heap's death was partly the cause of the lamentable failure of the choir-training that nearly led to disaster. This story should be a warning to festival committees.

When *The Dream of Gerontius* was in rehearsal an old chorister said to me, 'I call this a nightmare, not a dream.' It was probably a nightmare, too, to old Mr Stockley. Another elderly chorister, when I asked him what he thought of the new oratorio, said to me, 'What a queer finish! Surely it would have been better to end with something like the Hallelujah Chorus.'

Newman's poem was not then available in a cheap edition, and I remember going to the Birmingham Reference Library to read the work and understand what we were striving to express. If only an able young musician with a love of poetry and the power to explain it to us had been chosen as choir-master a very different tale might have been told of the first performance.

Instead of its being over-rehearsed, as Mr Maine suggests, many of the choristers went to Stockley as the date of the festival approached to try for further help in pages that had never been learned. 'Dispossessed, aside thrust,' was one of these. The cynical utterances in the demons' chorus were bound to shock Stockley, who, when conducting Berlioz's *Faust*, would hurriedly run through the mocking fugal, 'Amen', horrified, never attempting to dramatize it.

Richter, if my memory serves me right, took only one choral rehearsal of *Gerontius*. It was his usual course to devote one evening to each work before the final morning rehearsal with the orchestra. Elgar was present that morning, and I shall never forget his look of disappointment and how he railed, especially at the tenors, when he found that even the notes were not known. As for interpretation, it had never been thought about. Stockley had been the organist at a Congregational chapel, and he was much too anti-Catholic, I imagine, to have any sympathy with Newman's poem or the Catholic Elgar's music. The choir were aware that they did not know the work and the majority sincerely regretted it. I do not hesitate to question Richter's suitability as the conductor of the first performance of *Gerontius*, fine orchestral conductor though he was. What did he know of the subject of the work? Probably nothing. No wonder the performance was a failure. The composer should have been appointed conductor.

The Monthly Musical Record,
February 1933

A Memory from the Auditorium
by Mrs Richard Powell

Mrs Richard Powell (née Dora Penny) lived from 1874 to 1964 and first met Elgar when she was only 21. She became one of his youngest friends and made herself extremely useful by undertaking such tasks as collating his press-cuttings. In 1936 she published her memories of the composer who had immortalised her as Dorabella *in the* Variations, *where her slight stammer is translated into musical terms.*

Having heard Elgar play the music of *Gerontius* on the piano for hours together during the few months preceding the first performance, and having got to know a good deal of it fairly well, I was looking forward to hearing it properly performed, complete with chorus, orchestra and soloists. But it was not at all a good performance and was a dreadful disappointment. It lacked so much of what I knew was there. I could not make out what was the matter and I remember getting anxious and rather frightened, largely on account of the faulty intonation of so much of the choral singing.

Many people have asked me what happened and whether the performance was really as bad as was made out. Knowing that I was there in the Birmingham Town Hall that day, surely I could tell them what happened — and why?

I have never written about this or spoken of it in public. I really think that we all tried to forget it. But now, when nearly everyone connected with the performance, including players, singers and management, is dead, I feel it is almost a duty to set down my memory of it and explain some of the causes of the trouble.

A great many most unfortunate and tiresome things had happened. In the first place, Elgar had himself been to blame in being dilatory in getting the chorus parts corrected and returned to the printers. I am pretty firmly convinced that Elgar had not realized the difficulty the chorus was going to have to learn this music. Choruses in those days had been brought up on Handel and Mendelssohn and this music was what one might describe as a new language. How could they master it in just a few weeks? Elgar's mind was soaked in this music of his and therefore it must have seemed natural and easy to him.

An aunt of mine (wife of Archdeacon Hodgson, of Handsworth) who was a soprano in the chorus, wrote to me soon after some of the chorus parts had been received — 'How lovely this music is! but shall we *ever* learn it in time?' — and she was a fine sight-reader.

Then, in May 1900, soon after the combined rehearsals had begun, came the illness and sudden death of the beloved chorus-master Dr Swinnerton Heap (who was an enthusiastic admirer of Elgar's music) and his replacement by the former chorus-master, Mr Stockley (who was not). Mr Stockley was an elderly and rather old-fashioned man; he was also a strong Protestant and was not in sympathy with either the words or the music of *Gerontius* or with its composer, and I think he must have allowed his personal views to colour his actions to some extent. Dr Heap's death was a terrible blow, and the old proverb about changing horses while crossing a stream came to mind. Apart from the sorrow we all felt, and the loss Dr Heap was to many choral societies in the Midlands, it was undoubtedly a very bad stroke of luck for Birmingham at this particular time. Dr Heap was a very able musician, a splendid chorus-trainer and a delightful personality.

Dr Hans Richter, who conducted the Festival, was at that time pretty well beyond criticism, but in my opinion, and I was not alone, even he misjudged the difficulty of the work. His mind was not intimately familiar with this new music as was the composer's, and, moreover, he was both surprised and worried to find at his first rehearsal how ill-prepared the choir was to give him what he wanted. After what was to have been the final rehearsal the work was found to be so far from ready that he was obliged to ask for an additional long rehearsal.

I heard, years afterwards, that he spent half the night after his first rehearsal pacing up and down in his hotel bedroom with the full score stuck up on the mantelpiece — learning it! Another fact that will probably astonish choral singers of today was that at all rehearsals, and at the performance too, the chorus were using single chorus-parts, thus, the sopranos, for instance, could not see what the other sections were supposed to be singing. Of course, large choirs often use these single parts for familiar works as it saves a lot of turning over.

The lack of sympathy between Elgar and Stockley was responsible for the unfortunate fact that Elgar was not asked to attend any of the *Gerontius* rehearsals until Hans Richter took over. Elgar was then, naturally, asked to come.

All this happened nearly sixty years ago, and it is probably quite difficult for people now to realize that the music of *The Dream of Gerontius* came as something entirely new, and was like a new language for all performers, players as well as singers, to master in just a few weeks, when it really needed a whole season's work. In addition to this, there was, of course, other new music in the Festival programme to be learnt as well. The chorus was, I am told, dead tired before the Festival opened.

At the time of the 'Jubilee of *Gerontius*', in October 1950, the Birmingham City Choral and Orchestral Society kindly invited me to be present, and after a very fine performance I was fortunate enough to get in touch with an elderly tenor who had sung in the chorus in 1900, and he told me a lot of interesting things. He said that he and some of his friends in the tenor section of the chorus got together and rehearsed at home. Evidently they were very keen and enthusiastic and 'they knew their parts well and made no mistakes'. Far from having rehearsed at home, the basses did not know their parts properly and so, instead of being the reliable foundation to a chorus that basses usually are, they were a positive deterrent to correct singing.

Even one of the soloists, Plunket Greene, was not perfect in his part. In a place in Part 2 he came in a semitone wrong and stuck to it until the end of the piece! I heard that he was dreadfully upset and miserable afterwards. In later years I have heard the truth about that. The particular place in which he made that mistake (No 106) is rather difficult, but, if he had not been nervous, he would not have forgotten to wait for a certain lead given by one of the wind instruments.

Talking of soloists, how odd it is to note that Edward Lloyd sang the part of Gerontius. Of course, he was at the top of the tree in those days. He had a splendid voice, and it was said that he could read or sing anything at sight correctly, but he is not one's idea of Gerontius, fine singer of Handel arias and drawing-room ballads though he was. I do not remember anything particular about his singing that day. Marie Brema, the well-known opera singer, sang the part of the Angel very well and I am told that she saved the situation in Part 2 several times. Plunket Greene, again, is hardly one's idea either of the Priest in Part 1 or of the Angel of the Agony in Part 2.

I shall never forget leaving the Town Hall that day after the performance. I was so disappointed and miserable; I could not help thinking of poor Elgar and the intense disappointment he must be suffering. I avoided everyone who might want to ask me how I had 'enjoyed' it, and was thankful, that day, when I got home. However, there were some people in the audience who knew and understood. One was Professor Julius Buths, of Düsseldorf; Jaegar, of Novello's ('Nimrod' of the *Enigma Variations*), was escorting him and the two of them sat together. In his long letter to me, full of misery and disappointment, Jaeger told me that 'directly the performance was over, Buths grasped my hand (*coram publico*) and blurted out "ein wunderbares Werk"; eins der schönsten Werke die ich kenne" '. Immensely impressed by the work, he started on the translation of the words into German directly he got home. A very fine performance was given in Düsseldorf in 1902, to which the composer and his wife were invited. It was a brilliant success. I shall never forget the excitement on my next visit to the Elgars at Malvern when Mrs Elgar showed me the two huge laurel wreaths hanging up in the study ('like cartwheels,' Elgar said; 'what to do with them on the platform I did not know'). There were large red satin bows on each, inscribed in German. (I wondered how on earth they managed to get them home!) Mrs Elgar spoke German very well. After all these years I can fancy I hear her now; her light, high voice singing about the house — 'Preis Gottes Heiligkeit in der Höh'.

There was also a very musical connection of mine at the 1900 Festival, Mrs Meath Baker (wife of 'W.M.B.' of the *Enigma Variations*). She and I sat together that day. She knew the music pretty well and had done a good deal of 'turning-over' for Elgar too. When it was over she said: 'A very poor performance, but what a wonderful work!' What a pity a remark like that did not appear in the Press; it would have helped!

The Press accounts that followed were mostly concerned with pointing out all the mistakes, and one critic excelled himself by commiserating with Messrs Novello, 'whose philanthropy had risked overloading their shelves with more useless copies'. One or two of the writers actually had the penetration to see that they had been listening to something very much out of the ordinary. It makes one think that music critics, as a race, are much better at pointing out imperfections in performance than at assessing the value, or otherwise, of works that are new to them. There are many morals that could be drawn, but I think that by far the most important is that if a work is great enough it does not matter in the long run how poor the first performance is; the greatness will win through.

Far from being put off by the disappointment of the production of *Gerontius* at Birmingham in 1900, various cathedral choirs and musical societies studied and performed the work, and the beauty and value of it soon began to be realized. So the regrettable first performance was gradually forgotten.

Unfortunately, London did not hear *Gerontius* until 1903, but the West Country could not, and would not, wait. The Three Choirs Festival at Worcester in September 1902 gave it; Sheffield followed in October of the same year, and early in 1903 it was heard in Manchester, Wolverhampton and Hanley. So fine was this performance by the North Staffordshire Festival Chorus and Orchestra that they were asked to give it in Westminster Cathedral in June 1903. In the spring of 1904 *Gerontius* was heard at an Elgar Festival at Covent Garden and it won golden opinions there.

In 1957, the Elgar centenary year, *Gerontius* was performed at one of the Promenade Concerts under Sir Malcolm Sargent. I am told that the crowded audience listened spellbound throughout, and were obviously enthralled by the music. After a second or two at the end, when all performers stood motionless, the applause that followed was tremendous.

Elgar was a master of orchestration and it is often said how fine is the orchestration in *Gerontius,* but a thing that, oddly enough, is never mentioned, is the skill with which the words have been chosen from the poem and how beautifully they have been set to music. This work took Elgar a long time, but with the help of his great friend Father Knight, who had given him a copy of the poem as a wedding present in 1889, the work was done.

Finally, since it has become common practice to call *Gerontius* an oratorio, it is worth pointing out that Elgar himself was careful not to do so. On the title-page we find:

The Dream of Gerontius, by Cardinal Newman, set to music for mezzo-soprano, tenor and bass soli, chorus and orchestra, by Edward Elgar.

Both *The Apostles* and *The Kingdom* he called oratorios. You may be inclined to say 'What's in a name?' but I suggest that it really becomes important when misapprehension leads to the making of comparisons which are quite inadmissible. The principal characteristic of oratorios is that they are episodic, and usually have words that are taken from or based on, Holy Scripture. *Gerontius* has continuous dramatic unity, and this places it, as Elgar was well aware, in a different category.

The Musical Times, February 1959

Hans Richter and *Gerontius*
by Gareth H. Lewis

Without a doubt, Hans Richter deserves to be remembered with the deepest gratitude for his courageous championship of Elgar's music in the years around the turn of the century — when the composer was still experiencing difficulty in arousing the enthusiasm of his fellow countrymen. In particular Richter gave superb first performances of the *Enigma Variations* and the First Symphony. It is sad therefore that to many Elgarians the name of Hans Richter calls to mind chiefly the disastrous first performance of *The Dream of Gerontius*, which he conducted at Birmingham on 3rd October 1900. There are many puzzling features about Richter's part in this failure. We know that the chorus was ill-prepared and that their morale had been undermined by the sudden death the previous July of their chorus-master Swinnerton Heap. We also know that the soloists experienced difficulty both with the idiom and the vocal writing. One would have expected, however, that Richter, with his reputation for understanding new and unfamiliar music, would have grasped the essentials of the work sufficiently firmly to have been able to convey a sense of leadership and to guide the choristers to greater confidence and insight. When we look more closely at Richter's personality, however, it becomes clear that there was a deficiency in his emotional spectrum which put a surprisingly wide range of music outside his understanding — and it is probable that *Gerontius* came into this category.

Elgar, talking to Arnold Bax in 1901, bitterly blamed Richter for not knowing the score of *Gerontius*. This is hardly likely to have been the case. Richter's reputation as an interpreter of new music had been gained by careful and painstaking preparation of his performances. Richter had access to a copy of the full score early in September 1900 (giving sufficient time for a musician of his calibre to study it in detail) and it would seem, from Elgar's correspondence with Jaeger, that the composer and the conductor went through the work together at that time. We cannot therefore blame Richter for not having done his homework, and we must look more deeply for the reasons for the failure of

Gerontius. Hans Richter was Hungarian by birth, having been born at Raab in 1843. His mother was an opera singer with close associations with Wagner (she sang in the first performance of *Tannhäuser*) and she arranged for the young Hans to become a chorister in Vienna at the age of ten, and for him to study both the horn and the piano. It was presumably through his mother also that he became acquainted with Wagner — in the 1860s he assisted the composer by preparing fair copies of *Meistersinger* for the printers. As Richter's conducting career became established, he naturally emerged as one of the leading champions of Wagner's music, and he was invited to conduct *The Ring* at Bayreuth in 1876. Two years later he became chief conductor of the Bayreuth Festival.

It was as a Wagner conductor that Richter began his career in Britain, sharing with the composer the conducting of a Wagner Festival at the Royal Albert Hall in 1877. From 1879 Richter was an established part of London musical life, following the launching of the first of the very successful annual series of Richter concerts. After the death of Sir Michael Costa in 1885, Richter was invited to become the musical director of the Birmingham Triennial Festival. On the face of it this was an appointment difficult to justify; Richter's reputation in this country was exclusively as an orchestral conductor. Although he had conducted opera on the Continent, he had had little involvement with large-scale choral works — the main fare at the major British festivals. He was still unfamiliar with the work of those British composers kept busy providing the festivals with their regular 'novelties' and he had no experience in the administration of such large-scale festivals. On the other hand, the Birmingham committee no doubt recognised the commercial value of capturing a young conductor with a rapidly growing international reputation. There was, of course, considerable opposition to Richter's appointment. It was felt that a British conductor would have been more suitable in view of the nature of the Festival — and in particular the appointment was seen as a personal snub to Sullivan, who was generally considered to be the conductor most suitably qualified. Sullivan expressed his own dissatisfaction to his friend, the critic Joseph Bennett, tempering his disappointment with his characteristic generosity and magnanimity: 'I should certainly have considered it an honour if they had offered me the festival, whether I could have undertaken it or not. But it is not entirely selfish, for not a thought of envy or regret should I have felt if Cowen, Stanford, Barnby or

Randegger had been selected. They would have done the work well . . . I think it is an affront to all of us English.' In general the appointment of Richter to the Birmingham Festival was considered to be yet another example of a committee of businessmen failing to understand the musical problems involved.

Things seem to have started well, however. Many years later Stanford, in an essay on the great conductors of his youth, recalled the effect Richter had at Birmingham. He wrote: 'England had been, for long, in a condition of mezzo-forte in orchestral playing. The best material was there, but perform- ances were only pretty good. To make them super-excellent as players was the work of an authoritative man such as Richter. He swept away the ridiculous hash of everlasting items from opera . . . . He restored the orchestra to its proper balance . . . . He signalised his tenure at Birmingham by securing Joachim to play. He knew his value, and the personal effect the great violinist would have upon all the players who came into contact with him. With that Festival mediocrity disappeared.'

Undoubtedly Richter's influence on the standard of orchestral playing in this country was considerable. Stories abound of his patient coaxing of players to produce tone-colours from their instruments which were outside their previous experience. In particular, as a horn player himself, he laid great emphasis on improving the standard of tone production of horn players. He was not above stepping down amongst the orchestra in order to take the instrument from the player's hand in order to give a personal demonstration of his requirements. Stanford, on the evidence of the essay already quoted, and which was published in his collection *Interludes* in 1922, clearly held Richter in high regard — but he was by no means blind to his limitations, and it is from Stanford's picture of Richter's musical personality that we can obtain a glimpse of those blind-spots which inevitably led to the failure of the 1900 *Gerontius* performance:

> Richter was often stiff in his reading of an unfamiliar score. [He] was, and remained, a species of ideal bandmaster . . . for him, all music which was not German was foreign. Richter was all for straight- forwardness. He hated extravagance, and even took the 'diablerie' out of Berlioz. He took everything from the standpoint of commonsense; for this reason he was strongest in what he knew best — Beethoven, Weber and the *Meistersinger*. He was not often electric [although] he had magnetism . . . . He had an even temper, was always careful [and was] little affected by moods.

Despite this apparent equanimity, Richter was undoubtedly an authoritarian conductor of the old-fashioned type. Eugene Goossens who, as a young man in Liverpool, regularly attended Hallé concerts conducted by Richter, recalls in his autobiography *Overture and Beginners* an incident when an unfortunate cymbal player miscounted his bars in the finale of the Dvorák *New World* symphony. The resultant misplaced crash drew a glare of fury from the conductor — the full horror of which can readily be imagined by anyone who has seen a photograph of Richter's stern, imposing figure. Richter's eye remained fixed on the poor musician until the end of the movement, and at the end of the concert the man was instantly dismissed. Despite incidents like this, Richter was held in great affection by British orchestral players although Goossens goes so far as to describe him as 'a martinet'.

As far as Richter's conducting technique is concerned, Goossens gives a description which perhaps clarifies what Stanford meant by an 'ideal bandmaster':

> There is a tendency among my older colleagues to disparage his conducting powers in the light of flashier and more recent stick technique. Richter's technique was simplicity itself. He used a short, thick piece of cane with a padded grip, and indulged in few superfluous gestures . . . . The beat was a square one, vehement, simple and best suited to classic and romantic styles. Especially in long sustained rhythmic patterns did he preserve a marvellous continuity of style.

From these accounts we can conclude that Richter was a thoroughly sound, conscientious and painstaking musician, of the highest integrity, but ultimately perhaps just a little dull and emotionally contained as an interpreter. Against this, however, must be placed his indefatigable support for new music and he clearly regarded it as his duty as an internationally respected conductor, to use his position to give the works of young composers a fair hearing — whether or not he himself felt temperamentally in tune with their idiom. Goossens reminds us of his early championship of Richard Strauss 'and much other fairly provocative music' and says that only French impressionism 'utterly escaped him'. Yet his inhibitions sometimes prevented his getting close to the works of the more mature German composers of the latter half of the nineteenth century — Stanford tells a story of Brahms leaving a concert hall in anger at Richter's treatment of the slow movement of his First Symphony.

By the time of the preparation for the *Gerontius* performance,

Elgar had every reason to feel confident of Richter's ability to understand his work — after all Richter had already given two splendid performances of the *Enigma Variations. Gerontius,* however, occupies a totally different world — much further from the mainstream of European music of that time, and consequently further from Richter's safest ground. Perhaps if the preparations for the performance had been less disrupted, Richter's professional competence might have resulted in an adequate representation of the work. Under the circumstances only the inspiration that comes from total involvement could have pulled together the scattered threads. Elgar's friends shared his bitterness. The great Sheffield choral conductor, Henry Coward, not only attended the performance, but had been Elgar's guest at several of the choral rehearsals — including the one when Elgar's frustration allowed him to express his dissatisfaction with the quality of the choral singing in rather immoderate terms — succeeding only in alienating the singers still further. Coward was in no doubt that Richter should be held chiefly responsible for the failure of the Birmingham performance, and in his memoirs had this to say about the great conductor's limitations:

> Even the cleverest man has his prejudices and limitations in sympathies, outlook, and grasp of musical idiom. A striking case of limited attainment is afforded by Dr Hans Richter. He was undoubtedly a great orchestral conductor, but as a choral conductor he was quite ordinary. The worst performances of *Messiah, Faust* (Berlioz) and *Gerontius* were under his baton, and, though he was excused on grounds of his lack of sympathy with, or knowledge of, the idiom of the works, this did not make for the musical success of a festival. He, being a German, was not criticised, whereas, for a similar result, an Englishman would have been flayed alive.

Richter's career in Britain lasted little over a further decade after *Gerontius.* The regular seasons of Richter concerts in London ceased in 1897 when Richter succeeded to the conductorship of the Hallé concerts in Manchester, following the death of Charles Hallé. Interestingly this appointment aroused just as much opposition from the English musical establishment as his appointment to the Birmingham Festival. Again it was felt that Manchester should have a British conductor — an attitude hard to justify in view of Hallé's own German origins! Richter rarely conducted orchestral concerts in London after this time, although he became a familiar conductor at Covent Garden, where he conducted several complete cycles of *The Ring.* At Manchester he gave in 1908 the first performance of Elgar's First

Symphony — a completely successful occasion — thus making amends to the composer and his admirers for the Birmingham disappointment. By this time, however, Richter's health was failing, and in particular his eyesight was rapidly deteriorating to an extent that he found the reading of orchestral scores almost impossible. The following year he conducted his last Birmingham Festival and two years later terminated his association with the Manchester orchestra. He retired to Bayreuth where he remained for the last years of his life. Although the political climate after 1914 forced him to renounce the many academic and other honours awarded him during his career in Britain, Richter retained to the last an interest in the composers and other musicians who he had encouraged through his Birmingham, Manchester and London associations. In particular he would always ask any visiting British musician about 'Unser Elgar'. Despite the war, Richter was able to get occasional letters through to his British friends, and in one of the last of these, addressed to his son-in-law, Sydney Loeb, and written only a few months before his death in 1916, Richter movingly gives us clear evidence of how much the years spent in Britain had meant to him:

> Give my love to my friends and all the artists who worked with me, when you meet them. They are with me in my waking hours and in my dreams and my thoughts of them are always good and pleasurable. With thankfulness I think of the hours I spent with them. They were the happiest of my artistic life.

Based on an article in
The Elgar Society Newsletter,
January 1978

PART IV: ELGAR AT HOME

Elgar at 'Forli'
by R.J. Buckley

Robert J. Buckley, music critic of The Birmingham Gazette, *was Elgar's first biographer, his book appearing in 1904. Whilst being sketchy in details and telling us little about the music, it nevertheless has the distinction of the composer's seal of approval. One of Buckley's most interesting chapters is an account of Elgar's life at his home, Forli, Alexandra Road, Malvern Link, and for that reason it is reproduced here.*

A word of explanation is required concerning the date of this interview. Buckley's opening allusion to the Black Knight *period (1890-1892) is misleading, and later references to the forthcoming Worcester Festival at which* Lux Christi *is to be performed date the meeting as the summer of 1896.*

It was in the *Black Knight* period that I first visited the composer at *Forli*, a charming cottage under the shadow of the Malvern Hills, meet situation for the dreamy tone-poet, the creator of ravishing harmonies. It was the riotous summer. The hedge of the lawn before the house was in flower, and the wicket opened amid poetic blooms. Close at hand was a larger lawn, a pleasaunce of sloping banks and smooth-shaven turf, whereon was a sunny tent, the opening of which commanded a glorious valley, extending to the purple horizon. 'Forty miles and never a brick!' ejaculated mine host, as we took our seats in this ideal retreat, where were easy chairs, a table and a couch which reminded me of Rossini dashing off operas in bed. There, too, was a proof copy of *Lux Christi,* afterwards called *The Light of Life,* concerning which we held sweet converse together. The Worcester Festival was due in a few months, and the composer felt that much depended on the success of this, his first choral work to be heard at an important meeting. Overflowing with enthusiasm, he spoke rapidly and continuously of the state of musical art in England, deploring the fate of works commissioned for festivals, which, after painstaking and elaborate production, were heard no more. His bearing was that of one in deadly earnest, not wholly inaccessible to the jocular, but too intent on his aim to waste time on anything not directly leading to the goal. He laughed but rarely, and his mirth was soon checked. In the heat of the early struggle, and with the winning-post in sight, his mind seemed occupied with a fixed resolve to make the world aware of the power he believed to be his own. *King Olaf* was in hand, and the tent was littered with sheets of music-paper bearing myriad pencil marks, undecipherable to the stranger as the hieroglyphics on a blackbird's egg, and, like the proverbial lost pocket-book, of no use to any one but the owner. From the tent-pole a flag fluttered in the breeze, delicate hint that the composer was at work, and must not be lightly disturbed. But, as he explained, the restriction was more in jest than in earnest, and the flag was frequently struck.

Of a fugue in *The Light of Life* he said: 'I thought a fugue would be expected of me. The British public would hardly tolerate oratorio without fugue. So I tried to give them one. Not a "barn-door" fugue, but one with an independent accompaniment. There's a bit of canon, too, and in short, I hope there's enough counterpoint to give the real British religious respectability!' All this of course is badinage. Questioned as to his actual feeling for the perpetuation of the fugal style, he rose and walked rapidly about, as is his custom when interested. 'It has been done,' he said. 'Bach has done it. No man has a greater reverence for Bach than I. I play three or four preludes and fugues from the *Well-tempered Klavier* every day. No 33, in E major, is one of my favourites. No 31 is another, and No 29, a wonderful masterpiece, is constantly before me. But my veneration for Bach is no reason why I should imitate Bach. I certainly can't beat Bach in the Bach manner, and if any one asks me why I don't write in the Bach style, I think I shall say, "It has been done, once and for ever — by Bach!" You were talking of contrapuntal rules and restrictions. I have gone over them all: marked, learned, and inwardly digested everything available in theoretical instruction I could come across (and I think I have come across most of what has been written); and I cherish a profound respect for the old theorists. They were useful in their day, but they were not entitled to lay down hard and fast rules for all composers to the end of time.'

He paused and walked out into the sunshine. 'My idea,' he continued, 'is that there is music in the air, music all around us, the world is full of it and' — (here he raised his hands, and made a rapid gesture of capture) — 'and — you —simply — simply — take as much as you require!'

Truly a short compendium of the bookish theorick, and as satisfactory as short, the only important objection being occasional absence of the Elgarian grip.

Not music only, but books and literature, came under review on this occasion. The composer revealed himself as a book enthusiast, a haunter of the remoter shelves of the secondhand shops, with a leaning to the rich and rare. In the sitting-room was a grand piano, in the study a smaller instrument, surrounded by books, and books, and more books. He declared himself a devoted reader of all kinds of literature, and chuckled over a novel wherein an orchestra was described as awaiting the fall of the conductor's bâton, the trumpeters with their instruments pressed to their lips in eager anticipation, the piece being the introduction to the *Messiah* overture. Referring to his leaning to the *leitmotiv*, he said that his early studies in this direction were based on Mendelssohn, long before he had seen or heard a note of Wagner. His sketch-books of twenty years before contain experiments in all kinds of curious rhythms, 5-4, 7-4, 15-4, and even 11-4, of which the only published result seems to be the 7-4 Lament in *Caractacus*.

It was during this visit that Elgar spoke of a Malvern book club, a sort of literary federation, of which he was the first member, which enabled Malvern readers to know each other's libraries, the late Mrs Lynn Linton being an enthusiastic supporter. The surrounding piles of books were expressive of the man, but other features of the study spoke his many-sidedness. A large portrait of Wagner was conspicuous, and a board over the fireplace displayed in poker-work an ascending flash of chromatic semi-quavers. 'The Fire-motive', he said, 'from the *Ring of the Nibelungen;* one of my own attempts at decoration.' A cosy room, with quaint bric-a-brac from foreign lands; bits of carving from the Bavarian Highlands, then his annual summer resort. He showed the silver buttons of his waistcoat as specimens of Bavarian handicraft, described the character of the people, and pointing to the score of *The Light of Life* said he wrote the beginning of number three recitative and chorus, 'As Jesus passed by', six thousand feet above the sea-level.

'It has at least that claim to be called high art,' he remarked airily.

Tacked lightly to the wall was an uproarious illustrated joke cut from a German newspaper, and in a dim corner a photograph of a thirteenth-century panel sculpture of the Crucifixion from Worcester Cathderal. 'It shows a wonderful feeling', he remarked, as he looked upon it lovingly. Presently he spoke of recreations, and declared a liking for golf, remarking that if not of the first force he was certainly animated by the best intentions. He was for some time a follower of the American craze for kite-flying, with its aerial photography and its scientific aims, desiring to invent a compensating kite that should adapt itself to whatsoever currents it might meet in its celestial course. Kites, it seemed, were not to be relied on in unexpected emergencies. Sailing away in a suitable wind, and giving promise of irreproachable conduct, they were apt suddenly to jib, to fly in the wrong direction, to bolt, kick, plunge, buck, cavort, and to be guilty of other deplorable excesses. It was his hope to restrain these unregenerate tendencies, to break in and bridle the innate *diablerie* of the fiery untamed kite in a state of nature, and by taking much thought to compose a kite that might be useful. Nothing came of it except the fall of his neighbour's spouting, and the occasional employment of a powerful navvy to pull down the rebellious thing from the central blue.

Looking at Elgar's music, one may see in its general audacity the spirit of one who would invent a flying-machine. *Eripuit coelo fulmen* may surely be said of him. But if he has snatched fire from heaven, the feat was not accomplished by means of long-tailed, or square-tailed, or bob-tailed kites.

In these pleasant days at *Forli,* he declared his musical creed to be a love of everything that was good, whatever its style or period. He would go a hundred miles to hear a Wagner opera, and would enjoy a Haydn quartet, if a good example. Music, he thought, should be progressive; to stand still was to perish, or at least to degenerate. He would have enjoyed working on opera, but wanted both subject and libretto. Such was Edward Elgar three months before the production of *The Light of Life.*

Elgar at 'Craeg Lea'
by Rudolph de Cordova

Perhaps the main claim to fame of The Strand Magazine *is that it contained the first publication of some of Conan Doyle's Sherlock Holmes stories. It also included a series of* Illustrated Interviews, *of which the following was one of the most celebrated. It was conducted during the last months of the composer's residence at* Craeg Lea, *Malvern.*

'If ever this votary of the muse of song looked from the hills of his present home at Malvern, from the cradle of English poetry, the scene of the vision of Piers Plowman, and from the British camp, with its legendary memories of his own *Caractacus,* and in the light of the rising sun sees the towers of Tewkesbury and Gloucester and Worcester, he might recall in that view the earlier stages of his career, and confess with modest pride, like the bard in the *Odyssey:-*

Self-taught I sing; 'tis Heaven, and Heaven alone, Inspires my song with music all its own.'

It was in November 1900 that these words were spoken by the Orator when the University of Cambridge honoured itself by conferring the honorary degree of Doctor of Music on Dr Elgar, whom one of the most distinguished German writers on music declared to be 'the most brilliant champion of the National School of Composition which is beginning to bloom in England.'

The encomiums which Germany — the acknowledged leader of the world in music — has showered on Dr Elgar have at length been reflected in England, which has awakened to the fact that to him at least that much misapplied word 'genius' belongs by right divine. That awakening was marked by the three days' festival in the middle of March, when Covent Garden Opera House reverted to an old custom and for two glorious nights became the home of oratorio, with a concert on the third night. That festival is unique in the history of music, for it is the first time an English composer has been so honoured.

However gratifying the applause of the public may be to the worker in any art, his greatest pleasure must properly come from his fellow-workers, who know the difficulties which have to be surmounted before the desired effect can be produced.

'Was not Herr Steinbach, the conductor of the Meiningen Orchestra, among the others who said that you have something different from anybody else in the tone of your orchestra?' I asked Dr Elgar, as we sat in his study at Malvern, with a great expanse of country visible through the wide windows.

'I believe so,' he replied; 'and that remark has been one from which I have naturally derived great pleasure.'

'You know,' said Dr Elgar, as he settled down to talk for the purpose of this interview, in accordance with a long-standing promise made in what he came to regard as an unguarded moment — 'you know, since you compel me to begin at the beginning, that I 'began' in Broadheath, a little village three miles from Worcester, in which city my father was organist of St George's Catholic Church, a post he held for thirty-seven years. I was a very little boy indeed when I began to show some aptitude for music and used to extemporize on the piano. When I was quite small I received a few lessons on the piano. The organ-loft then attracted me, and from the time I was about seven or eight I used to go and sit by my father and watch him play. After a time I began to try to play myself. At first the only thing I succeeded in producing was noise, but gradually, out of the chaos, harmony began to evolve itself. In those days, too, an English opera company used to visit the old Worcester Theatre, and I was taken into the orchestra, which consisted of only eight or ten performers, and so heard old operas like *Norma, Traviata, Trovatore*, and, above all, *Don Giovanni*.

'My general education was not neglected. I went to Littleton House School until I was about fifteen. At the same time I saw and learnt a great deal about music from the stream of music that passed through my father's establishment.

'My hope was that I should be able to get a musical education, and I worked hard at German on the chance that I should go to Leipzig, but my father discovered that he could not afford to send me away, and anything in that direction seemed to be at an end. Then a friend, a solicitor, suggested that I should go to him for a year and see how I liked the law. I went for a year, but came to the conclusion that the law was not for me, and I determined to return to music. There appeared to be an opening for a violinist in Worcester, and as it occurred to me that it would be a good thing to try to take advantage of the opening, I had been teaching myself to play the violin. Then I began to teach on my own account, and spent such leisure as I had in writing music. It was music of a sort — bad, very bad — but my juvenile efforts are, I hope, destroyed.

'Although I was teaching the violin I wanted to improve my playing, so I began to save up in order to go to London to get some lessons from Herr Pollitzer. On one occasion I was working the first violin part of the Haydn quartet. There was a rest, and I suddenly began to play the 'cello part. Pollitzer looked up. 'You know the whole thing?' he said.

' "Of course," I replied.

'He looked up, curiously. "Do you compose yourself?" he asked.

' "I try," I replied again.

' "Show me something of yours," he said.

'I did so, with the result that he gave me an introduction to Mr, now Sir, August Manns, who, later on, played many of my things at the daily concerts at the Crystal Palace.

'When I resolved to become a musician and found that the exigencies of life would prevent me from getting any tuition, the only thing to do was to teach myself. I read everything, played everything, and heard everything I possibly could. As I have told you, I used to play the organ and the violin. I attended as many of the cathedral services as I could to hear the anthems, and to get to know what they were, so as to become thoroughly acquainted with the English Church style. The putting of the fine new organ into the cathedral at Worcester was a great event, and brought many organists to play there at various times. I went to hear them all. The services at the cathedral were over later on Sunday than those at the Catholic church, and as soon as the voluntary was finished at the church I used to rush over to the cathedral to hear the concluding voluntary. Eventually I succeeded my father as organist at St George's. We lived at that time in the parish of St Helen's, in which is the mother church of Worcester, which had a peal of eight bells. The Curfew used always to be rung in those days at eight o'clock in the evening, and I believe it is still rung. I made friends with the sexton and used to ring the Curfew, and afterwards strike the day of the month. My enthusiasm was so great that I used to prolong the ringing from three minutes to ten minutes, until the people in the neighbourhood complained, when I had to reduce the time. On Sunday the bells were supposed to go for half an hour before service, from half-past ten to eleven. The performance was divided into certain parts. With a friend, I used to 'raise' and 'fall' the bell for ten minutes, chime a smaller bell for ten minutes or so, and at five minutes to eleven I would fly off to play the organ at the Catholic church.

'You ask me to go into greater details about my musical education. I am constantly receiving letters on this point from all over the world, for it is well known that I am self-taught in the matter of harmony, counterpoint, form, and, in short, the whole of the "mystery" of music, and people want to know what books I used. To-day there are all sorts of books to make the study of harmony and orchestration pleasant. In my young days they were repellent. But I read them and I still exist.'

If only cold type could suggest the humour with which those words were spoken!

'The first was Catel, and that was followed by Cherubini. The first real sort of friendly leading I had, however, was from *Mozart's Thorough - bass School.* There was something in that to go upon — something human. It is a small book — a collection of papers beautifully and clearly expressed — which he wrote on harmony for the niece of a friend of his. I still treasure the old volume. Ouseley and Macfarren followed, but the articles which have since helped me the most are those of Sir Hubert Parry in *Grove's Dictionary.*'

'How did these various authorities mix?' I interrupted.

'They didn't mix,' was Dr Elgar's reply, 'and it appears it is necessary for anyone who has to be self-taught to read everything and — pick out the best. That, I suppose, is the difficulty — to pick out the best. How to forget the rubbish and remember the good I can't tell you, but perhaps that is where his brains must come in.

'It would be affectation were I to pretend that my work is not recognised as modern, and I hate affectation, yet it would probably surprise you to know the amount of work I did in studying musical form. Only those can safely disregard form who ignore it with a full knowledge and do not evade it through ignorance.

'Mozart is the musician from whom everyone should learn form. I once ruled a score for the same instruments and with the same number of bars as Mozart's G Minor Symphony, and in that framework I wrote a symphony, following as far as possible the same outline in the themes and the same modulation. I did this on my own initiative, as I was groping in the dark after light, but looking back after thirty years I don't know any discipline from which I learned so much.

'So you insist on my telling you some more of my early struggles and my early work? I was interested in many other things besides music, and I had the good fortune to be thrown among an unsorted collection of old books. There were books of all kinds, and all distinguished by the characteristic that they were for the most part incomplete. I busied myself for days and weeks arranging them. I picked out the theological books, of which there were a good many, and put them on one side. Then I made a place for the Elizabethan dramatists, the chronicles including Baker's and Hollinshed's, besides a tolerable collection of old poets and translations of Voltaire, and all sorts of things up to the eighteenth century. Then I began to read. I used to get up at four or five o'clock in the summer and read — every available opportunity found me reading. I read till dark. I finished by reading every one of those books — including the theology. The result of that reading has been that people tell me I know more of life up to the eighteenth century than I do of my own time, and it is probably true.

'In studying scores the first which came into my hands were the Beethoven symphonies. Anyone can have them now, but they were difficult for a boy to get in Worcester thirty years ago. I, however, managed to get two or three, and I remember distinctly the day I was able to buy the Pastoral Symphony. I stuffed my pockets with bread and cheese and went out into the fields to study it. That was what I always did. Even when I began to teach, when a new score came into my hands I went off for a long day with it out of doors, and when my unfortunate — or fortunate? — pupils went for their lessons I was not at home to give them.

'By the way, talking about scores, it will probably surprise you to know that I never possessed a score of Wagner until one was given to me in 1900.

'In the early days of which I have been speaking five of us established a wind quintet. We had two flutes, an oboe, a clarionet, and a bassoon, which last I played for some time, and afterwards relinquished it for the 'cello. There was no music at all to suit our peculiar requirements, as in the ideal wind quintet a horn should find a place and not a second flute, so I used to write the music. We met on Sunday afternoons, and it was an understood thing that we should have a new piece every week. The sermons in our church used to take at least half an hour, and I spent the time composing the thing for the afternoon. It was great experience for me, as you may imagine, and the books are all extant, so some of that music still exists. We played occasionally for friends, and I remember one moonlight night stopping in front of a house to put the bassoon together. I held it up to see if it was straight before tightening it. As I did so, someone rushed out of the house, grabbed me by the arms, and shouted, "It will be five shillings if you do." He thought I had a gun in my hand.

'The old Worcester Glee Club had been established as long ago as 1809 for the performance of old glees, with an occasional instrumental night. At these last I first played second fiddle and afterwards became leader, as, after a time, I used to do the accompanying. It was an enjoyable and artistic gathering, and the programmes were principally drawn from the splendid English compositions for men's voices. The younger generation seemed to prefer ordinary part-songs, and ballads also were introduced, and the tone of the thing changed. I am not sure if the club is still in existence.

'It was in 1877 that I first went to take lessons of Pollitzer. He suggested that I should stay in London and devote myself to violin playing, but I had become enamoured of a country life, and would not give up the prospect of a certain living by playing and teaching in Worcester on the chance of only a possible success which I might make as a soloist in London.

'The thing which brought me before a larger public as a composer was the production of several things of mine at Birmingham by Mr W.C. Stockley, to whom my music was introduced by Dr Wareing, himself a composer, and still resident in Birmingham. At that time I was a member of Mr Stockley's orchestra — first violin.'

In this connection it is interesting to break Dr Elgar's narrative to tell an anecdote which Mr Stockley relates. When he decided to do something of Dr Elgar's, he asked him if he would like to conduct it. 'Certainly not,' Dr Elgar replied; 'I am a member of the orchestra and I am going to stick in the orchestra. I am not recognised as a composer, and the fact that you are going to do something of mine gives me no title to a place anywhere else.' The piece was a success and the audience called for Dr Elgar, who came down from among the fiddles, made his bow, and then went back to his place.

To resume. 'Don't suppose, however,' Dr Elgar said, 'that after that recognition as a composer things were easy for me. The directors of the old Promenade Concerts at Covent Garden Theatre were good enough to write that they thought sufficiently of my things to devote a morning to rehearsing them. I went on the appointed day to London to conduct the rehearsal. When I arrived it was explained to me that a few songs had to be taken before I could begin. Before the songs were finished Sir Arthur Sullivan unexpectedly arrived, bringing with him a selection from one of his operas. It was the only chance he had of going through it with the orchestra, so they determined to take advantage of the opportunity. He consumed all my time in rehearsing this, and when he had finished the director came out and said to me, "There will be no chance of your going through your music to-day." I went back to Worcester to my teaching, and that was the last of my chance of an appearance at the Promenade Concerts.

'Years after I met Sullivan, one of the most amiable and genial souls that ever lived. When we were introduced he said, "I don't think we have met before." "Not exactly," I replied, "but very near it," and I told him the circumstance. "But my dear boy, I hadn't the slightest idea of it," he exclaimed, in his enthusiastic manner. "Why on earth didn't you come and tell me? I'd have rehearsed it myself for you." They were not idle words. He would have done it, just as he said. He never forgot the episode till the end of his life.

'Two similar occurrences took place at the Crystal Palace: rehearsals were planned which never came off, so I was no nearer to getting a hearing for big orchestral works.

'Mr Hugh Blair, then the organist of Worcester Cathedral, saw some of the cantata, *The Black Knight,* and said: "If you will finish it I will produce it at Worcester." I finished it, and it was produced by the Worcester Festival Choir. This cantata then came under the notice of Dr Swinnerton Heap, to whom I owe my introduction to the musical festivals as a writer of choral works. He had known me for a good many years as a violinist, but it had never occurred to him to talk to me about my composing, and he knew nothing of it.

'It was through Dr Heap that I was asked to write a cantata for the Staffordshire Musical Festival, and, shortly after, the committee asked me to provide an oratorio for the Worcester Festival. They were *The Light of Life,* performed in Worcester Cathedral, and *King Olaf,* at Hanley.

'Since then it has been a record of the production of one composition after another until we come to *The Apostles,* and my new overture *In the South,* produced at Covent Garden; the one great event that particularly stands out is the production of the *Variations* by Dr Richter, to whom I was then a complete stranger.

'For a long time I had had the idea of writing *The Apostles* in pretty much the form in which I hope it will eventually appear. As you know, there have been oratorios on many points of Jewish and Christian history, but none had shown how Christianity has

risen. I take the men who were in touch with Christ, the Apostles
in fact, and show them to be ordinary mortals rather than
superhuman men, as they are generally represented in art. I was
always particularly impressed with Archbishop Whately's
conception of Judas, who, as he wrote, "had no design to betray
his Master to death, but to have been as confident of the will of
Jesus to deliver Himself from His enemies by a miracle as He must
have been certain of His power to do so, and accordingly to have
designed to force Him to make such a display of His superhuman
powers as would have induced all the Jews — and, indeed, the
Romans too — to acknowledge Him King."

'In carrying out this plan I made the book myself, taking out
lines from different parts of the Bible which exactly express my
conception. How it was done the following chorus will show you,
for you will notice that the references to the text are printed in the
margin:

> The Lord hath chosen them to stand before Him, to serve Him. —
> *II.Chron. 29, 11.*
> He hath chosen the weak to confound the mighty. — *I. Cor. 1, 27.*
> He will direct their work in truth. — *Isa. 61, 8.*
> Behold, God exalteth by His power: who teacheth like Him? — *Job
> 36, 22.*
> The meek will He guide in judgement, and the meek will He teach
> His way. — *Ps. 25, 9.*
> He will direct their work in truth. — *Isa. 61, 8.*
> For out of Zion shall go forth the law. — *Isa. 2, 3.*

'You will notice that occasionally, as in the third extract, I have
used the words in their meaning that appears on the surface, and
not in the real meaning of the sentence which may be found in any
commentary. To keep the diction exactly the same I have not
gone outside the Scripture except in one sentence from the
Talmud in the case of the watchers on the Temple roof.

'It was part of my original scheme to continue *The Apostles* by a
second work carrying on the establishment of the Church among
the Gentiles. This, too, is to be followed by a third oratorio, in
which the fruit of the whole — that is to say, the end of the world
and the Judgement — is to be exemplified. I, however, faltered at
that idea, and I suggested to the directors of the Birmingham
Festival to add merely a short third part to the two into which the
already published work, *The Apostles,* is divided. But I found that
to be unsatisfactory, and I have decided to revert to my original
lines. There will, therefore, be two other oratorios.'

This definite pronouncement of Dr Elgar's cannot fail to evoke the warmest anticipations on the part of the music-loving world.

It is worth noting here that shortly after *The Dream of Gerontius* was produced at the Birmingham Festival, in 1900, Herr Julius Buths, the famous conductor of Düsseldorf, was so struck with it that he determined to produce it in Germany and himself translated the libretto. So great a success was this performance that *The Dream,* which one of the most celebrated German musical critics has declared to be 'the greatest composition of the last hundred years, with the exception of the *Requiem* of Brahms,' was repeated at the Lower Rhine Festival, a thing hitherto unheard of in the annals of English music, and at the Lower Rhine Festival on Whit Sunday *The Apostles* is to be given.

Dr Elgar has a delightful and most acute sense of humour, so that I was sure I should not be misunderstood if I ventured to ask a question about his 'musical crimes'.

He smiled. 'But which of my musical crimes do you mean? From the point of view of one person or another I understand all my music has been a crime,' he replied, lightly. Then he added, 'Oh, you mean *The Cockaigne, The Coronation Ode,* and *The Imperial March* especially. Yes, I believe there are a good many people who have objected to them. But I like to look on the composer's vocation as the old troubadours or bards did. In those days it was no disgrace to a man to be turned on to step in front of an army and inspire the people with a song. For my own part, I know that there are a lot of people who like to celebrate events with music. To these people I have given tunes. Is that wrong? Why should I write a fugue or something which won't appeal to anyone, when the people yearn for things which can stir them — '

'Such as *Pomp and Circumstance,*' I interpolated.

'Ah, I don't know anything about that,' replied Dr Elgar, 'but I do know we are a nation with great military proclivities, and I did not see why the ordinary quick march should not be treated on a large scale in the way that the waltz, the old-fashioned slow march, and even the polka have been treated by the great composers; yet all marches on the symphonic scale are so slow that people can't march to them. I have some of the soldier instinct in me, and so I have written two marches of which, so far from being ashamed, I am proud. *Pomp and Circumstance,* by the way, is merely the generic name for what is a set of six marches. Two, as you know, have already appeared, and the others will come later. One of them is to be a Soldier's Funeral March.

'As for *The Imperial March,* which was written for Queen Victoria's Diamond Jubilee of 1897, it would, perhaps, interest you to know that only on 22nd January last it was given in St George's Chapel, Berlin, at the unveiling of the memorials of Queen Victoria and the Empress Frederick, and Dr G.R. Sinclair, of Hereford Cathedral, played it on the organ.

'How and when do I do my music? I can tell you very easily. I come into my study at nine o'clock in the morning and I work till a quarter to one. I don't do any inventing then, for that comes anywhere and everywhere. It may be when I am walking, golfing, or cycling, or the ideas may come in the evening, and then I sit up until any hour in order to get them down. The morning is devoted to revising and orchestration, of which I have as much to do as I can manage. As soon as lunch is over I go out for exercise and return about four or later, after which I sometimes do two hours' work before dinner. A country life I find absolutely essential to me, and here the conditions are exactly what I require. As you see,' and Dr Elgar moved over to the large window which takes up the whole of one side of his study, 'I get a wonderful view of the surrounding country. I can see across Worcestershire, to Edgehill, the Cathedral of Worcester, the Abbeys of Pershore and Tewkesbury, and even the smoke from round Birmingham. It is delightfully quiet, and yet in contrast with it there is a constant stream of communication with the outside world in the shape of cables from America and Australia, and letters innumerable from all over the world.'

In the house itself there are not many evidences of Dr Elgar's productions, but prominent in a corner of the drawing-room is the laurel wreath presented to him at Düsseldorf when *The Dream* was first produced. The leaves are brown to-day, but the scarlet ribbon is as bright as the memory of the music in the enraptured ears of those who have heard it. In his study are two prized possessions, the one a tankard made by some members of the Festival Choir at Hanley at the time of the production of *King Olaf*. The inscription, taken from one of the choruses, is, appropriately, a Bacchanalian one:-

> The ale was strong;
> King Olaf feasted late and long. — Longfellow.

Next to this is a cup, also specially designed by Mr Noke, of Hanley, to commemorate the performance of *The Dream*. On one side is a portrait of Cardinal Newman and on the other a portrait of Dr Elgar, with the following inscription from the work itself:

Learn that the flame of the everlasting love
Doth burn ere it transform.

The Strand Magazine, May 1904

Elgar at 'Plas Gwyn'
by Gerald Cumberland

Gerald Cumberland was the pseudonym of Charles Frederick Kenyon, best remembered for a highly-outspoken book of essays on famous personalities of the time, published in 1919 under the title of Set Down in Malice. (*He went some way towards atonement with another volume,* Written in Friendship, *in 1923.) Elgar was one of the victims of the earlier collection, but Cumberland had previously published at least three other interviews with him, all dating from the* Plas Gwyn *period. The earliest of these, originally entitled* A Day with Sir Edward Elgar, *forms the first part of the present Chapter; the second is the relevant portion of the notorious book.*

To a superficial observer Sir Edward Elgar appears to be a man of many contradictions. He likes society, and loves solitude. He is a citizen of the world, and yet a child of Nature, devoted passionately to one corner of rural England. He is a dreamer of dreams and a seer of visions, and also is immersed in the secrets of his chemical laboratory. He is a mystic and a metaphysician, yet an ardent student of life, particularly the hidden life of the very poor and destitute. He is a composer of genius—yet one might pass a whole day in his company without discovering that he cared anything for music, so absorbed is he in the life around him, and in the literature and art of the past and present. But these diverse traits in Sir Edward Elgar's character are not in any way contradictory: they are merely the component parts of a nature that is at once extremely wide in its outlook upon life, and enthusiastically studious in certain directions. The variety of his interests, the comprehensiveness of his intellect, the depth and breadth of his nature—all these are revealed in his music: it is because they dwell in it, suffuse it, and quicken it to life, that his work has become a part of the intellectual and emotional life of the people. The influence of his work can be clearly traced in the trend of modern thought; it is the outcome of to-day's ideas, and consequently is the intellectual food of all to whom music makes appeal. To be a musician and nothing else is to work out of touch with the spirit of the age, and to make but an infinitesimal contribution to the development of thought in one's own generation.

A week or two ago I spent a day on behalf of *The Musical World* with Sir Edward Elgar, at his home in Hereford. I had already met him once before and conversed with him for five or ten minutes, receiving a very vivid impression of his personality; and this spring-like day at the end of December, spent on the banks of the Wye, was but a confirmation of the impressions previously stored up in my memory. I received an emphatic assurance that here was the man I had discovered and traced in his music, that here were the very qualities that had made him a force among the best intellects of his day. Elgar is primarily a child of the open, a veritable son of Nature. His tall, spare frame is well knit, supple, and strong; were it not for the 'student's stoop' one might take him for an athlete. He is an ardent cyclist, but he hates all forms of sport that involve killing anything. Born in the country, bred in the country, accustomed to receiving inspiration from the very smell of the delicious spring air or from the boisterous plunge and struggle of a wind from the north-west, he is not happy for long in cities: he longs for the wide horizon, the sense of space, the daily communion with Nature, who is always the same and always so different.

It is when out among the fields and meadows that Elgar is at his best: here his thoughts are free, and he gives expression to them. We discussed the subjects upon which he has been lecturing in Birmingham. These lectures have been very extensively reported in the daily Press: but, owing to the necessary condensation (and that by reporters having possibly no considerable knowledge of music), many extraordinary misconceptions have been propagated. Players of wind instruments, young and old composers, chorus-singers, conductors, and vocalists of established reputation, have all in turn become furiously angry at things that Elgar has never said: they have written to him, and to the newspapers, letters of remonstrance, argument, and abuse; and because the object of their anger has not replied to each and every correspondent, they have all taken it for granted that his or her letter is unanswerable and therefore more than justified! To have answered one would have meant answering all: for those whose complaints remained unregarded would very naturally assume that Sir Edward Elgar was unable to disown or modify the views and opinions fathered upon him by an undiscerning Press. All public men speedily recognise at the beginning of their careers that it is impossible to overtake a lie and kill it; and that to be misunderstood, misreported, and misrepresented in a thousand different ways is one of the penalties of eminence. It is to be hoped, however, that the Birmingham lectures will be issued in book-form, so that the public at large may take advantage of the privilege which the Midland citizens have already enjoyed.

I was anxious to have Elgar's views on the question of the many young and extremely talented composers who find it a matter of heart-breaking difficulty to secure a public performance of any of their works. It has always seemed to me that of all creative artists, the musical composer has the severest task before him if he desires his work to become known. In literature and art, fame is always holding out a hand to newcomers, and one must be a very indifferent poet or novelist if one cannot convince a single publisher of one's talent or genius. The British public is always on the look-out for a new novelist or new poet; every year dozens of young men and women step into prominence, eagerly invited and welcomed by the subscribers to Mudie's. It is the same in art. Jones paints a striking work and exhibits it: there is practically no difficulty in the way, for little money is spent on its production, still less on its exhibition, and—the public is waiting outside the gallery doors, impatiently longing to be let in! But in the world of music how different it all is! We simply do not *want* to hear the work of new men; it does not interest us; we prefer something we have heard twenty or thirty times before, like the Pathetic Symphony of Tchaikovsky, or the E flat Nocturne of Chopin. And withal, many of the really gifted composers of to-day place quite unnecessary difficulties in their own way. Sir Edward Elgar had a good deal to say on this matter. He pointed out that it was the custom for a young man in his early twenties to compose the most heavy and lugubrious music imaginable—music that was full of metaphysical subtleties and introspective questionings. The music may be good in itself—indeed much of it is; but the public has again and again refused to listen to the morbid self-revelations and mystical profundities of mere youths, who, howsoever great their musical talent may be, are certainly not yet sufficiently mature to originate philosophies and creeds of their own. It may be a pity that the public has assumed this attitude, but that it has done so there can be no manner of doubt. What the average man of musical tastes prefers is something frank, buoyant, hopeful, and inspiring; and it is precisely this that our young composers seem unwilling or unable to provide. When a composer has given unmistakable evidence that he has the root of the matter in him—that he is so far master of the medium in which he is working that he can express himself clearly and unhesitatingly—then probably the public will be glad to hear his more intimate and serious work. Just at present it seems to be the habit of young men to take the whole world *au grand sérieux*; it is a desperately melancholy place, without hope, without joy, without dignity or grandeur! The spirit of Omar Khayyam is upon them, and they pour out the borrowed pessimism of Tchaikovsky through the medium of orchestral effects weakly imitative of Richard Strauss. Is it likely that the public will clamour to enter concert-halls to hear the metaphysical moanings of men who in experience are little more than children? We Englishmen have in our naval and military history, in our religious struggles and traditions, in our national temper and qualities, in our literary and social achievements, and in our legends and tales, sufficient material to inspire and hearten the weakest and most cold-blooded of men. It is impossible for us Englishmen to do great work and have a school of music of our own, until we embody in it our national characteristics.

There is another point to be considered. While unwilling to speak of his own career, Sir Edward showed me that whatever he may have achieved—and I must confess he under-rates considerably the value and significance of his own work—his success has been very gradual, and a matter of slow development. He was content that his early compositions should be performed by amateur societies; it was neither his intention nor his desire that his music should receive the careful attention of the critics while he was yet feeling his way towards his own particular method and idiom. It would perhaps be not altogether to the disadvantage of the present-day young genius is he would adopt a similar method; to begin one's career by storming the Queen's Hall, or Covent Garden, or the Manchester Free Trade Hall may be valour, but it is not discretion. People who have no personal knowledge of Sir Edward Elgar, and who are particularly obtuse in penetrating below the surface of character, have on more than one occasion accused him of doing nothing to assist obscure talented composers; from my own knowledge, and from the experience of one of my friends, I know this to be false. In the case I have in mind Elgar has given generously of his time, experience, and advice, in the assistance of a young composer of obvious talent but equally indisputable obscurity; he has helped him in a dozen different ways, and in so quiet a manner that the object of his aid was scarcely aware whence it came.

We talked a good deal on the vexed question of programme

7 Two photographs of Elgar as he puts the finishing touches to the score of the *Dream of Gerontius*.

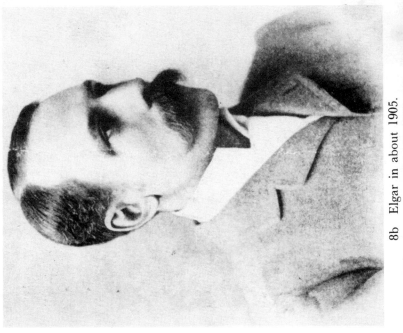

8b Elgar in about 1905.

8a Elgar in his study at 'Craeg Lea'.

music. Elgar is of the opinion that absolute music is the true form of the art—that is to say, the highest and purest form in which it can be presented. He regards programme music as a side-path branching off from the main road of absolute music: a path leading one to much beautiful country, and revealing much exquisite landscape: but that it is a natural development in which the whole art of music is about to be centred—a main road along which music must travel if it is to make legitimate and natural progress—he very strongly denies. If you point out to him that much of his own work is programme music, he laughingly acknowledges that you are quite right: he has written programme music because he cannot write anything else! He did not for one moment agree with the theory that absolute music had now exhausted its possibilities, and that the art of music was at this very moment on the borderland separating the two forms under discussion. It seemed to him that programme music was essentially the literary man's attitude towards an art with which he had sympathy, but of which his knowledge was comparatively small. As much as anything it was brought into existence through the influence of the critics, and, needless to say, it pleased them.

I should like to give you an impression, as vivid as may be, of what I regard as the real Elgar. In bearing, in physique, in temperament, in the calibre of his mind, in everything pertaining to him, he is an aristocrat. He seems to me to have wandered out of an early novel of Meredith's—say *The Ordeal of Richard Feverel*. He is that rarest of all human beings, a frankly modest genius. He sees himself in his right place in the picture, though even that is not strictly true, for he is apt to underrate the value of his work. He is intellectually equipped at all points. Chemistry is his favourite science, and his laboratory (into which I had a surreptitious peep) presents an imposing array of bottles, dishes, flasks, Bunsen burners, pestles, mortars, retorts, and all the paraphernalia of a serious chemist. As a young man he drove round with a baker's cart delivering bread to the houses of the very poor, in the hope that in this manner he might see something of the way in which they lived; and for weeks together he accompanied a doctor in the slums, eagerly in search for anything typically human. A man of the world, he is at home in the house of both prince and peasant. His wit is lambent and constantly flowing; it plays about all subjects discussed with the caressing touch of a purely sympathetic yet extravagant fancy. One does not care to dwell upon the private life of a public man, but it is a truism that one cannot obtain an exact portrait of anyone until he has been seen in the bosom of his family. One perceived in a moment that in his family life Sir Edward Elgar always exercises an extraordinary delicacy of perception, a sympathetic and affectionate give-and-take, and a charming comradeship which so seldom exist between a father and his child. In the house of father, mother, and child it was as though a gentle, kindly, and hopeful music were always to be heard—if not in the corridors and rooms, then in the hearts of their inhabitants.

The Musical World,
15th January 1906

The weaknesses that seem to be inseparable from genius—and, most particularly, from artistic genius—are precisely those one would not expect to discover associated with greatness of mind. It would appear that few men are so great as their work, or, if they are, their greatness is spasmodic and evanescent. Works of genius, it is sometimes stated, are created in moods of exaltation, when the spirit is in turmoil, when the mind is lit and the nerves are tense. In some cases it may be so. It was so, I believe, in the case of Wagner, who had long spells, measured by years, of unproductiveness, when his creative powers lay fallow; and it was so in the case of Hugo Wolf, Beethoven, Shelley, Poe, Berlioz and many other men whose names spring to the mind. But it certainly was not so with Balzac and Dickens, any more than it is to-day with Arnold Bennett.

There is in Sir Edward Elgar's work a strange contradiction: great depth of understanding combined with a curious fastidiousness of style that is almost finicking. Many aspects of life appeal to his sympathies and to his imagination, but an innate and exaggerated delicacy, an almost feminine shrinking, is noticeable in even his strongest and most outspoken work.... It is this delicacy, this shrinking, that to the casual acquaintance is at once his most conspicuous and most teasing characteristic.

My first meeting with Elgar was ten years ago, when, being commissioned to interview him for a monthly musical magazine, I called on him at the Midland Hotel, Manchester, where he was staying for a night. On my way to his room I met him in the corridor, where he carefully explained that he had made it a strict rule never to be interviewed for the Press and that under no circumstances could that rule be broken. His firm words were spoken with hesitation, and it was quite obvious to me that he was feeling more than a trifle nervous. I have little doubt that this nervousness was due to the fact that in an hour's time he was to conduct a concert at the Free Trade Hall. However, he was kind enough to loiter for some minutes and talk, but he took care, when I left him, to remind me that nothing of what he had said to me must appear in print.

I, of course, obeyed him, but, in place of an interview, I wrote an impressionistic sketch of the man as I had seen him during my few minutes' conversation at the Midland Hotel. Of this impressionistic sketch I remember nothing except that, in describing his general bearing and manner, I used the word 'aristocratic'. At this word Elgar rose like a fat trout eager to swallow a floating fly. It confirmed his own hopes. And I who had perceived this quality so speedily, so unerringly, and who had proclaimed it to the world, was worthy of reward. Yes; he would consent to be interviewed. The ban should be lifted; for once the rule should be broken. A letter came inviting me to *Plas Gwyn,* Hereford—a letter written by his wife and full of charming compliments about my article.

So to Hereford I went and talked music and chemistry. It was Christmas week, and within ten minutes of my arrival Lady Elgar was giving me hot dishes, wine and her views on the political situation. The country was in the throes of a General Election, and while I ate and drank I heard how the Empire was, as Dr Kendrick Pyne used to say, 'rushing headlong to the bow-wows.' Lady Elgar did not seem to wish to know to what particular party (if any) I belonged, but I quickly discovered that to confess myself a Radical would be to arouse feelings of hostility in her bosom. Radicals were the Unspeakable People. There was not one, I gathered, in Hereford. They appeared to infest Lancashire, and some had been heard of in Wales. Also, there were people called Nonconformists. Many persons were Radicals, many Nonconformists; but some were both. The Radicals had won several seats. What was the country coming to? Where was the country going?

Where indeed? I did not allow Lady Elgar's rather violent political prejudices to interfere with my appetite, and she appeared to be perfectly satisfied with an occasional sudden lift of my eyebrows, and such ejaculations as: 'Oh, quite! Quite!' 'Most assuredly!' and 'Incredible!' If she thought about me at all—and I am persuaded she did not—she must have believed me also to be a Tory. After all, had not I called her husband 'aristocratic', and is that the sort of word used by a Radical save in contempt?

After lunch Elgar took me a quick walk along the riverbank. For the first half-hour I found him rather reserved and non-committal, and I soon recognised that if I were to succeed in obtaining his views on any matter of interest I must rigidly abstain from direct questions. But when he did commit himself to any opinion, he did so in the manner of one who is sure of his own ground and cannot consider, even temporarily, any change in the attitude he has already assumed.

I found his views on musical critics amusing, but before proceeding to set them down I must make some reference to his relations with Ernest Newman. Newman, it is generally agreed, is unquestionably the most brilliant, the fairest-minded and the most courageous writer on music in England. His power is very great, and he has done more to educate public opinion on musical matters in England than any other man. For some little period previous to the time of which I am writing he and Elgar had been close friends, and their friendship was all the stronger because it rested on the attraction of opposites. Elgar was an ardent Catholic, a Conservative; Newman was an uncompromising free-thinker and a Radical. Elgar was a pet of society, a man careful and even snobbish in his choice of friends, whilst Newman cared nothing for society and would be friendly with any man who interested or amused him.

Up to the time Elgar composed *The Apostles* he had no more whole-hearted admirer than Newman, but this work was to sever their friendship and, for a time, to bring bitterness where before there had been esteem and even affection. Newman was invited by a New York paper—I think *The Musical Courier*—to write at considerable length on *The Apostles*. As his opinion of this work was, on the whole, unfavourable, he may possibly have hesitated to consider an invitation the acceptance of which would lead to his giving pain to a friend. But probably Newman thought, as most inflexibly honest men would think, that, on a matter of public concern, silence would be cowardly. In the event, he wrote his article and sent it to America, also forwarding a copy to Elgar himself, telling him that, though it went against his feelings of friendship to condemn the work, he thought it a matter of duty to speak what was in his mind. That letter and that article severed their friendship, and the severance lasted for some considerable time.

My visit to Elgar took place during his estrangement from Newman, and when I mentioned the subject of musical criticism to him it was, I imagine, with the hope that the name of the famous critic would crop up. It did. 'The worst of musical criticism in this country,' said Elgar, 'is that there is so much of it and so little that is serviceable. Most of those who are skilled musicians either have not the gift of criticism or they cannot express their ideas in writing, and most of those who can write are deplorably deficient in their knowledge of music. For myself I never read criticism of my own work; it simply does not interest me. When I have composed or published a work, my interest in it wanes and dies; it belongs to the public. What the professional critics think of it does not concern me in the least.'

Though I knew that Elgar had on previous occasions given expression to similar views, his statement amazed me. So I pressed him a little.

'But suppose,' I urged, 'a new work of yours were so universally condemned by the critics that performances of it ceased to take place. Would you not then read their criticisms in order to discover if there was not some truth in their statements?'

'It is possible, but I do not think I should. But your supposition is an inconceivable one: there is never universal agreement among musical critics. I think you will notice that many of them are, from the æsthetic point of view, absolutely devoid of principle; I mean, they are victims of their own temperaments. They, as the schoolgirl says, "know what they like." The music they condemn is either the music that does not appeal to their particular kind of nervous system or it is the music they do not understand. They have no standard, no norm, no historical sense, no—'

He stammered a little and waved a vague arm in the air.

'There are exceptions, of course,' I ventured. 'Newman, for example.'

'No; Ernest Newman is not altogether an exception. He is an unbeliever, and therefore cannot understand religious music— music that is at once reverential, mystical and devout.'

' "Devout"?' whispered I to myself. Aloud I said: 'A man's reason, I think, may reject a religion, though his emotional nature may be susceptible to its slightest appeal. Besides, Newman has a most profound admiration for your *The Dream of Gerontius.*'

Elgar was silent for a few minutes. Then, with an air of detachment and with great inconsequence, he said:

'Baughan, of *The Daily News*, cannot hum a melody correctly in tune. He looks at music from the point of view of a man of letters.

So does Newman, fine musician though he is. Newman advocates programme music. Now, I do not say that programme music should not be written, for I have composed programme music myself. But I do maintain that it is a lower form of art than absolute music. Newman, I believe, refuses to acknowledge that either kind is necessarily higher or lower than the other. He has, as I have said, the literary man's point of view about music. So have many musical critics.'

'And so,' I interpolated, 'if one has to accept what you say as correct, have many composers, and composers also who are not specifically literary. And, after what you have said, I find that strange. Take the case of Richard Strauss, all of whose later symphonic poems have a programme, a literary basis. Do you, for that reason, declare that Strauss regards music from the literary man's point of view—Strauss who, of all living musicians, is the greatest?'

He paused for a few moments, and it seemed to me that our pace quickened as we left the bank of the river and made for a pathway across a meadow. But he would not take up the argument; stammering a little, he said:

'Richard Strauss is a very great man—a fine fellow.'

But as that was not the point under discussion, I felt that either his mind was wandering or that he could think of no reply to my objection.

A little later, on our way home, we discussed the younger generation of composers, and I found him very appreciative of the work done by his juniors. He particularly mentioned Havergal Brian, a composer who has more than justified what Elgar prophesied of him, though perhaps not in the manner Elgar anticipated.

Apropos of something or other, Elgar said, I think quite needlessly and a little vainly:

'You must not, as many people appear to do, imagine that I am a musician and nothing else. I am many things; I find time for many things. Do not picture me always bending over manuscript paper and writing down notes; months pass at frequent intervals when I write nothing at all. At present I am making a study of chemistry.'

I think I was expected to look surprised, or to give vent to an exclamation of surprise, but I did neither, for I also had made a study of chemistry, and it seemed to me the kind of work that any man of inquiring mind might take up. I did not for one moment imagine that I was living in the first half of the nineteenth century when practically all British musicians were musicians and nothing else and not always even musicians.

When we had returned to the house we sat before a large fire and, under the soothing influence of warmth and semi-darkness, stopped all argument. In the evening Lady Elgar accompanied me to the station, and all the way from Hereford to Manchester I turned over in my mind the strange problem that was presented to me by the fact that, though I was a passionate, almost fanatical lover of Elgar's music, the creator of that music attracted me not at all. I saw in his mind a daintiness that was irritating, a refinement that was distressingly self-conscious.

Some years later Sir Edward Elgar moved to London, and when I saw him in his new home he tried to prove to me that living in London was cheaper than living in the country.

His attitude towards me on this occasion was peculiarly strange. I represented a Labour paper, but Elgar did not know that I was at the same time writing leading articles for a London Conservative daily. He treated me with the most careful kindness, a kindness so careful, indeed, that it might be called patronising. It soon became quite clear to me that he imagined I myself came from the labouring classes, but I cannot boast that honour, and as he, the aristocrat, was in contact with me, the plebeian, it was his manifest duty and his undoubted pleasure to help me along the upward path. I was advised to read Shakespeare.

'Shakespeare,' said he, 'frees the mind. You, as a journalist, will find him useful in so far as a close study of his works will purify your style and enlarge your vocabulary.'

'Which of the plays would you advise me to read?' asked I, with simulated innocence and playing up to him with eyes and voice.

The astounding man considered a minute and then mentioned half-a-dozen plays, the titles of which I carefully wrote down in my pocket-book.

'And Ruskin,' he added as an afterthought. 'Oh, yes, and Cardinal Newman. Newman's style is perhaps the purest style of any man who wrote in the nineteenth century.'

'I do not think so,' said I, thoroughly roused and forgetting to play my part. 'The *Apologia* is slipshod. My own style, faulty though it may be, is more correct, more lucid, even more distinguished than Cardinal Newman's.'

He turned away, either angry or amused.

'It is true,' said I, with warmth. 'Anyone who has tried for years, as I have done, to master the art of writing, and who examines the *Apologia* carefully will perceive at once that it is shamefully badly written. For two generations it has been the fashion to praise Newman's style, but those who have done so have never read him in a critical spirit. I would infinitely prefer to have written a racy book like—well, like *Moll Flanders*, where the English is beautifully clean and strong, than the sloppy *Apologia*.'

'*Moll Flanders*,' he said questioningly; '*Moll Flanders*? I do not know the book.'

'It is all about a whore,' said I brutally, 'written by one Defoe.'

And that, of course, put an end to our conversation. I rose to leave.

The impression left on my mind by my two visits to Elgar is definite enough, but I am willing to believe that it does not represent the man as he truly is. He is abnormally sensitive, abnormally observant, abnormally intuitive. Like almost all men, he is open to flattery, but the flattery must be applied by means of hints, praise half veiled, innuendo. If you gush he will freeze; if you praise directly, he will wince. His mind is essentially narrow, for he shrinks from the phenomena in life that hurt him and he will not force himself to understand alien things. His intellect is continually rejecting the very matters that, in order to gain largeness, tolerance and a full view of life, it should understand and accept. Yet, within its narrow confines, his brain functions most rapidly and with a clear light.

I have been told by members of the various orchestras he has conducted that when interpreting a work like *The Dream of Gerontius* his face is wet with tears.

He has a proper sense of his own dignity, and it is doubtful if he exaggerates the importance of his own powers. Many years ago, as I have related, I employed the word 'aristocrat' in describing him, and to-day I feel that that word must stand. He has all the strength of the aristocrat and many of the aristocrat's weaknesses.

Elgar at 'Severn House' — I
(unsigned)

Those who climb the steep hill which leads from Finchley Road soon find themselves in a land of perfect peace which it is hardly possible to imagine existing within three miles of Oxford Circus. In the very heart of this delectable country is Netherhall Gardens, where Sir Edward Elgar now lives in a house that is a fitting home for a creative artist. It is one of three which were built by Edwin Long the painter. As soon as the door is opened we realise that it is no ordinary house. A Reinhardtesque portal of brass with the royal lion of Scotland boldly embossed on each side, and a mosaic pavement said to be a relic of ancient Carthage, greet the visitor. Then through a door on the left, and we are in a long, lofty corridor, with a delightful alcove on one side, and on the other the door of the dining-room. At the end is a staircase over which hangs a wonderful lamp, the gift of some friends, which must have shed light on the hall of some palace by the Grand Canal. Upstairs are the principal rooms of the house: first, a drawing-room which is pure Louis Seize. Then we open the door, and we seem to step from the Trianon to a Georgian mansion — with a white ceiling of austere simplicity and oak panelling that reaches a long way up. In the room everything, even to the blotting-paper on the writing-table, is of a rich dark blue. Over the vast fireplace an Italian landscape with a ruined temple, and everywhere light and air and perfect quiet. To the left is another study, more for use than display, in which much of the composer's work is done. Here is the composer's portable typewriter, and he explains that he is devising a new scheme for the making of letters likely to be more needed than the commercial symbols which the manufacturers provide. He handles it with affection and the skill of an expert, for why should not a typewriter have as much romance in it as a steam-engine or an electric-power plant? On the floor repose Sir Edward's violin with which he fought his way through the world in his youth, and — incongruously enough — a trombone which he used to play. On the walls are memorials of more brilliant phases of his career — wreaths, all faded, given to him on various occasions now historical. Chief among them is that which was the tribute of the authorities of the Lower Rhenish Musical Festival on the day when *The Dream of Gerontius* was performed at Düsseldorf and made an epoch in the history of English music. It has a history attached to it. When it reached the composer's house in Malvern, the gardener took a cutting from it and planted it, and it flourished exceedingly, and now the laurel grows in the Hampstead garden — a plant of good augury. On the walls, too, are reminders that Sir Edward is an antiquary as well as a musician. He is fond of drawing special attention to three maps of a great age of the counties of Worcester, Hereford, and Gloucester, with quaint drawings of historical scenes — one a single combat between a Saxon and a Danish king in seventeenth-century dress, with the rival armies drawn up in battle array and looking on. Another has written on it a eulogy of the city of Bristow (which is Bristol) and the cleanliness of it, for it 'has not in its streets any sinke,' 'but everything is conveyed under ye grounde.' He has also what is probably the most varied assortment of pencils of all colours, shapes, and sizes that ever a musician has collected; and each kind has its special use in the marking of his scores.

The manuscripts of nearly all his works are in his house, but the most precious of all, that of *The Dream of Gerontius*, has been given to the Oratory at Birmingham, the home of Cardinal Newman, who wrote the text. The original score of *Cockaigne* was given by him to one of his earliest friends.

Another room that leads from the studio is a most delightfully cosy book-room in which one can be completely shut off from the world. The shelves give evidence of the owner's catholic and most fastidious taste in literature. They bear witness also to various hobbies which have beguiled his leisure hours. On one shelf is a collection of books on heraldry, on another are works on chemistry, for which he has also a great passion. In his house at Hereford he used to have a well-fitted laboratory.

To anyone who wishes to cross-examine him, Elgar is the most fascinating and elusive victim. He will with the utmost adroitness direct the conversation into another channel just when you think he is on the point of answering questions which are of particular interest. When asked what he is going to do now, he invariably replies that he has given up composition for good. A few minutes later he will tell you that he is still hunting for a libretto for an opera, and that he has studied seventy within the last few months; and when questioned as to the prospects of national opera in

England, he will say vaguely that the people will get it when it
wants it. On the day when the present writer saw him, he was
moved to speak of choral singing and his experiences in the
North. He was led to refer to his now-historial remarks, which
he made nine years ago, and which created no little stir at the
time. They have been so frequently misquoted that he suggested
that it might be well to reproduce his very words. On that
occasion, speaking of the Morecambe Festival he said: 'I cannot
well express what I feel as to the immense influence your Festival
must exert in spreading the love of music: it is rather a shock to
find Brahms' part songs appreciated and among the daily fare of a
district apparently unknown to the sleepy London Press; people
who talk of the spread of music in England and the increasing love
of it rarely seem to know where the growth of the art is really
strong and properly fostered; some day the press will awake to the
fact, already known abroad and to some few of us in England,
that the living centre of music in Great Britain is not London, but
somewhere further north.'

He recalls with amusement the fact that on the day when this
particular Festival was in progress a leading London paper
printed a page of news from Morecambe, which did not mention
the Festival, but devoted a good deal of space to the dead body of a
sailor which had been washed ashore on the beach.

Of the various works which are supposed to be occupying his
mind — the completion of the trilogy which began with *The
Apostles,* and a second important work for violin and orchestra —
he refuses to speak for the present. He is devoting time at the
present moment to the unravelling of certain literary problems,
of which the authorship of *The Letters of Junius* is apparently
uppermost in his thoughts. All the same, the writer left him with
the conviction that he might expect something new and
important from him in time for next year's Musical Festivals, and
he is looking forward with pleasurable anticipation to the first
London performance of *The Music Makers.*

The World,
22 October 1912

Elgar at 'Severn House' — II
by Percy Scholes

Toilsome is the ascent of Parnassus. In other words, to attain Severn House, you have a stiff pull up Netherhall Gardens. This is one of those Hampstead corkscrew-roads that seem to crawl up an incline of at least forty-five degrees on a cool day — and more than eighty degrees on a hot one. In time of frost it must be like an Alpine pass; one can imagine the inhabitants climbing home with mountaineer's spikes in their shoes and Alpenstocks in their hands — roped together for safety.

Once at the summit, and admitted into the house, the interviewer is happy. He sinks back into an arm chair, Sir Edward sits up to his library table ready for business and the questioning begins.

It is not difficult to get Sir Edward to talk. He appears to like talking, which is very natural, for he is a good talker. Ideas flow forth in language that you would call 'well-chosen,' but that it comes so naturally and without effort. All you have to do is listen, now and again interjecting a note of query or of mild dissent in order gently to deflect the stream of thought in one direction or another. Music, literature, politics, the War — one after another these subjects come under review and are disposed of. It is a pity Sir Edward does not write books as well as music, for he has much to say. And as next year will see his sixtieth birthday, is it not time we had a volume of reminiscences — just to go on with, pending a fuller one twenty-five years later?

It is with reminiscences we begin. Here is one of the earliest.

A summer's day. A little boy of five sitting on the ground with paper and pencil. The boy's face is serious. He is engaged, as he feels, on a great task; a musical composition of sorts is being brought into the world. One by one the black dots with tails are pencilled into the score. The paper is gradually covered with a wandering string of notes, as the great work takes shape. Still the boy plods on with the task.

So much for the young artist, now for an older one. For sister arts have enterprises on foot. The youngster, in a vague childish way, is busy fashioning tone; close at hand another Worcester resident is adorning shape with colour. The elder artist is at the top of a ladder, the younger one at its foot.

By-and-by the painter comes down. He glances over the work of the musician. The boy had drawn a four-lined stave, on which, by some method of notation, partly imitated, partly self-invented, he is recording his musical ideas. 'But music has *five* lines,' says the colour-artist. This is something new to the tone artist. Here is his first lesson. He takes the hint; five lines are ruled in future. The information is not forgotten. To this day the boy remembers it — and to this day he writes his oratorios, symphonies and violin concertos on staves of five lines.

To Elgar music came early and quite naturally and instinctively — as it did, of course, to every great composer, with the possible exception of Wagner.

Then, too, Elgar was brought up in an atmosphere of music, for his father was a musician and the owner of a music shop. As he puts it, 'A stream of music flowed through our house and the shop, and I was all the time bathing in it.' You can still see that shop, in the High Street of Worcester, and the name 'Elgar' is still there over the window.

There is one point Sir Edward makes in telling this. Music to him was never the keyboard. It was just 'music.' He never evolved his musical thoughts in a keyboard shape, as the early training of so many composers impels them to do. His thoughts came to him, and still do, as abstractions — just music, but clothed in one colour or another, determining their disposition on one line or another of the orchestral score.

The real awakening to the possibilities of music came on this wise. One day there came into the young musician's hands a copy of Beethoven's First Symphony. He turned over the closely printed pages of the old Wolfenbüttel Edition. The first movement made no particular impression. The slow movement was already familiar as an organ voluntary. The last movement seemed perfunctory. But the Scherzo — he glanced through this and rushed to a place of solitude. With six active children in the house there was little opportunity for the quiet enjoyment of the treasure. Out he went! and once by himself, he examined it. Here was a relevation — a revelation of romance, fire, poetry. He looked at the page before him —

> . . . like stout Cortez when with eagle eyes
>> He star'd at the Pacific — and all his men
> Look'd at each other with a wild surmise
>> Silent, upon a peak in Darien.

A new ocean was in view, and he longed to sail it. An ocean on which you might set forth from the safe harbour of Natural Quay, touch rapidly and momentarily at such adjacent ports as the Quays of One Sharp and Two Sharps, and then, with a sudden favouring breeze find yourself making for the Coast of Flats — passing quickly from port to port, resting nowhere and, almost before you realised the distance you had travelled from home, find yourself casting anchor for a time and swaying gently on the tide in the harbour of Five Flats.

How Elgar learnt to play he hardly knows. He played the piano, and in later years gained a reputation as accompanist. He played the organ, and was able to help his father, and later, to take an organist's post of his own. He played the violin, and that proved his main entrance into the practical world of music, and was for long years of early manhood his source of income. He played the 'cello and the double-bass well enough to take his part in the Haydn and easier Mozart Symphonies that were then the staple fare of amateur orchestral societies. The bassoon he played in a wind quintet and in later years he played the trombone. So keyboard, strings, wood-wind and brass all claimed his attention at one time or another — and had we only probed a little deeper with our questions, we should doubtless have dug up memories of percussion.

Perseverance is one quality that must have gone to the making of the long list of instruments on which Elgar was a performer given above. And perseverance came to the support of natural instinct also in the study and practice of composition.

Mr R.J. Buckley, in his bright and informative little book, gives an account of the boy's eager efforts to assimilate such old-fashioned books of theory as he could lay hands on. Some of them he still has, and very dear to him they are. Some of the early compositions, too, have lately come to light and have just been sent down from Worcester to London.

We turn over a pile of these lying on the top of the grand piano, and beg permission to take away with us an unfinished fugue, written about the age of fifteen. Sir Edward looks it over with interest, and opening the piano, plays it through. 'Quite good stuff,' he murmurs approvingly.

As we turn over these old papers we come across a volume of Schobert's sonatas, and volumes of music by Kozeluch and Emanuel Bach. Very thin, old-fashioned music it looks now, this work of the eighteenth-century Versailles organist, the famous harpsichordist who for so long gave the Parisians pleasure by his playing, and at length died, as the chronicler solemnly records, 'by eating some fungi which he gathered near Paris and which killed his wife, his children, a friend, the servant and himself!' Schobert is nearly forgotten nowadays, but the Elgar family played him, and here, with the dust of years upon it, is the volume from which they did it.

We talk of piano playing as it was forty years ago and as it is to-day. Sir Edward has a tender memory of the past. The Mozart tradition lingered in the Elgar household, for Elgar's father had been a pupil of Sutton of Dover, and Sutton had been a pupil of Michael Kelly, and Michael Kelly, the Dublin boy who became a famous operatic singer and composer, was the intimate friend of Mozart.

'Mozart is rarely or never, played to-day as he was in my boyhood,' says Sir Edward. 'Nowadays the players play either too rigidly or with sentimentality. The tradition seems to be dead.'

It is, by the way, interesting to realise that Sir Edward is, in a way, a musical great-great-grandson of Mozart.

This leads us to a chat about the great pianists of to-day. Some of them Sir Edward praises; others he condemns heartily. Brainless pieces of machinery, mangling whatever passes into their heads and out of their fingers, he thinks them. Applause and gain are their ends, and brilliancy and display their means. 'Paderewski and Busoni in their best days meet my ideal, I suppose, of piano playing. As for the violent and fireworky school, I'd far rather have a Pianola!'

'Indeed,' he goes on, 'I'm not sure that the pianola is not our best means of hearing piano works well performed to-day. Paderewski and Busoni are not always at hand, but we can domesticate good pianism in the pianola. The state of things as it used to be has been curiously reversed. Some years ago the pianists had the beautiful touch and the pianola the hard one. The pianola maker in those days was trying to imitate the touch of the pianist. Nowadays the pianist seems to be trying to cultivate the touch of the early pianolas.'

'Complaints are sometimes heard,' we reply, 'that the pianola touch is hard and unvarying.'

'That,' says Sir Edward, 'is a matter of control. Properly used the pianola can play with a very beautiful touch — the Schumann things, for instance; some of these come out magnificently.'

'The gramophone also is of the greatest possible service. It puts on permanent record the readings of the best performers. The violinist, the pianist, and the vocalist, for instance, may take a lesson from the very greatest artists, and best of all, the lesson can be repeated indefinitely, and remains for all time a benefit to musicians of coming generations.'

As is well known, Sir Edward has himself conducted many of his works for recording purposes.

Music, Sir Edward fears, is tending to become an art of sight rather than sound. People go to see a famous performer rather than to hear him. Or they go to watch his actions, if he is noted either for acrobatics or eccentricity. A recent incident at Queen's Hall comes to mind and we feel we can to some extent confirm Sir Edward's view. [The anecdote is our own and we do not commit Sir Edward to acceptance of it as an illustration of the view he has just expressed.]

Pachmann was announced to play. He had a large audience, as he deserves to have, for of all the pianists before the public he possesses the most charming touch and the most delicate sense of finish in playing. But for once (the only time within our experience) Pachmann played badly. Yet the audience applauded just as vigorously as usual. It really did seem as though sight rather than sound was what had brought them.

Worse than this, in Chopin's Nocturne in G, Op. 27, No. 2, where a few bars before the end there occurs an 'interrupted cadence' followed by a pause, a very large section of the audience broke into applause. A musical child who had never heard the piece before would have felt this could not possibly be the end of it. This audience, then, was not musical! So much in confirmation of Sir Edward's view. But it is only fair to say that arguments could, of course, be brought on the other side.

From this subject the conversation naturally turns to the cognate one of British support of British composers. 'We are not a patriotic people,' says Sir Edward. 'We think we are, of course, but in the sense in which one might call the French or Russians patriotic, we are not. Perhaps we are a little too much afraid of that awkward self-conscious feeling, that so readily attacks the Briton, to let ourselves go in the matter of patriotic expression. And so, when public occasion calls for music, we do not make a point of using British music for British expression of emotion. We stick to the music that has become traditional in that particular connection, as for instance when we play Chopin's Funeral March at Lord Kitchener's memorial service. Surely a people who were at the same time patriotic and naturally musical would demand their own music on such occasions.

'The fact that we are not an intensely musical people necessarily reacts on the composer.'

Speaking of provincial music, Sir Edward alludes in passing to Mr. Rutland Boughton's Glastonbury Music Drama Festival scheme. He has the greatest hope of this, considering its basis a thoroughly sound one. Some day he thinks it will be a big thing. We have so often given accounts of the admirable work of Mr. Boughton's 'Festival School' that we need not dwell on this here, but it is gratifying to hear Sir Edward's very emphatic good opinion on an enterprise that has always had the warm sympathy and support of *The Music Student*.

Sir Edward also alludes in glowing terms to the excellent municipal orchestra at Bournemouth, and the truly excellent work so long carried on there by Mr. Dan Godfrey.

'Why have we never had a music-drama from you?' we are bold enough to ask.

'Because I have never found a libretto,' is the reply. 'But, if you mention that, the only result will be that I shall get a hundred-and-fifty libretti sent to me the day after *The Music Student* appears, and it will take one person a whole day to send them all back.'

We think quite as much of the poor postman toiling with his load up the precipitous slope of Netherhall Gardens, as of Sir Edward's dismay as a sackful of bulky packages is poured out on the floor of his library, and we beg the poets and dramatists among our readers to take our hint and refrain.

'I suppose,' says Sir Edward, as the conversation turns on his own plan of life, 'that the public imagines the composer rising early and sitting over his music paper the whole day long. That is nowhere near the truth, as a matter of fact.

'In my own case, an idea comes to me, perhaps when walking. On return I write it down. Weeks or months after I may take it up and write out the movement of which it has become the germ. The actual labour of writing this, with the complete scoring, takes perhaps eight or ten hours. But the piece has gradually shaped itself in my mind in the meantime, and the actual writing is thus a small matter. Later comes the writing out with care for the printer, and this, of course, is a more laborious business.'

At this point Lady Elgar comes in, and, as we chat, she humorously alludes to an institution of some interest in the Elgar household. This is the 'Freak Box' in which are stored the strange letters Sir Edward receives from time to time.

Here is one, for instance, received shortly after return from America. The writer charges Sir Edward with being the guilty party in the notorious Tarrytown murder, and goes on to the ominous information that he knows where is buried the axe with which the dreadful deed was performed. We watch the composer closely as this matter is discussed. No sign of a guilty conscience shows itself on his face and so far as we are concerned we are convinced that the American Sherlock Holmes is on a wrong trail.

Some Americans think rather better of Sir Edward than does this one. He has even been asked to lead a great meeting for prayer in New York. It was at the time when Strauss's *Salome* was to be given, and as Elgar was at the time conducting his oratorios there, it was taken for granted that his sympathies would be with the good people who made it a matter of public prayer that New York might be saved from the calamity of a performance of the dreadful work. Elgar is, however, an old friend of Strauss, and he did *not* 'lead the prayers.'

As we turn to leave, Sir Edward alludes to the large number of musicians who are fighting the country's battles. 'I get letters from some of them,' he says, 'and from what I have learned I think British music should be very proud indeed of them.'

The Music Student,
August 1916

PART V: MEMORIES OF THOSE WHO KNEW HIM

Memories of a Pupil
by Mary Beatrice Alder

Mary Beatrice Alder was born in 1878 and became a violin pupil of Elgar when he was living at 'Forli'. The following is a transcription of a radio interview she gave to Michael Pope, Chairman of the Elgar Society, shortly before her 95th birthday. Incidentally, it was Miss Alder's brother, George Alder, a horn-player, who first introduced Bax to Elgar at Birchwood.

When I was about twelve my parents began looking about for the best teacher of the violin that they could find in the neighbour-hood of Malvern. Elgar was clearly the best and he was invited up to our house for an interview. I remember standing, very unsophisticated and very childish, by the grand piano with a very cheap violin in my hand awaiting him. He came in and had about five minutes' conversation with my parents and then they went out, leaving me to get to know him myself. He put me at my ease by taking me up to a picture of the Sistine Madonna above our mantelpiece and said 'The German students, you know, make paper hats for the two cherubs at the bottom of that wonderful picture.' That cheered me up and then he took me to a mirror and said 'Now I want you to look at yourself when you play in this so that you stand quite properly'. I don't remember any more conversation but it was arranged that he would give me lessons and we started immediately.

At first he held his lessons in a music room at the local music shop in Malvern and came there once a week. I don't remember his forcing exercises on me, though it sounds inevitable, but I remember very well many of the things he taught me, including at the beginning his own *Salut d'Amour*. I learnt that very young and liked it.

He made many wise remarks all through the years, the first one being 'Never make an ugly sound, only beautiful'. We soon advanced from that music, simple music, to Beethoven's Sonatas and he was rather shocked, I think, to find that having got the whole book of Beethoven, I hadn't run through the whole lot. Little he knew the lure of the tennis court!

I knew, almost from the beginning, that he was great, simply because when I went home after my lessons my ribald elder brothers used to say in mocking voices 'How was the great man today?'; a remark I had never made of the piano Mus. Doc. who had given me my piano lessons. Quite a different influence, but I don't remember how he did it. I was probably not quite like his other pupils as I had never been to school and I remember his quizzical, amused look when I calmly handed my violin to him whenever I wanted it retuned. He seemed now very amused and slightly quizzical — I can see that now.

The lessons appear to me now to have been really more like recitals in which he occasionally made remarks. He was never impatient, never. He always lured me on, I think, to do things. Of course he did stop me, no doubt, but there was very little of the 'Oh, you mustn't do that and you should do that' that I can remember at all. I never felt thwarted, in fact. All the time he very much wanted you always to have an accompanist. At the very first meeting with him he said 'Please, as far as you possibly can, have an accompanist the whole time'. As I told him I had five brothers and sisters and a mother who all played the piano, I thought I could do that. When he thought I was mature enough we went to those earlier people like Nardini and then on to a man I had never heard of called Rode, which was very advanced in technique.

He was so unusual, I think I found him. I can't tell you exactly why. His remarks were most unusual. He said to me one day 'Great musicians are things to be ashamed of.' What he meant by that was that they were much too simply stuck into their musicianship and nothing else. I'm sure he meant that.

As I grew into the teens he invited me to join a school — I don't know whether to call it a class or little orchestra or band — with about six pupils and two headmistresses, which was most enjoyable. He played the piano and we played some of his music yet unpublished, and then I remember going down to his house, *Forli*, later on, and his suggesting at the end of the class that we should go and play with kites in the garden together!

I was very much struck, of course, by his looks when he came into the room when I saw him first. Instead of being, of course, dressed in black striped things like my piano man who didn't interest me at all, I expected the same thing, I suppose, of him. I have never seen him dressed in anything but plus fours, never — and gaiters. That was a new thing to me. He was always the same, always dressed like that, always the same and I very much admired his long, thin hands, I remember, sensitive hands, very.

Very expressive eyes, very sensitive, long hands. I should think he hated giving lessons, shouldn't you? But I think his mind was so on music I should think he hated it probably, but he never showed it. All about him was so different, completely different to me but I knew he was great and I knew I liked him and I knew he was very nice, and he was very nice to me.

Very soon after we began I suppose he thought it was rubbish having a childish violin and he said 'Don't you think we should have a better violin?' and my parents said 'Oh yes, rather,' and he said 'I don't mind getting it for you. Would you like a very great name or would you like a sweet tone?' and we all said 'A sweet tone,' and he got me a very nice old French one. Very nice indeed. It must have been much more pleasant for him, mustn't it?

He really did try to give me an all-round time, I think, with the orchestra and with the class and with all the lessons and so on. He never seemed bored and I had the great feeling that he was a very great and a very good person to teach. But, of course, one didn't sit down at that time of life and think about it, especially when you were very interested in tennis and things like that. And then, of course, later on I suppose, they said you must do some Classics or you will not get into Oxford, so my life was not entirely bound up with music, but I did go on with his lessons almost till the time I went to Oxford, I think.

He was very keen on fritillary flowers: flowers that grow in very few places and always by the water and I remember very well as soon as I went up to Oxford, sending him a bunch and getting a nice letter from him with 'Wach' auf!' at the top. It was after that, of course, Oxford and London took me right away from him and I never saw him again.

Elgar as I knew him
by Sir Richard Terry

Thirty-three years ago Edward Elgar had attracted some notice as a 'young' composer of promise. His name had not yet appeared in *Grove's Dictionary*, but *The Black Knight* and *King Olaf* were comparatively well known, and *Caractacus* had engaged the attention of choral societies, with whom the less distinguished *Banner of St. George* soon became a favourite. 'Musical' England was in those days dominated by a coterie who shepherded us along the paths of correct taste. We took them at their own valuation; consequently when Hans Richter (then the idol of musical England) performed the *Enigma Variations* (in 1898) we felt that he had conferred a great honour, of which we trusted the 'young man' would be sufficiently conscious. This attitude was crystallised when Madame Clara Butt sang *Sea Pictures* in 1899. We again expressed hopes that the composer would appreciate the honour that great artists were continuing to accord him. Taking our cue from our self-constituted mentors, we were all very kindly and strictly non-committal.

Then came 1900, and with it the first performance (at the Birmingham Festival) of *The Dream of Gerontius*, on which work, we understood, Elgar had been busied for ten years. That deplorable 'first performance' is now a matter of history. Richter, at the conductor's desk, demonstrated a strange inability to grasp the subtleties of Elgar's thought, and the famed Birmingham Festival Chorus floundered pitifully through a work which proved itself completely beyond their powers. When the dismayed composer was stung into telling them that they did not understand his music, he was soon reminded—both in the Press and out of it—that it was an impertinence for a comparatively obscure composer to criticise an august choral body which had produced with *éclat* such master-works as Mendelssohn's *Elijah*, Costa's *Naaman*, and Gaul's *Holy City*.

Public opinion of that day (by which I mean the clique of musical mandarins and their following) pronounced the work to be dead. And dead it remained until 1902, when it was brought to a hearing in Germany. The Germans gave it an ovation, and its composer received the warm congratulations of Richard Strauss. It was only then that we began to feel uncomfortable about *Gerontius*, and to wonder whether it really *had* received justice at Birmingham.

I was present at the Birmingham 'first performance' and found myself unable to share in the 'public opinion' of the work. In spite of its wretched rendering, one felt one's self in the presence of something new in English music. The sincerity and dignity, the picturesque imagery, the lofty serenity, and the deep spritual significance of the music caught one (as it were) by the throat. The choral effects (both new and startling in those days) were as far removed from the accepted canons of oratorio as is Heaven from Hades. The orchestral technique one felt to be that of a master. With its rich, warm, and varying colour it moved on a higher plane than British music had known up to that time.

It is therefore (to me) a deep and abiding happiness to remember that it was my privilege to be one of those instrumental in securing for *Gerontius* (in 1903) its first hearing in London (within the bare walls of the then unfinished Westminster Cathedral), with the further privilege of taking a humble part in the performance.

That performance took place before the present generation was born. The latest edition of *Grove's Dictionary* alludes to it casually and incidentally as a 'private' one. I find that, in consequence, every young musician of my acquaintance believes (on the authority of *Grove*) that the undertaking was some sort of hole-and-corner affair, conducted by the Cathedral choir behind closed doors. In view of this serious misapprehension it may not be out of place here to recall the real facts.

The performance was a public one; the Cathedral was packed to the doors. Elgar himself conducted; the Hanley Choral Society formed the chorus; the band was recruited from the leading orchestral players in London. Both band and chorus were (as regards numbers) of full Festival proportions. Two of the three soloists who had sung in the German production of 1902 (Muriel Foster and Ludwig Wüllner) repeated their respective *rôles* at Westminster, and Ffrangçon Davies was the baritone.

It would be outside the scope of this article to trace the career of *Gerontius* or to criticise its composer's later works. It is enough to say that since the festival of his compositions in 1904, at the request and under the personal patronage of King Edward VII, the position of Edward Elgar as our foremost composer has been unchallenged. But I might add that the nation owes much to Sir

Landon Ronald and the conductors of the Three Choirs Festivals for the faithfulness with which, in an age of rapidly-changing fashions, they have kept Elgar's works before the public.

My acquaintance with Elgar began with the performance of *Gerontius* in that (to me) memorable June of 1903. It would be hardly correct to say that it 'ripened' into friendship, for Elgar was one of those rare souls whose heart opened into friendship from the very beginning. After he left Hampstead, where we were near neighbours, my actual meetings with him were infrequent and fitful, but time and space matter little in such friendships as men of Elgar's stamp have to give.

In my intercourse with him three things struck me with great force—the wide range of his interests and of his reading outside music; his great modesty respecting some branches of music which I knew he had studied, but about which he protested he knew nothing; and, lastly, his deep human sympathy and understanding. I had early experience of the last-named when I was beginning my work at Westminster. (*Gerontius* was produced there before the Cathedral was opened for public worship.) Out of the plenitude of his experience he 'put me wise' to some of the difficulties I should have to face, and events proved him a true prophet. Big men do not always extend such sympathy to mere beginners.

In Plainsong and Polyphony he made no pretensions to knowledge, but his use of the fourth mode in *Gerontius* showed that whatever might be the extent of his technical equipment he was steeped in the spirit of Plainsong to a degree that no mere technician could have acquired. On the question of polyphony he used to embarrass me by his persistent attitude of a listener and a learner. I found out the depth of his knowledge (which I had long suspected) by the merest accident. Hearing that I had lost my volume of Rochlitz, he asked me to accept a copy which he had bought in early youth 'to try and get the hang of those old fellows' (as he put it). His notes in the book and across the music showed me that his had been no superficial study. He had noted all that was worth noting about the characteristics (contrapuntal and harmonic) of the old Polyphonists from Dufay and Josquin to Goudimel Lasso, Palestrina and his school.

At another time, when he found I was interested in metrical psalmody, he gave me an early edition of the Huguenot Psalter (also purchased in his youth, like the Rochlitz, and for the same reason). This I found most useful for reference when preparing Calvin's *Strassburg* collection of psalms for the press.

Elgar's many-sidedness would provide material for many articles, but space is running short, and one more instance must suffice. A number of years ago the council of 'The Union of Graduates in Music' were considering whom they should invite to be their President for the following year. Most of our prominent musicians had served their term, and it was felt that Elgar ought to be approached. Everyone agreed on this point, but there were some suggestions of misgiving as to how far an 'idealist' composer would accommodate himself to business routine. Elgar was invited; he accepted the post; he proved himself such an ideal chairman at council meetings (from the business point of view) that we took the unprecedented step of re-electing him (in succession) for *four* years.

Intercourse with 'the leading musicians' of any country is an interesting psychological study. One becomes curious to note, at a first meeting, whether one's new acquaintance regards fellow composers as brothers in art or mere rivals. Whether some of his prominent contemporaries were entitled to the term brothers in art, Elgar never disclosed. But one thing is certain—he was devoid of any feeling of rivalry. From my first meeting with him until my last I never heard him speak a disparaging word of his contemporaries or their works. He was a stranger to anything ignoble.

With the passing of Edward Elgar we mourn the passing of a great soul, a great artist, and a great Englishman, whose music will stand for all time as the expression of all that is finest in the English character.

The Radio Times
9th March 1934

Elgar: Some Aspects of
the Man in his Music
by Ernest Newman

What will be Elgar's ultimate place in musical history it must of course be left to the future to determine. As we of to-day see him, he is almost the last of a great line. That he ends an epoch rather than begins one will, as all history demonstrates, be in his favour rather than to his disadvantage; for musical experiments along totally new lines, fascinating as they are to students of evolution, have as a rule not proved to be rich in survival value. Elgar's task has been less to innovate than to complete, not to make a new musical language but to distil what may prove to be the last drop of expression out of the old.

He was in all respects a man of the great culture-epoch that settled down into its last phase in the early years of the present century. I think it was Remy de Gourmont who pointed out, quite justly, that there are certain thinkers and artists whose mission it is to say what was left unsaid by their great forerunners: it is not that they row in other men's boats but that, in a boat unmistakably their own, they discover fresh currents in the great river that was first opened out to them and us by their mighty predecessors, and explore creeks and islands which, but for them, would have remained for ever unknown. It may be true, for example, that, without *Parsifal, Gerontius* would never have been written; but it is equally true that *Gerontius* gives expression, and the final expression, to certain things that may indeed have been implicit in Wagner but never became explicit in him. The Elgar symphonies and concertos, again, though they are nourished both in form and in content by Wagner and Beethoven, are a progeny that are independent of their parents, with a build of their own and a life of their own.

In the present article, however, I propose not to go once more over ground that will be already familiar to my readers and to students of Elgar, but to say something about the man and his art that is derived from my personal knowledge of him. One of the commonplaces of criticism is that we ought to try to see a work as its creator saw it. It is a precept easier to lay down than to follow; and my intercourse with Elgar has convinced me that there will always be something in a man's work to which it is impossible to find the key unless we know the man—and perhaps not even then. I would cite, in support of this theory, Elgar's so frequent use of the term *nobilmente* in his scores. That marking has been greatly misunderstood. It was not that Elgar was saying, in effect, 'This musical theme is a noble one,' but that he himself had seen his subject in terms of nobility.

He was a man of enormous vitality, for all his sensitiveness and occasional valetudinarianism. That nose of his, with its boldness and mass, and the exceptionally large nostrils that, even when he was lying pitiably weak in his last illness, seemed to be distended in a passionate effort to draw all life into them and make it part of himself, were the outward symbol of a constitution and a mind of unusual strength. He saw the outer world as a magnificent pageant, every line and colour of which thrilled him. I remember the passion of delight with which he would describe a piece of superb horsemanship at a military display; the sculpturesque figures of man and horse had etched themselves upon a brain that revelled in any manifestation of life at its strongest and proudest. It was the sight of the ruins of the monument of Augustus on the hill at La Turbie, with their imperial glance over space and time, that moved him to one of the most splendid passages in the *In the South* overture. It was this gusto for life at its strongest and quickest that enabled him to express the very soul of our race in the military marches, in the *Cockaigne,* and in the *Falstaff.*

The great leaps with which he was so fond of filling his melodies were the unconscious expression of this delight in energy. They invariably have the same spiritual significance: the upward leap to which, during the war, he set the words *Spirit of England* is only a later expression of the same noble pride that we find in the similar melody of the slow movement of the *Serenade for Strings,* written in his youth. It was characteristic of him, again, that for epigraph to the *Froissart* Overture he should have chosen the words of Keats,

> When chivalry
> Lifted up her lance on high

It was one of the paradoxes of his rich nature that, although inclined to moods of the profoundest pessimism, he mostly saw life in terms of chivalry, of brave pageantry, of a line that was at once bold and sensitive.

This quick nervous response to life at its most salient and most energetic had a curious way of betraying itself in his gestures: the spiritual thrill had to find expression in physical movement. I

never stood or sat by him when he was listening to music—
especially his own—that soared upward on the wings of its own
ecstasy without finding him gripping my arm convulsively. He
could rarely listen to fine-souled music without the tears coming
into his eyes. Yet he was anything but a sentimentalist or a
weakling; his emotions were under the control, for purposes of
art, of a powerful and critical mind. He was a man of great
knowledge, of wide and curious reading in matters that lay rather
off the beaten track, with a curious interest in subjects, such as
heraldry, that have a note of their own, even if it be only one of
quaintness. He found life perpetually interesting.

My talks with him, as I have hinted, convinced me that there is
always something in a great man's art to which few but himself
will ever have the true key. He did not readily talk about his own
music, perhaps because of the feeling that nobody who was not
made precisely like himself could possibly hear it as he had
conceived it; but when he did talk, it was clear that his music had
come straight out of some highly vitalised experience or other.
Many a passage in it has only revealed its true meaning to me
after I have heard him talk about it. During his last illness he gave
me some of the sketches for the adagio of his third symphony, with
written remarks that show from what profound depths of thought
and feeling this music had welled.

It is more true of him than of most composers, perhaps, that the
key to his music is to be found only by those who, being by nature
one with him, already possess it. Without for a moment
disparaging his interpreters, one or two of whom have shown
admirable insight into his mind, it remains true that the best
conductor of Elgar's works was generally Elgar himself. He alone
knew that his music needed no emphasis, for all the emphasis
required is implicit in the sounds themselves. The emotional
exaggeration with which he has been sometimes charged was
never in the music itself, but only in some of the interpreters of it.
More than once he protested to me that all his music required was
to be left alone to say what it had to say in its own way: the
expression was *in* the music, and it was not merely unnecessary
but harmful for the conductor to add to it an expression of his
own.

The full intensity of an Elgarian idea is in the melodic lines and
the harmonic complexes, and in the special colour given them by
the composer; to supercharge this inner intensity with a factitious
intensity from the outside is only to achieve that over-emphasis
that has done Elgar so much harm, because the uninstructed

listener has attributed to the composer an effusiveness that was merely the unwarrantable and unwanted contribution of the conductor. The ordinary performance of an Elgar symphony always sets me thinking of the old Greek story of the ass who loved his master so much that in his transports he threw his front legs round the poor man's neck and brought him to the ground. The ass, it is said, received a beating for his misguided display of affection; in this country, in our time, he would have received a musical knighthood.

I would cite, as a cardinal example of an Elgar complex that simply requires to be left alone to say to the full all it has to say, the theme for the 'cellos in the first movement of the second symphony (at No. **11** in the score). This is almost invariably *over-*expressionised by the conductor, with the result that it is made to sound maudlin. The truth is that all the expression required is in the notes and the sounds themselves—in the high pitch at which the 'cellos are playing, that of itself conveys all the nervous tension that is intended, in the fall of the melody in the second bar, in the slight (it can hardly be too slight) ebb and flow of the volume of tone at this point and that.

Elgar knew perfectly well what he was putting on paper and how it would sound: he knew that a pianissimo in the 'cellos near the extreme higher point of their range would suggest all the wistfulness, the complaint, that were implicit in his idea. His careful marking of *dolce e delicato* is as a rule flagrantly disregarded, the conductor, knowing that here is a theme that is meant to be 'expressive,' being unable to refrain from larding it with a conventional concert-room 'expression' of his own, the extra little that is far too much. It is because of this excess of zeal on the part of some of his interpreters, not because of anything in the music itself or in the constitution of the composer's mind, that Elgar's music is too often credited with a 'vulgarity' that is completely alien to it.

The Sunday Times, 25th February, 1934

Sir Edward Elgar
by Sir Compton Mackenzie

The writer Compton Mackenzie (1883-1972) penned two major essays on Elgar: the first chapter of his book Echoes *(Chatto & Windus, 1954) and a centenary tribute to open the June 1957 issue of* The Gramophone, *the magazine which he founded and edited. Here the two have been compounded together, the first four paragraphs coming from the magazine and the remainder from the book.*

As a matter of interest the concert to which Sir Compton refers took place at the Queen's Hall on 18th November 1929, with Albert Coates conducting the London Symphony Orchestra.

I met Elgar first in 1921. He was then sixty-four, and when one is thirty-eight that seems a venerable age; it seems rather less venerable when one is seventy-four. It was Robin Legge, the music editor of *The Daily Telegraph,* who introduced me to him when the bow-windowed Savile Club was still housed at 107 Piccadilly. Later Robin Legge told me that Elgar had behaved ungratefully to Charles Stanford and Hubert Parry, but I was never able to extract from him the reasons for this accusation. I had been devoted to Parry, but by this date Stanford was so infernally disagreeable to younger men that I should not have felt the slightest indignation, however badly Elgar might have behaved.

It may be difficult for us to-day to think of Elgar as a revolutionary figure in music at odds with the academic and conservative figures of his art, but it is important (and perhaps it was never so important as it is for the young critics of to-day) to recognise who have been the genuinely creative artists of the near past. The critics of to-day suffer from an excess of influence with a lack of equipment to justify such influence. The reason for their influence is the vast uncritical and comparatively uneducated public of intellectually *nouveaux riches* whom they serve as guides. Contemporary criticism has much in common with the books of etiquette that were a feature of late Victorian times when social barriers were beginning to fall.

Elgar himself was for a man of genius strangely sensitive about being considered old-fashioned, so sensitive indeed that as a kind of protective armour he used to protest continually that he had lost all interest in music. To hear him talk sometimes one might suppose that he regarded his own musical achievement as a youthful indiscretion. When I started *The Gramophone* in 1923 Elgar said to me one day that he supposed all the young critics of the paper would be sneering at him.

'Not that I care,' he growled quickly. 'I take no more interest in music. You'll find as you grow older that you'll take no more interest in literature. The secret of happiness for an artist when he grows old is to have a passion that can take the place of his art. I have discovered the joy that diatoms can give me. This miraculous world of beauty under the ocean revealed by the microscope is beyond music,' and he went on to expatiate on the exquisite patterns formed by these fossilised algae and the spiritual comfort that observation of them brought to his mind.

And as he spoke, there was a note in his voice which has remained vividly in my memory as a revelation of a mystical beauty to which he had penetrated and to which he was showing me the way. I have never since listened to any of his music without remembering the world of exquisite miniature he evoked that afternoon, or the subtle variety of the pattern he wove in that London club, as exquisite and various a pattern indeed as his own music.

Warned by our first conversation I never attempted, when I had the privilege of talking to him on other occasions, to mention of my own accord the subject of music. But on another afternoon while we were sitting in the billiard-room of the old Savile Club I heard from the further end of the long settee the voice of W. J. Turner say that he was going to the Queen's Hall to hear the *Symphonie Fantastique* of Berlioz. Suddenly and sharply Sir Edward said to me:

'What's that about the *Symphonie Fantastique*?'

When I told him that it was being played that afternoon in the Queen's Hall, he asked me if I had ever heard it, and on my telling him that I had not he asked me if I would like to hear it, and that if I would, he would take me with him to hear it, because it was a piece of music which one ought to hear and appreciate for its importance in the development of the art.

'There is one thing in it,' he added, 'which is really tremendous, and that is the *March to the Guillotine*.'

It was a Saturday afternoon, and as we drove along Piccadilly in the taxi to Queen's Hall I was aware while I listened to Sir Edward talking about Berlioz and Berlioz's world of music that I was enjoying a momentous occasion in my life. I was indeed listening with such absorption that the taxi with Sir Edward and myself inside it seemed to be standing still while the houses of Piccadilly and Regent Street flowed past on either side until Queen's Hall reached us, and it would have taken Dante to describe the awe I felt when following my Virgil upstairs to the first circle.

The concert opened with Strauss's *Don Juan*, but who the conductor of the concert was I cannot remember, for to my fancy the whole of the orchestra and the whole of the audience was being conducted by my companion. It was not until the Berlioz symphony began that I became aware of the emotion to which Sir Edward was exposed by the music. He was like a man in a strong gale of wind. Once or twice when tiresome people in front turned round and stared curiously at him I wanted to pick them up and pitch them over into the stalls, because they looked so idiotic staring at one who was himself music and yet whom they were only supposing to be a rather fidgety colonel. When the long third movement was over Sir Edward turned to me and said:

'Now I am going to mark for you the rhythm of this astounding march to the guillotine.'

And mark it he did most vigorously on my ribs. Then he got angry because the cymbal player was not handling his cymbals in the way they ought to be handled, and ejaculated under his breath several uncomplimentary remarks about him, whereupon some floppy young woman in front turned round and said 'Hush!' She might as well have tried to hush Vesuvius in full eruption as Sir Edward Elgar that afternoon, for the merciless rhythm of that march was having such an effect upon him that I should not have been surprised if he had suddenly leapt from his seat, vaulted over the floppy young woman in front, and landed down on the conductor's dais in order to make that cymbal player handle his cymbals in the way he thought they ought to be handled. The crisis, however, was reached just as the oboist put his instrument to his mouth to play that ghastly phrase which signified the last agony of the man about to be executed. He must have caught sight of Sir Edward Elgar in the circle at that moment, and whether he thought it was his wraith or his ghost or Sir Edward Elgar himself I do not know. I have never seen on any man's face an expression of such horrified surprise, but when I

9 Elgar, Carice and Alice on the steps of 'Plas Gwyn' in 1910.

10   An early, unfinished fugue by Elgar, originally illustrating
Percy Scholes's article.

turned and saw Sir Edward's eyes flashing down to where he was sitting I wondered that he was able to emit a sound from his oboe.

During the last movement the great man who had given me such a memorable experience sat back, apparently exhausted by the emotion of the music; and at the end of the symphony he rose abruptly.

'You are not going to stay to hear the Rachmaninoff Concerto?' I asked.

'No, no,' said Sir Edward. 'As I have told you, I do not take the slightest interest in music any longer, but you'd better stay and hear it.'

With this he hurried away up the aisle, the glances of the floppy young woman in front, who had only come to Queen's Hall to adore Rachmaninoff, following him indignantly.

With Sir Edward's departure the atmosphere became so ordinary as to seem heavy, and though Rachmaninoff himself was playing, and though I have no doubt he gave a splendid performance of his last Concerto, I have never been bored so intensely by music, and I have never wished so much for a concerto to come to an end. I have told this story at length and for the first time, because I feel that it may do more to suggest to those who are hearing Sir Edward's music some of the dynamic force of his personality in the art of to-day than any amount of pretty programme writing about his works.

'When I was a small boy,' Sir Edward once told me, 'I said to my mother that one day it would be enough to write my name on a letter for it to find me, and a little while ago I did get a postcard from the other end of the world simply addressed to me by name with no place or country.'

Those who have followed with him that elusive spirit of delight in the Second Symphony, who have pondered with him the sombre agony of the war in the Violoncello Concerto, who seem to hear, nay, more than hear, to be a veritable part of the sea as he, most utterly English of composers has let them hear and be, in his *Sea Pictures*, who have dreamed through the gracious romance of his Piano Quintet, who have failed to solve the lovely riddle of the *Enigma Variations*, who have been carried out of their dull selves by the *Dream of Gerontius*, who have seen his fame grow not as a fashion but as a mighty tree, those will not be astonished that so simple an address was sufficient.

Elgar — as I knew him
by Sir Malcolm Sargent

Greatness in men is a quality hard to define, but easy to recognise. It is an unconscious virtue which is self-revealing. I have lived a full life with friendships and acquaintances gathered from many continents, but my 'gleanings' of great men have been few; I could count them on the fingers of my two hands.

Elgar I place unhesitatingly in this limited number. Like all providential occurrences in one's life — it appeared to be accidental. It certainly was unexpected.

I first met *The Dream of Gerontius* in 1912; it was literally 'thrown at me' by my tutor, who hated 'modern' music. It was a case of love at first sight; I devoured every word of the poem, and every note of the music, with a youthful passion which was fanatic. A war intervened, and it was not until 1921 that I was able to organise and conduct a performance of the work in Leicester, combining the choral resources of Leicester and of Melton Mowbray, where I was organist. The Leicester Symphony Orchestra (which I had formed) accompanied, led by Woodhouse from the Queen's Hall Orchestra of London.

The circumstances were unforgettable for me. A relation to whom I was devoted was dying, and I had had to rush out of a preliminary choral rehearsal so that I might sob in private; and during the final rehearsal in Leicester a telegram was handed to me which could have announced a death. The news was not so bad, and I continued the rehearsal and conducted the performance. All of which may have helped.

John Coates, who sang the rôle of Gerontius and Woodhouse, who led, both wrote to Elgar of me, and he invited me to visit him in London. I went to his flat in the Adelphi, and there met the greatness which was Elgar. My impression of him may have been due to the youthful enthusiasm of hero worship, but I don't think so. He was kindness itself, and from the first moment of our meeting we were obviously friends with an accepted mutual understanding. I have never experienced shyness, but have often had to combat it in other people. I found Elgar the most natural of men, one who could not feel that self-consciousness with strangers which can be so embarrassing.

All great artists are of 'no class' — that is to say they are equally at home with any class, and cannot themselves be labelled as belonging to any particular stratum. Elgar annoyed some not-very-discerning acquaintances by appearing to wish to be mistaken as belonging to the 'racing', 'landed-gentry' class. My impression of him — and I do not pretend to know the whole Elgar — is quite the reverse. He was not at home with the so-called 'intellectuals' in the music profession; he had little reason to like them. They were not of his class musically, and belittled his genius. He had to endure criticisms that his honest expressions of patriotism and loyalty — and how good they are — were 'jingoism'; and his inspired spiritual outpourings were labelled as 'sentimental' or 'stinking of incense'.

I was present at the Queen's Hall in 1930, when Toscanini performed the *Enigma Variations* with the New York Phil-harmonic Orchestra. I had known the work well for many years and had conducted it many times — but this performance was overwhelming to me and to the audience. Everyone, having recovered from the emotional impact, stood up and shouted, recalling Toscanini time after time. I walked the Thames Embankment until four in the morning.

I lunched with Elgar a few days later, and told him of the ovation, and how we all shouted for 'the composer'. But Elgar was that night at a variety entertainment! He was very 'cool' about the audience's enthusiasm, pointing out that Toscanini had toured the *Variations* with the Vienna Philharmonic Orchestra 25 years earlier, and that Rimsky-Korsakov had written to him proclaiming these *Variations* 'the best since Brahms', and that Richter had compared the Wagner crescendo in the *Meistersingers* Overture with that in the Nimrod Variation, stating that Elgar's was the better. Elgar then turned to Kipling, who was on his other side, and praised the music of Sousa!

I met Elgar many times in his own flat, where we went through most of his works — singing, gesticulating, making those strange noises which are only intelligible to the musician, and taking it in turns, or sitting side by side, at the piano. They were some of the happiest and most memorable moments in my life.

There is a famous club, the Beefsteak, which I am told is 'exclusive' in its election of members — Elgar was the only musician in its company, and was loved and respected by all. Distinguished members of the House of Lords, Cabinet Minis-ters, admirals and others would offer him the head of the table at lunch or dinner, and rejoice in his companionship and gentle wisdom. One of his many kindnesses to me was to insist that I should be elected as a very young and quite unworthy member. Also through him I had on several occasions the honour, and great thrill, of being the only civilian to conduct the Massed Bands of the Brigade of Guards by special Sovereign's permission.

As Master of the King's Musick, Elgar was often responsible for the music at pageants, Empire Day celebrations and other similar occasions, and usually called me in as his lieutenant. No work has given me greater pleasure than that of working with and for him.

I cannot attempt here to write of his music. During the first week in Lent, at my suggestion, the Royal Choral Society have 'plugged' *The Dream of Gerontius* for many years. It has become a 'best-seller'. I know *The Apostles* and *The Kingdom* to be works equally great, but more difficult to comprehend. If I wished for a long life, it would be that I might see these two works as fully appreciated by music-lovers. The greatness of Elgar's music, and its immortality, lies in its fundamental religious mysticism and faith. *The Apostles* and *The Kingdom* are the direct descendants of the Bach *Passions*. The strange but inspired sequence of text — incomprehensible except through Biblical foreknowledge — is parallelled by that of Handel's *Messiah*.

It has been suggested that Elgar's religious convictions weakened towards his end. I had a grave illness at the time Elgar was dying. We exchanged many letters. I do not believe he had any doubts whatever as to the Redemption and the Hereafter. It is true that in *The Kingdom* he suddenly blazes in anger against an unworthy priesthood — an expression of scorn unique in Elgar, except when in *The Spirit of England* he derides the enemy with the music from the Demon's Chorus of *Gerontius*; but in this work we have music of a Bach-like sublimity when revering the Sacraments, and of a child-like simplicity unexpectedly murmuring the Lord's Prayer.

The greatness of Elgar is ours for all time. May our performance, and our listening, be worthy of our heritage.

Music & Musicians, June 1957

Memories of my Father
by Carice Elgar Blake

I have always read with great interest about centenaries of famous people, but I have obviously never been involved personally in such a celebration, and I never knew what a thrilling and unique event it would be.

To realise that every musical organisation, from the largest to the smallest, is preparing to honour my father this month with special performances of his work is most gratifying and inspiring. It would be interesting to look back on the career of the hero of this particular centenary, and think about the hard work and even drudgery that went to its making, in a period when there was no radio or television, or even gramophones, and certainly no 'Easy Way' to theory for harmony.

The little house where he was born is three and a half miles from Worcester, and his father — who had come to Worcester from Dover to tune the pianos for the Dowager Queen Adelaide, who was living in the county at Witley Court — had to drive in and out in a pony cart. My grandfather set up a music shop in the High Street, and when that began to flourish, he found the daily drive back and forth took too much time, so the family moved to Worcester. The children were sent to a dame's school, and later my father went to a small private school.

When he was about 13 it was decided that one member of the family must earn some money, as my grandfather's artistic temperament came between him and the business side of shop-keeping. So my father was apprenticed to a lawyer, where he remained for nearly two years. But, though he gained consider-able knowledge of the law and developed an exemplary copperplate handwriting, it was not congenial, and he gave it up, to cope with the accounts at the shop.

Here he was able to learn all about pianos and any other musical instruments which happened to be about, and all the music in stock; and he was close to the Cathedral, where he could study the Church of England services. Meanwhile my grand-father had been appointed organist at the Roman Catholic church, so of course my father was expected to blow the organ.

But he not only blew, but learned to play it and to know the liturgy of the Catholic church. I would like to stress that this, with lessons on the violin with local teachers whom he soon outstripped in knowledge, and a week's tuition with Adolf Pollitzer, was the only musical education as such that he received.

In his early twenties he succeeded my grandfather as organist at the Catholic church, and he had built up a large teaching connection all over the county. All this left little time for composition, but he managed to write a few small pieces which were performed in Birmingham by Stockley's orchestra.

He took a room in Malvern for teaching and advertised it in the local paper. This notice reached a certain lady living in the depths of the country nine miles away on the borders of Worcestershire and Gloucestershire, and she decided to have lessons. After the old coachman had driven her to Malvern for two or three months, he was heard to say that he thought there was more in it than music, which turned out to be perfectly true. Miss Roberts and my father were married in 1889, in spite of opposition from her family. She was the daughter of Sir Henry Gee Roberts, one of General Napier's most trusted generals in India, and she gave up her own ambition to become a writer of repute in order to devote herself entirely to furthering my father's career. After an unsuccessful year in London, they returned to Malvern where he still had his teaching connection, and the first event was a commission to write an Overture (*Froissart*) for the Worcester Festival of 1890. The cantatas *King Olaf* and *Caractacus* followed, and made his name known further afield to the Potteries.

Then came the extraordinary success of the *Enigma Variations*, which rapidly extended his fame to London. A commission for the Birmingham Festival was a great step forward in 1900, and I can remember the hard work and spiritual emotion that went into the writing of *The Dream of Gerontius* and the bitter disappointment when it was neither well performed nor understood. Time has put that matter right, but it was a cruel blow. But, in spite of it, we all know how the great works succeeded one another year by year — *The Apostles, The Kingdom*, the Symphonies and the Violin Concerto, to mention the most important. The recognition of his genius in the bestowal of the Order of Merit in 1911 was the crowning joy for my mother after all her care and solicitude.

During the 1914-18 War my father was absorbed in so many

other ways that he wrote only occasional pieces for special events for war charities. But in 1919 he turned his mind to chamber music, which he had only attempted before very early in life, and what he had written then did not satisfy him and he destroyed all his attempts.

The Violin and Piano Sonata, the Quartet and the Quintet are full of the sadness and poignancy of the preceding years, and the anguish of the 'Cello Concerto was perhaps a foreshadowing of the sorrow that was to come to him in 1920 when my mother died. Without her, inspiration seems to have died, for the works he wrote after her death were either transcriptions or, as in the case of the *Nursery Suite* and the *Severn Suite*, themes taken chiefly from old sketch books.

So, after thinking back over his life, it is deeply moving to hear of the celebrations which are to mark the culmination of his strenuous work, and I can but rejoice, with great thankfulness, at being permitted to take part in the celebrations on this wonderful national occasion.

Music & Musicians, June 1957

Some Personal Memories of Elgar
by Alan Webb

I have always been rather proud of the fact that I was born in Worcester in 1900, the year of *The Dream of Gerontius*. In fact, *Gerontius* seems to have had an early effect on me; for at the age of five I was overheard picking out, in a somewhat elementary form, the Angel's Farewell on the piano. From then onwards I was immersed in an Elgarian atmosphere. My father and three of his sisters had been string pupils of Elgar in the eighties and nineties of the last century, and frequently joined in chamber-music lessons at their home in Worcester. Elgar himself sometimes took part, playing the violin in trios and quartets by Mozart, Haydn and Mendelssohn. And they were all, even at that early period, convinced of his future greatness. My father also played under Elgar's conductorship in the Worcester Amateur Instrumental Society. He had a number of autographed first editions of the early violin and piano pieces, including one dedicated to him — *Virelai*, Op.4, No.3. When asked by my father why the dedication was in French ('A mon ami Frank Webb') Elgar replied in a letter: 'It is only done so that it may sell abroad: if you put an English title only you confine the sale entirely to the English market, while a French title secures its circulation in France ... anywhere in fact'. Some discouragements facing Elgar in his early career appear in his letters: 'The average taste in music is extremely low — the majority of amateurs are satisfied in playing an ordinary march tune ... and I fear it is useless asking them to devote their energies to something higher and more difficult'.

'My overture (it was *Froissart*) is finished and I do not think it will be liked. I find that one's own friends are the people to be most in dread of'.

I believe the first time I ever set eyes on Elgar was at a Three Choirs Festival rehearsal in Worcester Cathedral, before the first World War. A great-uncle of mine had taken me, and as we sat, a tall military figure with an iron-grey moustache passed us, and walked rapidly up to the conductor's rostrum, where he gesticulated to the (then) Mr. Ivor Atkins. My great-uncle turned to me, saying: 'Do you know who that is?' And instinctively I did.

Much later, during Elgar's last five years, one would encounter him at the railway-station on his way to catch the Paddington train, or smiling mischievously on the doorstep of Sir Ivor Atkins' house at a Festival, or sitting with Bernard Shaw at a performance of a Shaw play in Malvern. His car, I remember, was a rather tall, old-fashioned looking limousine, with the initials 'E.E.' painted on the door-panels. He was conscious of his dignity in those last days. He would walk down High Street with slow and stately stride, one gloved hand behind his back, and hat pulled down over his forehead. His eyes were fixed on some point ahead of him, and one would have said his thoughts were far away with the Third Symphony. But no. He would suddenly turn into Woolworths, where he bought odd little toys and trinkets, and where he once compelled Sir Ivor Atkins to eat an ice with him. On occasion he would visit my father in his office. Once he pulled some manuscript sheets out of his pocket and said: 'Here, would you like these?' 'These' were sketches for the *Introduction and Allegro for Strings*. Another time he dangled the insignia of the G.C.V.O. in front of my father, as who should say: 'See what they've given me?' In actual fact he was not at all pleased, as he was hoping for the peerage he never got . . . .

But more important than any of these things was the sight of Elgar conducting his own works. To watch that dignified, silver-haired figure slowly mount the conductor's rostrum was something never to be forgotten. He was immaculately dressed, and aristocratic in appearance and bearing. He looked as though he had stepped out of a different century.

In his last years his beat became a little stiff and jerky. There was economy of gesture; he never threw himself about, and for that very reason the great 'fff' outburst of 'Praise to the Holiest' in *Gerontius* was all the more marvellous. He was an erratic conductor and could become too emotionally involved in the music; and his *tempi* changed from performance to performance. But there was always energy and *drive* (which is quite clear from the records he made); and he was able to impart his meaning to the performers, so that the music somehow sounded different under him. He enjoyed conducting his own works. I once saw him, in a performance of the *Nursery Suite,* put down his baton at the end of 'The Waggon Passes' and give a happy little chuckle. He was an extremely sensitive man. I recall one of his last appearances in Queen's Hall. The whole audience rose to greet him when he came on to conduct the Second Symphony; and he visibly flushed with pleasure.

As a young man I had never dared to hope that I would meet
Elgar. But suddenly it happened; and on January 13th, 1931, my
wife and I were invited (by telephone) to spend the evening at
Marl Bank, the house in Worcester where Elgar lived his last five
years, and which the City Council shamelessly allowed to be
demolished in 1969, to make way for blocks of flats. It is
something, I think, which could not have occurred in any other
country but England. I felt somewhat overawed at the moment of
introduction. But there was no need for apprehension. Elgar was
in one of his most genial moods (which was perhaps fortunate for
us). What struck me at once was his normality. He was a typical
hospitable old English gentleman, with nothing of the remote
genius about him, so that as I watched him I had to ask myself:
'Can this man really be the creator of *Gerontius,* the Symphonies,
and the Concertos?'. His conversation was easy, natural, and
amusing. It was the first time I had heard his voice. Rich and
pleasant, with now and again a distinct trace of the old
Worcestershire accent. One of his Grafton nieces was keeping
house for him, and his favourite spaniel 'Marco' was brought into
the conversation immediately. ('You've kept Marco waiting for
his bone. He hates you like poison!'). He went into the drawing-
room and I noticed some freshly-written pages of manuscript on
the piano.

I looked at him closely. What magnificent features . . . . The
forehead with the silky white hair growing far back over it was
veined and intensly sensitive in appearance. The nose, mouth,
and chin were so heavy as to be almost coarse; and yet the general
effect was one of outstanding distinction and refinement. It was
the abrupt downward break in the curve of the nose which
seemed to give the whole face its character. The eyes were not big,
and of no particularly striking colour, yet they were astonishingly
expressive and lighted up, now with a merry twinkle, now with a
beautiful happiness at the sound of well-loved music. And they
looked at us so directly. He blinked slightly as he talked, and
moved his head from side to side. Sometimes he chuckled rather
thickly behind his moustache when talking. Although not
absent-minded in the accepted sense of the term, he gave the
impression of being intensely occupied with his own thoughts and
feelings, and his voice seemed to come from some inner life.
Nevertheless the general impression was that he enjoyed his
fellow-men thoroughly and felt that the world was full of
wonderful things to think and do. His sense of humour bubbled

over. His hands were rather small, neatly-formed, and hairy. His back was extraordinarily humped. It looked almost a deformity. He held his hands up a little in front of him as he walked, almost as though he might at any moment raise an invisible baton.

He suddenly turned to me, offered cigars and cigarettes, and said: 'So you're interested in gramophones?' Whereupon we crossed the hall to the dining-room; and there was his gramophone — one of those huge cabinet models of the period. And at once began what turned out to be a fascinating evening of records. Elgar put on an advance copy of the newly-recorded 'March of the Mogul Emperors', from his own Suite, *The Crown of India*. He was delighted with the reproduction. Like an enthusiastic child, he turned the volume-control on full, and strode restlessly about the room. Then came his new *Pomp and Circumstance March No.5*. We had rather expected the Verdi *Requiem*, and presently he asked his niece to find it. (She did so promptly, but she was obviously the only person who knew where things were. For Elgar was gloriously capricious, seeming to want everything at once, and often changing his mind just after having made a choice. There seemed to be only one list of records, on rough paper, in pencil, with many crossings-out and additions. There were several record-cabinets, but the table was littered with his immediate favourites, all piled one on top of another, without their envelopes. He seized them as he would cheap crockery. Then, when they were playing, he would want to hear a favourite passage again and would stab with a vicious-looking 'Tungstyle' until he found it.) He gave us one score of the *Requiem*, he took another, and we sat down together at the table. 'Let's have the full power on', he said to his niece. We jumped from one section to another, and some records he insisted on having twice. 'That's one of the most superb passages in all music', he said, and his finger came down on to our score. At one point he raised both his arms in the air and burst out with: 'Oh my *God*, isn't that beautiful?' And again, that expression of sublime happiness on his face. At the end he turned to us; 'What d'you think of that? Did you ever hear anything like it?' After that came the *Siegfried Idyll*, and while the music was in progress he hummed the theme half to himself. It was all so exciting that I found his restlessness infectious. Then came one of the biggest thrills for me. Elgar put on another advance copy of a record, without saying anything — and it was the opening of his own First Symphony, as yet unissued. He was delighted with the great technical progress in recording. I asked to hear the final pages of the work, and we listened to it together out in the hall, which he said was the best place to hear from. The next record he put on was — suprisingly — Saint-Saëns' *Le Rouet d'Omphale*.

Between records came entertaining stories of all sorts. Elgar was a first-class 'raconteur', laughing heartily and infectiously. Another record he played to us was his rehearsing of the Rondo of the Second Symphony with the L.S.O., made without his knowledge. He then said: 'Now let's have something frivolous', and put on the Ballet Music from Gounod's *Faust*. My wife at this point boldly asked for 'The Tame Bear' and 'Fairies and Giants' from *The Wand of Youth*. 'Oho!' said Elgar, obviously pleased .... So we heard those and also 'The Wild Bears', in the middle of which Elgar produced the original manuscript and, guided by his forefinger, we rushed through the pages. Then from him: 'Oh! we *must* have 'Fairies and Giants' again. I love to hear the three Giants coming on one after another.' His excitement at his own music was completely unselfconscious and unaffected. One just felt excited too.

'But did you ever see a full score, with the chorus as well?' he asked. 'It makes you wonder how the poor devil who wrote it can still be alive.' And we went back to the drawing-room to see the score of *The Apostles, Falstaff, The Music Makers,* and others. I confessed to being ignorant of *Falstaff*. 'What!' he exclaimed; and then, with real enjoyment: 'Don't you know the Interlude in the orchard?' (The work had not then been recorded.)

Among many subjects he talked of was conducting, and he was somewhat indiscreet about two of his fellow-conductors, mentioning them by name. 'The Press knows nothing and always lauds the man who makes a great show of gesture in order to bring in this or that instrument; whereas the man who really counts has everything arranged beforehand and has no need of dramatic flourishes, because there is an understanding between him and the orchestra', (which was exactly true of Elgar's own conducting.)

He produced a little Woolworth toy which greatly intrigued him. You pressed the rubber tip of a glass tube and a little imp moved up and down in the water inside. He was at a loss to understand how it worked, 'although', he said, 'I am something of a scientific man'.

He suddenly looked at me and asked: 'What are you a professor of?' It was an odd word to use, and I wondered if there was perhaps a hint here of his well-known anti-academic bias.

About publishers and their conventionalities: 'When I used to send things to Schott's in the old days, they never did anything so undignified as to *pay* me; they used to write and say they had "set a sum aside" for me!' He was most entertaining about religion in England. Talking without malice about the Church of England ('Most of my friends are Churchmen') he said: 'The English are the most moral and the most hypocritical race on earth'. 'What the people like is an aristocratic parson, not the hard-working type', (this was of course 1931), and he quoted the case of a Worcester parish priest in his young days who had an added distinction in the eyes of his parishioners because he was believed to be one of George IV's illegitimate sons. Bemoaning the decline of church music he said: 'Music in England was ruined by *Hymns Ancient and Modern.*'

He showed us a little old print of the cottage where was born, (it is now in the Elgar Birthplace at Broadheath), and some quaint daguerreotypes, one of them showing himself as a little boy, resting his head against his mother's knee. 'My mother', he said simply, 'was one of the most beautiful women alive'. Which launched him into fascinating family history about his father, the piano-tuner. 'He used to ride a thoroughbred mare when he went to tune a piano'.

The hour was already late, and we made several attempts to leave, fearful of outstaying our welcome. But Elgar's conversation flowed on almost without a break. (He quoted amusingly from Lowell's *Essays.*) And furthermore, he insisted on our having some more music 'to finish up with'. So back we went to the dining-room and he got out an overture by Suppé, whom he admired tremendously. 'You know', he said 'dear old Sullivan was all very well, but he didn't write for a big orchestra, like Suppé and Offenbach and Johann Strauss'. And he started the record, and at once became infectiously enthusiastic again. We must all listen attentively. 'This is one of the most divine tunes ever written', he exclaimed. He straightaway put it on again, singing to the music, and watching our faces as we listened.

When at last we emerged into the freezing night we heard Elgar already playing something else on his gramophone . . . .

His niece told me later that after we had left he said to her: 'Do you think they really loved my music?' The humility of the truly great . . . . I never met Elgar again, but when he lay dying in Worcester I wrote to him to try and tell him what his music meant to me. A postcard of thanks came back, dictated to his daughter, but bravely signed 'Edward Elgar' in a shaky hand.

It was a great privilege for me to have been brought up in

Worcester, within sight of Elgar's Malvern Hills; to have been closely connected with his music as conductor of choral societies in different parts of the world; finally, to have spent the six happiest years of my life as Curator of Elgar's Birthplace, surrounded by his scores and personal possessions. It was there, with thousands of people going through the little house, that I realised to the full the world-wide interest in the man and his music.

PART VI: ELGAR AND OTHER COMPOSERS

Elgar and Handel
by W. J. Turner

The recent Elgar festival given by the B.B.C. was the occasion of a performance of his oratorio, *The Kingdom*, Op. 51, which was composed about the year 1906, when it was first performed at Birmingham. It is not often that one has a chance of hearing this work, and it was particularly instructive on this occasion, since its performance at the Queen's Hall on Wednesday, December 14th, by the B.B.C. Symphony Orchestra, the B.B.C. Chorus and the Wireless Ladies' Chorus under Dr. Adrian Boult was followed two nights later by a performance of *The Messiah*, with the Philharmonic Choir and the London Philharmonic Orchestra under Sir Thomas Beecham.

There is a good diversity of opinion about Sir Edward Elgar's music. There are few who, with Mr. Bernard Shaw, think him the greatest symphonist since Beethoven, but even those, like myself, who consider his two symphonies to be among the weakest of his works, are glad to hear that Sir Edward has written a third symphony which we may hear this year. The academic world has been inclined to look askance at Elgar because he did not go through any of our official schools of music, but learned to compose in the more haphazard style of natural musicians. Then there are the enthusiastic patriots who pretend that Elgar is the quintessence of England and his music 'English' music — perhaps the first English music since Purcell. No doubt Elgar is the most gifted composer we have had in this country since Purcell, but in many respects he is far from being typically English in character and outlook, whilst the actual idiom of his music derives so directly from German music of the nineteenth century, from Wagner and Brahms, that I cannot understand what some musicians mean when they talk about the 'Englishness' of the Violin Concerto, for example. I cannot see how this concerto is more in the blood of Albert Sammons than of Yehudi Menuhin or vice versa. It seems to me neither Jewish nor Christian music, and yet I think it would be possible to find more points in common in the Violin Concertos of Max Bruch and Elgar than we should ever find in the music of Vaughan Williams and Elgar.

To me *The Kingdom* has something of the atmosphere of *Parsifal*; but — to continue our doubtful nationalistic distinctions — it is *Parsifal* written by a gentleman. It is doubtful whether any German can be a gentleman, because the Germans have themselves declared that under the rank of baron they don't exist; but there can be no doubt that *The Kingdom* is the work of a gentleman, and I mean this as a serious compliment. The text of *The Kingdom* is biblical and has its source in the New Testament. The text is very dexterously and tactfully put together, and describes the Pentecost and other incidents of the early Christian Church. Unlike *The Dream of Gerontius*, which is definitely Catholic, *The Kingdom* has no sectarian bias but is broadly Christian. Nevertheless, the music has the same definite flavour of what I hope I may call, without offence, erotic religiosity as *Gerontius*, though more temperately and discreetly expressed. I find it hard to define this particular kind of religious sentiment without seeming to decry it. In order not to do this I will choose the best example of it I know, which is in some of the poetry of Coventry Patmore. Patmore was also a Catholic, and there are many other points of resemblance between these two artists who are in some ways so very English and so extremely un-English. The music of *The Kingdom* is a rich haze of a particular kind of religious sentiment. I have an enormous admiration for Patmore as a poet, and to rank Elgar as an artist with Patmore is to give him high praise indeed. The religious sentiment they both share may be illustrated by two lines out of Section II of *The Kingdom*, described as 'At the Beautiful Gate.' You may distinguish infallibly two main types of English religious feeling by using these words 'At the Beautiful Gate' and the following lines:

This man lame from his mother's womb
is carried daily to the Beautiful Gate

as a touchstone. Those who like this phrase 'At the Beautiful Gate' are of the religious type of Elgar, Patmore, Alice Meynell, Francis Thompson and a large band of thoroughly English artists and mystics going right back through our history. Those who dislike this phrase intensely belong to the other religious type, the type of Milton, Blake, Cromwell, and Shelley.

As I think Patmore a far finer poet than Swinburne, and one of the few real poets of the last hundred years, I hope I may not be misunderstood when I say that *The Kingdom* is as un-English as the *Messiah* is English. In the *Messiah* I always seem to hear the authentic voice of my own country, although it was composed by a German. But I don't think this has much to do with any religious standpoint. It is rather a matter of genius, and yet when one says that *The Kingdom* is a work of great talent and the *Messiah* a work of genius, one does not say all that needs to be said. We have no right to say that the voice of Milton is the voice of England, and that the voice of George Herbert or Patmore is not the voice of England. And the complexity of the matter is made startling by the fact of the *Messiah* being composed by a German, and being from beginning to end as utterly English and non-German as our imaginations can conceive.

I should like to be able to go on to the conclusion that irresistibly thrusts itself forward, namely, that all genius is English. There is a sense in which I really believe this to be true, and to me there is something foreign about the music of Elgar and the poetry of Patmore which I also recognise in the music of Brahms and Wagner. All these artists are in some sense alien. But Beethoven, Haydn, Schubert, Handel and Mozart are not alien: they are English — as English as Job, Jeremiah, Isaiah and Abraham. Now that I have mentioned these ancient Hebrews, we can see more clearly where our English affinity lies. It lies in the religious purity of monotheism. The *Messiah* is monotheistic, *The Kingdom* is not. The *Messiah* is passionate, *The Kingdom* is sensual. The *Messiah* is thrilling, sublime, and radiant. *The Kingdom*, like *Parsifal* — only, I repeat, it is the work of a gentleman — is dim, rich, warm, languorous and enervating.

Naturally, if any German likes to say that the quality I call English he calls German and cites Luther, not to mention the great composers I have named, I have no quarrel with him. But I might point out that it will be more difficult for him to lay claim to the great Old Testament Jews as being German. There is no doubt at all that they are entirely English. Not all Jews are English. Schnabel is English, but the Jews you will find in the Regent Palace Hotel are not English. Saint Paul was English, but I am not at all sure about Jesus. That is why I, as an Englishman, am reluctant to describe myself as a Christian. I am a member of the Church of England and not a Christian. But Coventry Patmore was a Christian, so is the composer of *The Kingdom*, and therefore not, in my opinion, wholly and most characteristically English like Handel, Abraham, Moses, and St. Paul.

Elgar, Parry and Stanford
by Vincent Waite

In one of his early letters to Jaeger, Elgar wrote, 'These great men seem to be busily employed in performing one another's works,' and then tartly added, 'no-one else will.'[1] The three men he referred to were Parry, Stanford and Mackenzie, all of whom together with Sullivan and Cowen represented the contemporary musical 'establishment'. Elgar's associations with Mackenzie were never pariculary close although Basil Maine describes them as friendly towards the end of their careers, and as proof of this he mentions that it was then 'Elgar's custom to send at intervals a basket of flowers from his country home to the older musician' living in retirement in London.[2] With the other two musicians Elgar's relationships were much closer and are of no small interest and value in throwing sidelights on the characters of all three.

Both Parry and Stanford were older than Elgar and both were distinguished in the academic field; indeed Elgar acknowledged the help he had obtained in his 'teens from Parry's articles in *Grove's Dictionary*. The backgrounds of Parry and Elgar could scarcely have been more different. Elgar came up the hard way to become the outstanding British composer of his age; virtually self-taught, entirely without financial resources, he also had the additional disadvantage in the Victorian era of being the son of a tradesman who kept a music shop and tuned pianos. This was a handicap which seemed to rankle throughout his life: Dr. Jerrold Northrop Moore quotes from a letter Elgar wrote in 1900 in which he said, 'As to the whole "shop" episode . . . I know it has ruined me and made life impossible until I what you call made a name — I only knew that I was kept out of everything decent, "cos his father keeps a shop".'[3] Parry, on the other hand, the Old Etonian, was the son of a wealthy Gloucestershire land owner with a great country house and estates at Highnam. It may be

---

[1] Elgar to Jaeger, 4 February 1898.
[2] Basil Maine, *Elgar, His Life and Works* (Bell, 1933).
[3] Elgar to F.G. Edwards, 19 September 1900.

added that Parry had the other great advantage (perhaps the almost indispensable qualification for an Englishman) that he was prominent 'in almost every branch of athletics and sport and constantly ran into every kind of danger that land and water afford, suffering almost every possible injury short of the immediately fatal.'[4] In fact every game was played by Parry with impetuous vigour, and even an innocent pastime like billiards became for him something of a battle. As in many country houses of the period the Highnam billiard-room was surrounded by glass cases containing stuffed birds, and one of them was nearly always smashed when Parry played a game.

Yet no-one could have been less of an athletic philistine: indeed he went out of his way to deprecate the undue worship of sport, saying in one of his College addresses, 'But don't imagine because I am an advocate of wholesome activity, of bodily exercise and the invigorating influence of friendly emulation of open-air games and sports, that I cast in my lot with the extravagant estimates put upon sport by the world. There is no doubt that the worship of sport is carried to a very excessive pitch in this country, to the injury and depreciation of the higher pursuits of art and literature and the achievements of mind and imagination.'

In 1892 after two years of unrewarded struggle and fruitless rounds of music publishers in London, a disillusioned Elgar was once again among the first violins at the Gloucester Festival when Parry's *Job* was having its first performance. Perhaps with a pardonable sense of hopeless despondency in the face of the well-entrenched musical establishment, Elgar wrote bitterly on his copy of the programme: 'I played first violin for the sake of the fee, as I could obtain no recognition as a composer.' However, it was not until six years later, in the year he wrote the letter to Jaeger quoted above, that he first met Parry. It was at the Leeds Festival and it is clear that Elgar at once took to the older man. Indeed it would have been difficult for anyone to feel anything but warmth towards someone so utterly honest, generous and transparently honourable as Parry. Even the anti-Parryite Jaeger told Elgar that 'Parry of all men in England is the one who would not take offence at one's opinion if sincerely stated.'[5] At the same time Jaeger rarely lost an opportunity of gratuitously disparaging Parry as a composer. Thus he wrote of a new Parry *Te Deum*: 'Parry, oh Parry! Very much Parry! Toujours Parry! Fiddles

---

[4]   *The Oxford Companion to Music.*
[5]   Jaeger to Elgar, 28 February 1898.

sawing all the time! Dear old Parry!' — and then added sarcastically, as if on purpose to arouse Elgar's jealousy, 'Now if you could compose a skoughre [sic] like that.'

A year after their meeting, Elgar's *Enigma Variations* had their first performance. Parry was vastly impressed and was heard to say afterwards, 'Yesterday I heard Richter perform the *Enigma Variations* by a Mr Elgar which is the finest work I've listened to for years. Look out for this man's music; he has something to say and knows how to say it.' Later he sent Elgar 'a rapturous letter', as Alice Elgar described it. 'Most nice of him', commented Elgar, obviously more than just pleased, as was shown by the letter he later sent Parry with a copy of the *Enigma* score: 'When Richter produced my *Variations* you sent me a very kind letter; this naturally you will have forgotten — but I have not and never shall.'

As it happened, two years before the appearance of the *Enigma Variations* Parry had conducted the first performance of his own *Symphonic Variations* which have been described by Michael Pope as 'the first notable set of orchestral variations by a British composer.' Even Jaeger went so far as to say he thought them very good, and then added 'but as usual, badly scored.'[6] Fortunately an excellent record (Lyrita SRCS 48) is available of some of Parry's music, including the *Variations,* so that we can judge for ourselves whether they are 'badly scored.'

Parry continued to show his regard for Elgar in a number of ways: he was among the group of musicians who subscribed towards the cost of Elgar's robes when he received the honorary Doctorate of Music at Cambridge; and he was one of his sponsors (Stanford was the other) when Elgar was elected to the Athenæum Club. In 1905 Elgar received an honorary Doctorate of Music at Oxford and it was Parry who made 'a fine oration', as Alice Elgar reported in her diary. By this time Parry was to Elgar 'a dear good man', and on a postcard to Jaeger he was 'an angel as ever, God bless him.' In a letter to Frank Schuster he paid him a different kind of compliment saying, 'All professors, except Parry, neglect to wash.' On another occasion he wrote to Parry who had done him some unspecified kindness, and offered to relieve him in some way in his administrative work — copying, transposing or adapting; — 'anything in fact that an ordinary copyist could, or could not quite, do, I would take the greatest pride and pleasure in doing it for you.' Another instance of his

---

[6]   Jaeger to Elgar, 8 March 1898.

high regard for Parry was shown when he withdrew his offer to write the preface to a book when he saw that it contained things against Parry. 'I could not give my name to this,' was his terse comment.

Two years later Elgar burst into enthusiastic praise of Parry's new work for the Gloucester Festival, his Symphonic Poem *The Vision of Life*. 'I say,' he wrote to Jaeger, 'that *Vision* of Parry's is fine stuff; you *must* hear it one day'; and added that the words (Parry's own) really were 'literature'.[7] I find Elgar's praise of this libretto especially interesting because I think it shows how even in 1907 his philosophy of life was moving away from the dogmas of the Roman Catholic church. For Parry, as he grew older, departed from purely biblical texts for his cantatas, and instead used secular words, especially his own, to express a vague kind of Walt Whitmanish humanism.

But Elgar, in spite of praising *The Vision of Life*, was still severely critical of Parry's orchestration. 'No,' he said to Jaeger, 'I cannot stand Parry's orchestra: it's dead and is never more than an organ part arranged.' No-one will deny that Elgar, the superb master of the orchestra, had every right to pass his own personal judgment of Parry's orchestration, but his criticism of Parry's song-writing is more difficult to justify. 'There is one dear good man against whom I would think nothing but the greatest admiration, and that is Parry,' he wrote to Jaeger, 'but he almost, if not quite, annoys me in the way he sets the words which swarm in our English — two syllables, both short, the first accented, e.g. petal.'[8] This is an odd criticism from one who has himself been taken severely to task for his own shortcomings in solo-song writing, by displacements of stress, etc. Diana McVeagh says bluntly that Elgar 'was insensitive to word values,' and that the example 'of Parry's English Lyrics was lost on him.'[9] An earlier critic, Ernest Newman, drew attention to the weakness of Elgar's solo-song settings 'which always seemed to follow the line shape instead of the meaning. His ear is plainly insensitive to defects of phrasing; his tune is conceived for its own sake, and the words have to be made to fit as best they can.'[10] In Thomas Dunhill's opinion even Elgar's better songs are 'far below the less significant songs of Parry.'[11] Again, even an Elgar admirer like

---

Elgar to Jaeger, 8 October 1907.
Elgar to Jaeger, 26 April 1908.
Diana McVeagh, *Edward Elgar, His Life and Music* (1955).
[10]   Ernest Newman, *Elgar* (Music of the Masters Series, 1922).
[11]   Thomas Dunhill, *Sir Edward Elgar* (1938).

Dyneley Hussey is forced to admit that 'for an assiduous reader of poetry, Elgar was curiously insensitive to the niceties of poetic rhythm, and even to the simpler problems of accentuation.' Very properly he hastens to add that no such reservations need be made about Elgar's choral works 'where his technical mastery is absolute.'[12]

On the other hand, as regards Parry's songs Fuller-Maitland considers that (apart from two early songs written while he was still at Eton) he shows 'wonderful skill in accentuation; the words always seem to have suggested the framework of the vocal phrase.'[13] R.O. Morris takes the same view saying that 'in the scrupulous observance of the verbal rhythm Parry is, as ever, a model to composers.'

In his inaugural lecture as Professor of Music at the University of Birmingham, Elgar went out of his way to give special praise to Parry, 'a name,' he said, 'which shall always be spoken in this University with the deepest respect, and I will add, the deepest affection . . . with him no cloud of formality can dim the healthy sympathy and broad influence he exerts and we hope may long continue to exert upon us.' He referred to Parry as 'the head of our art in this country' and spoke of *Blest Pair of Sirens* as 'that English masterpiece'; and Parry is of course best known for his choral mastery, his skill in handling large masses with seemingly effortless ease, obtaining climax after climax with noble simplicity of effect. For many of his contemporaries, however, it was his work as an inspiring teacher and administrator which earned their gratitude and admiration. Sir Hugh Allen, who succeeded Parry as Director of the Royal College of Music, said that 'Parry's teaching and influence, throbbing with infectious energy, were almost miraculous.' Dr. Douglas Fox recalls that 'for many of us, Sir Hubert Parry's dynamic personality seemed to direct and inspire our College life in an extraordinary and indefinable way, though we rarely saw him except at concerts and on the first morning of term, when after a characteristically genial welcome he would deliver one of his sequence of College Addresses.'[14]

The Oxford Companion to Music concludes its article on Parry with the words: 'His geniality, generosity, moral character and artistic ideals were of the greatest influence; indeed, he was everything that one would like the world to consider as implied in

---

[12] *The Musical Companion*, Ed. A.L. Bacharach (1934).
[13] Fuller-Maitland, *The Music of Parry and Stanford* (1934).
[14] Winifred Fox: *Douglas Fox; A Chronicle* (1976).

the description "English gentleman".' His ashes were buried in
St. Paul's, 'as was only fitting, because he was a national figure
who had made through music a contribution to the public and
social life of his country.' The Cathedral was packed for the
occasion, so packed that Thomas Dunhill, who was then acting as
a steward, had the greatest difficulty in finding a place for Elgar
and his wife. And, at the service they sang perhaps the most
beautiful motet of Parry's *Songs of Farewell:*

> There is an old belief
> That on some solemn shore,
> Beyond the sphere of grief,
> Dear friends shall meet once more.

Four years later Elgar was present at the unveiling of a
memorial tablet to Parry in Gloucester Cathedral, and the
occasion led to a token reconciliation between Elgar and
Stanford who, as we shall see later, had been estranged for many
years. Parry himself would surely have been happy that it was this
ceremony which brought the two together, for like many other
friends of Elgar and Stanford, he had long felt distress and
embarrassment at their antagonism. Indeed, such bitter ill-
feeling, harboured for so long, would have been impossible in the
warm-hearted, generous Parry who, in Sir Hugh Allen's memorable phrase, 'carried the stimulus of sunshine wherever he went.'

Elgar's relationship with Stanford was of a very different
character, but the real reason for the estrangement which existed
for so long between them still remains something of a mystery.
According to Lady Elgar the real hostility between the two began
with an 'odious letter' which Stanford sent to Elgar in December
1904, the contents of which have never been revealed. In fact
differences had arisen before, and it seems only fair to trace the
course of their previous relationship so that neither party shall be
unjustly blamed for any part of the mutual antagonism.

The two men first met in 1896 when Stanford and his wife came
to lunch with the Elgars in Malvern in order to meet Swinnerton
Heap, the conductor of the Birmingham Festival Choral Society.
Although only five years older than Elgar, Stanford was already
Professor of Music at Cambridge and on the staff of the Royal
College of Music. With their fiercely definite characteristics,
some of them similar, it was perhaps inevitable that these two
personalities should ultimately clash. Elgar was shy, suspicious,
abnormally sensitive and quick to take offence. In many ways
Stanford was even more difficult: although kindly and generous

in spirit he was quick-tempered, intolerant and emotional. As Scott Goddard has perceptively expressed it, 'he wore his nerves so near his upper skin that they were easily exposed and his temper Celtically aroused . . . . His was the strange case of a man full of wit and with an abundant sense of fun, but with little sense of humour, a lack of which turned his wit bitter when circumstances became intemperate.'[15]

At first relations were amicable enough to encourage Elgar to write to ask if the Bach Choir (of which Stanford was conductor) would welcome a new choral work. In his reply Stanford regretted that 'this is a very inopportune moment financially', but he promised to recommend a work from Elgar directly the right moment came. In the same year Elgar sent him the score of *The Banner of St. George* asking his opinion of the work, only to receive a typically forthright crushing reply: 'It's all very well having fine raiment, but there must be a fine body to put it on.' It is difficult to imagine what the prickly Elgar (to say nothing of his wife) thought of this tactless snubbing sarcasm. In return Elgar expressed his opinion of Stanford's own music in a letter to Jaeger, describing it as 'neither fish, flesh, fowl nor good red herring.'[16]

Outwardly at least there still seems to have been a veneer of cordiality between the two, and there is certainly no doubt about the genuineness of Stanford's admiration for the *Enigma Variations*, although Plunket Greene's claim that throughout this time there was no ill-feeling at all is scarcely borne out by a letter from Elgar in January 1900 telling Jaeger that he 'saw Stanford in Manchester the other day . . . and we are quite as before — this between ourselves: we smoked and supped together.'[17] Similarly a later letter from Jaeger certainly suggested that there had been some previous disagreement, for he announced that 'the result of your Stanford *entente cordiale* is that he is going to do your *Variations* at the College. They have bought scores and parts already.'[18] In return Elgar performed Stanford's *Last Post* with the Worcestershire Philharmonic, and Stanford became an honorary member of the Society.

It was undoubtedly on the earnest recommendation of Stanford as Professor of Music that Elgar was offered an honorary

---

[15] Article in *Grove's Dictionary of Music and Musicians* (1954).
[16] Elgar to Jaeger, 11 December 1898.
[17] Elgar to Jaeger, 28 January 1900.
[18] Jaeger to Elgar, 4 February 1900.

Doctorate of Music at Cambridge in 1900, the first of all the academic tributes to be paid to the composer. It was unfortunate that Stanford could not be present at the ceremony but he had already warned Elgar of this possibility and sent a telegram on the day regretting his absence which was due to unavoidable commitments at Leeds where he was to be conductor-in-chief of the forthcoming festival. He had certainly been among the group of fellow musicians who had contributed towards the cost of the academic robes which Elgar confessed he could not afford to buy.

The first London performance of *Gerontius* did not take place until June 1903. Apparently when Stanford heard that it was to be given in Westminster Cathedral he went out of his way to regret the choice saying, as Elgar reported bitterly, 'It is a *great pity* for *my* sake, etc., etc., all on account of the deadly bad acoustics of the building, etc., etc.' Stanford undoubtedly meant it kindly and indeed his fears afterwards proved amply justified, but Elgar put the worst possible construction on it. 'I quite appreciate Stanford's kindness in pointing out that the performance must be disastrous,' was his sarcastic remark to Littleton of Novello's. 'They say that about anything I do or compose . . . if anything can be said or done to throw cold water on the thing it will be done.'[19] Yet so far there had been no open breach between the two. It is true that as regards the music there was an ambivalence in Stanford's attitude towards *Gerontius:* on one occasion he could exclaim that he would have given his head to have written Part I and then at another time describe it as 'stinking of incense.' This did not prevent his writing in generous terms to Elgar congratulating him on the success of the *Variations* at Düsseldorf in 1901; and in the following year he was (together with Parry) a sponsor for Elgar's membership of the Athenæum Club. In 1903 Stanford had to use his influence to extricate Elgar from the result of an unpleasant contretemps with the Leeds Festival committee when Elgar's procrastination had badly mismanaged arrangements regarded as settled by the committee.

We now come to what was apparently the flashpoint of their estrangement, the 'odious letter' received by Elgar on December 27, 1904. Plunket Greene has described how Stanford had a passion for writing letters which, generally with a stinging postscript, would provoke trouble. ' "I took up me pen, me boy," was the recognized prelude among his friends to some inevitable row with a temporary antagonist.'[20] In March of that year the

[19] Elgar to Littleton, 20 April 1903.
[20] Plunket Greene: *Charles Villiers Stanford* (1935).

Stanfords had been present at a dinner party given for Elgar by his adoring friend Leo Schuster in honour of the forthcoming festival of Elgar's music at Covent Garden which was to have royal patronage. The party was held in Schuster's house and was a sumptuous affair with no expense spared; even the panels of the dining-room had been decorated with emblems 'referring to various phases of Elgar's works in order to pay tribute to the composer.' According to Sir Henry Wood's autobiography *My Life of Music,*[21] what should have been a happy occasion was completely spoiled by Elgar's churlish and unmannerly behaviour: far from showing pleasure at this generous tribute he appeared utterly bored by the whole proceedings. The crowning discourtesy came when Schuster, to quote Alice Elgar's diary, 'proposed E.'s health in the most touching way with his heart in his voice.' The guests were by now thoroughly uncomfortable but, to quote Wood, 'naturally expected Elgar to make a suitable reply. Instead he went on talking to an old friend and probably had no idea his health had been drunk at all.'

As someone who was always a convivial guest and never so happy as when in congenial company, Stanford must have been especially incensed at this strange lack of courtesy. After all, Elgar had with surprising speed caught up with the musical establishment with his honorary degrees, his three-day Festival and his forthcoming knighthood; surely he might have shown suitable decorum, appreciation and gratitude at a dinner party in his honour. Percy Young has pointed out that Elgar was not well at the time, having suffered one of his severe headaches in the morning, but Stanford could not be expected to know that. Perhaps, among other things which rankled, Stanford's suppressed anger at this unhappy social *gaffe,* together with the ill-feeling created by the unfortunate blunder Elgar committed over the Leeds Festival commission had been secretly bottled up until there was a final explosion in the 'odious' December letter.

From then on there was little real pretence of friendship. In 1910 Stanford 'fled' when he saw Elgar in Bournemouth to avoid speaking to him, and certainly during his tenure of the Peyton Professorship of Music at the University of Birmingham, Elgar seemed purposely to have made the breach wider in his inaugural lecture. Then among several derogatory remarks about contemporary English composers he referred scornfully to those of them who called some work of theirs a rhapsody. 'Could anything be

---

[21] Henry Wood: *My Life of Music* (Gollancz, 1938).

more inconceivably inept?' he asked. 'To rhapsodise is one thing Englishmen *cannot* do.' As Stanford had already written some of his successful *Irish Rhapsodies,* it seemed obvious against whom the remark was directed, and was another example of Elgar's tactlessness. His devoted friend W.H. Reed admitted that even in an ordinary short speech Elgar had an unhappy knack of letting 'a word or phrase drop which had the effect of annoying someone and which, if he had stopped to consider it, he might have left unsaid.'[22] It was a pity that Stanford descended to the same rather childish level by satirically using one of Elgar's favourite musical directions, *nobilmente,* and applying it to a passage in his *Ode to Discord.*

The scene of the strangest episode in the Elgar/Stanford disagreement was at Lady Elgar's funeral at Little Malvern in 1920. In *Elgar as I Knew Him* and in a letter to Plunket Greene, W.H. Reed relates that as he was following the coffin to the graveside, 'a hand was placed convulsively on my arm and a voice said, "Tell him I had to come. I dare not go to the graveside as I am not well and my doctor absolutely forbids me to stand bareheaded in the open air; but I felt I must come: do tell him from me".'[23] It was Stanford who then 'buried his face in his hands and walked away in tears.' Far from being touched by Stanford's gesture in toiling 'all the way contrary to the doctor's orders', Elgar was if anything even more implacably hostile when he heard of it after the funeral. He regarded it as 'a cruel piece of impertinence', and in a letter to Schuster[24] he bitterly described it as 'a very clever trick' to make it appear that 'after all, he is really a decent fellow etc . . . and that *I* am the culprit — that the fault (if any) of our difference (which only exists by his manufacture) is wholly *mine* and not his. As to his wanting to show respect and the like, I do not believe a word of it and never shall do: it was a mere political trick. He is an old friend of yours, older than I am, and probably more trusted, but that cannot alter my opinion.' But even in this unforgiving mood Elgar felt constrained to add 'For the good things he has done in the past I still hold respect.'

Not until another two years had passed was there at last some sort of reconciliation. It was at the 1922 Gloucester Festival when a Memorial to Parry was unveiled. Granville Bantock or Brewer — accounts differ — brought the two men face to face. Stanford

---

[22] W.H. Reed: *Elgar* (Dents' Master Musicians Series, 1939).
[23] W.H. Reed: *Elgar as I knew him* (1936).
[24] Elgar to Schuster, 18 April 1920.

with his usual impetuosity exclaimed, 'Let's forget all about it', and held out his hand. Afterwards Elgar mentioned that he had no idea what 'it' was that they had to forget, but at least some sort of *rapprochement* had been effected. A photograph of the occasion shows Elgar staring ahead with a kind of uncompromising cool aloofness, and with his morning coat tightly buttoned up. When chaffed by Sir Hugh Allen about this he retorted tartly, 'I always keep *everything* buttoned up when I am in *this* company,' which scarcely struck a very cordial or conciliatory note.

Stanford died two years later and thus the unhappy discord came to an end except for that kept flickeringly alive by a few misguided members of a Stanford clique who, as Michael Kennedy puts it, 'not such big men as C.V.S. himself, were responsible in the 1920s and 1930s for ensuring a cold climate for Elgar's music in circles where they had influence.'[25] Now even they are forgotten.

In July of 1976 the BBC broadcast on the same day Stanford's *Clarinet Concerto* and Elgar's First Symphony. It seemed to me a happy, even if unintentional, symbol of the reconciliation in harmony of these two men, both of whom in their own ways made imperishable contributions to the musical history of this country. And as I listened to the splendid music I felt that perhaps under the benignity of 'the master of all Music, the Master of all Singing' the spirits of Elgar and Stanford, too, came together on that day as friends and fellow musicians.

The Elgar Society Newsletter,
January and May 1978

---

[25] Michael Kennedy: *Portrait of Elgar* (O.U.P, 1968).

Elgar and Delius
by Christopher Redwood

The St. James's Hall, London, named after the Church which stood opposite one of its entrances, occupied land lying between Regent Street and Piccadilly, access to the larger of its two concert-rooms being gained from the former thoroughfare. Built in 1858 to replace the Hanover Square Rooms, compared with which it was twice as large, it was nevertheless extremely modest by the standards of 20th Century concert-halls. Notwithstanding this fact, it played host to all the famous soloists and orchestras of Europe until 1905, when it was superseded as the centre of orchestral music-making in London by the Queen's Hall, and the Piccadilly Hotel built on its site.

In the spring of 1899 two concerts took place at the St. James's Hall, each of which introduced to London a new and important composer who was to dominate British music for the next thirty-five years. The first was on 30th May when 37 year-old Frederick Delius spent about half of a £1,000 legacy left him by a fond uncle in mounting a concert of his most prized compositions; it was the first time that any of his orchestral music had been heard in London. Neither had the capital yet heard the *Variations on an Original Theme for Orchestra* by 42 year-old Edward Elgar, which were conducted by Hans Richter three weeks later, on 19th June. Besides being the senior of the two composers, Elgar was also the better-known, although his reputation had until this time been mainly confined to the West Midlands. The concert in question set the seal on his fame in London, and five years later he was a Knight.

On the face of it these two men had little in common. The one was a true and patriotic Briton who is often considered to epitomise the era of his greatest attainments; the other, born of German immigrant parents, thought so little of the country of his birth that he made his home in France and was proud to describe himself in the phrase of his idol, Nietzsche, as 'a good European'. The one was a devout (though not straight-laced) Roman Catholic, who found his greatest inspiration in the Holy Bible and associated writings; the other a wicked atheist who never tired of tilting at Christianity. Nevertheless the fact remains that they were the leading British composers of their generation and alone re-established British music on the continent of Europe. A comparison of their lives is therefore of value, not least on account of a number of parallels, some perhaps coincidences, which may be found.

Their backgrounds, to be sure, were very different. Elgar's father, as is well-known, was a modest music-seller whose trade immediately stamped his offspring as members of the lower middle-class. Delius's father, on the other hand, was a highly successful wool and noil importer who occupied a distinctly higher social status in Bradford. The fact that both sons were largely self-taught was the result of quite different causes. Elgar was compelled to acquire virtually all his knowledge of the theory of music from books in his father's shop because family finances would not stretch to formal musical education. Delius's father, by contrast, while actively supporting amateur music-making, was determined that his son should follow a respectable business career and only agreed to finance professional musical training reluctantly, belatedly and under great pressure.

Elgar studied the violin, for some of the time under Pollitzer, but the nearest he approached to his ambition of studying at the Leipzig Conservatorium was a fortnight's holiday spent in the city in 1883. Delius also specialised in the violin, some of his lessons being under Hans Sitt. These *were* at Leipzig, where he studied for eighteen months between 1886 and 1888, leaving of his own accord. Later in life he affirmed that the Conservatorium had taught him nothing, all his technique having been learned from Thomas Ward, the New York organist who had given him intensive tuition in early days on his Florida plantation. Much of his craft, nevertheless, and particularly his orchestration, was learned from his own studies of the works of composers who interested him.

In the nineteenth century it was customary for the aspiring young composer to seek out a wealthy benefactor who would provide him with an allowance until he obtained sufficient recognition to support himself. The possibilities of the teaching profession were much more limited than they are to-day, and it is therefore worth remarking that both Elgar and Delius made their earliest livings in this way. Most of their pupils were female, Delius teaching at a young ladies' finishing college in Virginia and Elgar at various girls' private schools in the Worcester and Malvern areas. There is nothing to suggest that Delius was anything but successful as a teacher and he is not recorded to have complained about the work. With his handsome, dashing appearance he cut a popular figure among his pupils and was sorely missed when he departed for Europe. By contrast Elgar found teaching extremely irksome, describing it as 'like turning a grindstone with a dislocated shoulder' and, far from charming his female charges, he seems more often to have reduced them to tears.

The greatest benefit which teaching brought to Elgar was meeting Caroline Alice Roberts, a pupil five years older than himself, whom he married a month before his thirty-second birthday. She proved to be a wife in a thousand, providing him with inspiration as well as shielding his over-sensitive nature. Delius made no attempt to resume his teaching career after returning to Europe, for the simple reason that he managed to persuade his father and uncle to provide him with an allowance sufficient to live on in Paris. At the age of thirty-five he met Jelka Rosen, a talented painter, and another mature love-affair commenced. They began living together at Grez-sur-Loing a year later and regularised their relationship five years afterwards. Like Alice, Jelka belonged to that small band of totally devoted wives, as is particularly exemplified by her attentions in his long and painful final illness, although there is evidence to suggest that Delius's admiration for her was more cool and balanced.

These selfless wives were of inestimable benefit to the two composers in their long waits for recognition. Delius was even less widely-known than Elgar at the time of the 1899 concert: only a small album of his songs had been published in England, while there had been a couple of orchestral performances on the Continent. Unlike Elgar, though, he did not suffer from any self-pity; indeed, on at least one occasion he had actually stood in the way of a public performance of a major work over which he apparently had misgivings. Throughout his life he maintained an aloofness and studied indifference to the promotion of his music which was in stark contrast with Elgar's nervous insecurity, even when world-famous.

Eighteen months after the 1899 St. James's Hall performance, Elgar's *Variations* reached Germany, when they were conducted at Düsseldorf by the city's musical director, Julius Buths. Buths (1851 - 1920) had a few months previously attended the ill-starred première of *The Dream of Gerontius* at Birmingham, had apparently been one of the few people present to perceive its genius and had prepared a German translation. He not only produced the work at Düsseldorf in December 1901 but repeated it at the Lower Rhine Festival of May 1902; as the musical world knows, the success of the composition was thereafter assured. Richard Strauss was in the audience and said afterwards, 'with that work England for the first time became one of the modern musical states.'

Buths had also discovered the music of Delius: in January 1904 he gave the first performance of the second version of *Lebenstanz*, in October that year he travelled to nearby Elberfeld (where he had previously been Director of Music) to play the solo part in the first performance of the Piano Concerto under the baton of his successor, Hans Haym, and in June 1905 he conducted *Appalachia*, a work dedicated to him by the composer. Along with Haym and another German conductor, Fritz Cassirer, he established Delius as a major composer in Germany. Strauss in this case also showed his admiration — a feeling which was reciprocated — and was reported on a later occasion after hearing Beecham conduct Delius in Berlin to have made the characteristic remark: 'I never dreamt that anyone except myself was writing such good music'.[1] Later, rival factions were to idolize Strauss and Delius in the way they had Brahms and Wagner in the previous century; the present rivalry was only cut short by the outbreak of the First World War. It was as well that Delius did become established in Germany, for after the 1899 concert not a note of his orchestral music was heard in the British capital for more than eight years, the silence being broken when *Appalachia* was performed in 1907 — under the baton of a visiting German conductor.

It is worth remarking that Elgar also received help from a number of German musicians, Frank Schuster, Alfred Rodewald of Liverpool and Alfred Jaeger of Novellos prominent among them. Indeed, it is salutory to reflect that the resurgence of British music in the early twentieth century owed not a little to Germans.

Not only composers and conductors championed both Elgar and Delius in their early days, but critics, too, including the percipient Edward Algernon Baughan. Baughan's writings on Elgar appear elsewhere in this volume; it will not have escaped the reader's attention that his notice of *Caractacus* in *The Musical Standard* in 1896 led Elgar to describe that journal as 'the first to

---

[1] Quoted by Percy Grainger in *The Personality of Frederick Delius*, reprinted in *A Delius Companion,* ed. Redwood. (Calder, 1976), p.123.

11 Elgar and Carice in the garden at 'Marl Bank'.

12 British Musicians at Bournemouth in 1910. From left to right (standing): Parry, German; (seated): Elgar, Godfrey, Mackenzie, Stanford

give me the place I've fought for'. (A pity, therefore, that he should also have gone on record as saying 'Baughan . . . cannot hum a melody correctly in tune'. [see p.133] The remark may, for all we know, have been true; it was certainly not tactful.) After the 1899 concert of Delius's works Baughan devoted two pages of *The Musical Standard* to it, commenting:

> Personally, I admit that some of Mr. Delius's music sounded discordant to my ears, harsh, uninviting and ugly. But I could hear that he made it so with a definite purpose in view, and I can quite imagine that I might get to like those discords if I knew them better. This is what happened with Wagner's music.

As late as 1908 the magazine *Truth* (which might loosely be described as a kind of nineteenth-century *Private Eye*) was reporting on a 'campaign to puff Delius, apparently led by EA Baughan' and referring to his attack on the critic of *The Times* for not whole-heartedly worshipping *Brigg Fair*, first produced by Bantock at Liverpool on 18th January of that year.

Another critic who championed both composers and whose writings appear elsewhere in this volume was Ernest Newman, and it was he who was probably indirectly responsible for the first meeting between them. Newman was the instigator of the Musical League of 1908 - 13, backed enthusiastically from the start by Delius and Bantock. It was natural that the movement should elect Elgar as its President; Delius accepted the Vice-President's rôle and other committee members included Bantock, Mackenzie, Percy Pitt, Norman O'Neill, Henry Wood, Thomas Beecham and William McNaught (editor of *The Musical Times*). Neither Elgar nor Delius was fond of committee work and the minute-book indicates that of some twelve committee and general meetings held, Elgar attended five and Delius only two. There was but one occasion when both were present, this being a committee meeting on 14th October 1908, held for some reason at the London offices of *Punch*, and incidentally EA Baughan was also invited to attend. The date may well have been arranged to suit the convenience of Delius, who was on his way back to France after attending the British première of *Sea Drift* under Wood the previous night at the Sheffield Festival.

Almost a year later, on 8th September 1909, both composers conducted at the Hereford Three Choirs Festival. In this field of activity they were in sharp contrast for, while Elgar's conducting talents have seldom been questioned and are the subject of a separate chapter in this book, Delius on the podium might best be described as less than competent. On this occasion he was handicapped by a severe chill and disconcerted by having had his wallet stolen; he may, therefore, have left the concert immediately after directing the first performance of his *Dance Rhapsody No. 1* and before Elgar conducted *Cockaigne*. Nevertheless it is highly probable that they met at rehearsals.

The next time that they both appeared in public was at the Birmingham Triennial Festival of 1912. Elgar conducted the first performance of *The Music Makers* on Tuesday, 1st October and *The Apostles* on Friday 4th, while on Thursday 3rd Sir Henry Wood conducted *Sea Drift* in the presence of the composer. This time it was Elgar's turn to be in poor health and he directed *The Apostles* from a recumbant position. It has been recorded that the two composers saw one another but avoided speaking,[2] circumstances which might suggest a rift. The imagination turns to speculate as to the possible cause. After one concert the Musical League was beginning to flounder: there had been a lapse of nearly two years between the last two committee meetings, and Elgar was on the point of resigning. Did he hold Delius's poor attendance at meetings against him? Or did Delius resent the committee's (and therefore, by implication, its President's) spurning of his offer to use his continental connections to persuade Mahler, Schillings and D'Indy to come over and conduct their works at the 1909 Festival? The cause of the rift, if indeed there was one, remains for the present a mystery.

Years later Delius remembered the 1912 première of *The Music Makers* and commented: 'I didn't care for it — it was too rowdy and commonplace'.[3] As with most of his musical opinions he expressed his feelings on Elgar's music outspokenly. To C.W. Orr he wrote:

> ... I find Elgar's musical invention weak; whenever he gets hold of a good theme or nice harmonies they remind me of *Parsifal* or Brahms. He never seems to have outlived his admiration for the Good Friday music; he has it also in *Gerontius*. His manner of composition is also Brahms's. And then the Symphony is very long, and the orchestration thick and clumsy, as is also Brahms's, and the musical matter in the last three movements very meagre. I heard the Violin Concerto in London, and found it long and dull ...[4]

---

[2]   P.M. Young, *Elgar OM*, p.227, and A. Jefferson, *Delius (Dent, 1972)* p.71.

[3]   *Delius as I knew him,* Eric Fenby (Bell, 1936) p.123.

[4]   Delius to C.W. Orr, in *A Delius Companion*, p.60.

(If the second sentence is true, then it is only fitting to add that Delius never outgrew the *Liebestod*.)

Delius loathed development in music, and one suspects that he would have supported his great friend and champion, Sir Thomas Beecham, who was reported to have cut part of the exposition and the whole of the development section from the first movement of Elgar's 1st Symphony, reducing the length of the complete work to thirty-eight minutes![5] Years later Delius claimed that Elgar's attitude to his music was 'slightly censorial as if he considered it not quite proper!'[6]

All the evidence suggests that there was no contact between Delius and Elgar from 1912 to 1933, for when they met in that year in the presence of Fred Gaisberg, Chief Recorder of the Gramophone Company, he wrote of 'this notable meeting after a period of twenty-one years'.[7] The occasion was Elgar's flight to Paris to conduct his Violin Concerto with the 15 year-old Yehudi Menuhin as soloist. Percy M. Young[8] gives the impression that Elgar made the visit reluctantly and out of a sense of duty, apparently referring to a letter to him from Gaisberg dated 17th May 1933:

> You could hardly go to Paris and return without having seen Delius. There is no question at all that this is a duty which ought to be carried out, if Delius is in good enough health to receive your visit.

Dr. Young seems to have been unaware of Elgar's letter of two days earlier, to which the above was a reply:

> I do not know how far away Delius lives, but I should like to see him: it may be that he does not care to see people, even an old friend like me — I have written to ask him . . .[9]

The words 'an old friend like me' and Delius's prompt reply, dictated to his wife, make it clear that time, the great healer, and age, the great mellower, had obliterated all traces of any rift there might have been:

> Your kind letter gave me the greatest pleasure, and I should like

---

[5] Letter from H. Brian to *The Musical Times,* Dec. 1909. The performance discussed is alleged to have taken place on 28th October 1909.

[6] *Delius* by Eric Fenby (Faber, The Great Composers, 1971) p.90.

[7] *Elgar on Record,* Gaisberg, p.204.

[8] Young, op. cit., p.227.

[9] Gaisberg, op. cit., pp.200-1.

nothing better than to welcome you here at Grez — In spite of my infirmities, I manage to get something out of life, and I should love to see you.

On Tuesday 30th May Elgar spent the morning rehearsing, after which he and Gaisberg were driven by Menuhin *père* out to lunch at Ville d'Avray (where Delius had lived before his marriage). After a short rest they set out again in the new Buick for Grez, but before long ignition trouble forced them to continue the forty-mile journey by taxi. It was well after 5pm when they arrived.

With him Elgar had brought a number of gramophone records: Sibelius's 5th Symphony, *Tapiola* and *Pohjola's Daughter*, and an album of songs by Hugo Wolf. Gaisberg described the conversation between the two great men as reminding him 'somewhat of a boasting contest between two boys'. (Could this have been at the root of that rift: nothing more complicated than the rivalry of the country's two most talented composers, which still smouldered but mattered no longer?)

When he returned to England Elgar wrote an account of his visit to Delius for *The Daily Telegraph*, in which it appeared on 1st July. After stressing the energetic interest that Delius was taking in all that was going on in contemporary art, even to the point of continuing to compose, Elgar continued:

Delius has been re-reading Dickens, and remarked on his rich humanity and uncertain art; this led to a discussion of the comparative merits of his novels. Apart from *The Tale of Two Cities* and *Barnaby Rudge* (which are historical), and of *The Pickwick Papers*, which stands apart, I have always held *Bleak House* is the best of his writings. Delius thought *David Copperfield* might claim the first place, but agreed that the picture of Dora was, to say the least, overdrawn. Then the talk went round to older writers and I mentioned Montaigne, whose translation by Florio Delius does not know. He became at once tremendously interested.
'Elgar has new ideas', he said to his wife, and, throwing up his left arm outstretched (his characteristic gesture when making a decision), 'we'll read Montaigne', he declared.

Elgar went on to enquire what the prospects were of seeing Delius in London, and on learning that travelling was the obstacle he suggested the pleasant alternative of flying.

The prospect attracted him. 'What is flying like?' he asked. 'Well,' I answered, 'to put it poetically, it is not unlike your life and my life. The rising from the ground was a little difficult; you cannot tell exactly how you are going to stand it. When once you have reached the height it is very different. There is a delightful feeling of elation in sailing through gold and silver clouds. It is, Delius, rather like your music — a little intangible sometimes, but always very beautiful. I should have liked to stay there for ever. The descent is like our old age — peaceful, even serene.'

My description must have pleased Delius. Up went the left hand: 'I will fly', he said determinedly.

Mention of whisky — the smell of which they both abhorred — led Delius to propose a toast, and champagne was sent for, accompanied by sandwiches of home-baked bread and home-cured ham. They talked of old friends — Buths, Bantock and Percy Pitt, of their likes and dislikes in music and of what would and would not grow in each man's garden. Eventually it was time to go, and they bade one another an affectionate farewell, Delius holding both of Elgar's hands. 'To me,' Elgar concluded, 'he seemed like the poet who, seeing the sun again after his pilgrimage, had found complete harmony between will and desire.'

The following day, before leaving France he wrote:

> Before boarding the plane for England I send a note to thank you and Mrs. Delius for your charming welcome. It was a great privilege to see you and I was delighted to find you so much better than the newspapers had led me to expect.

This was the beginning of a fascinating correspondence that has survived and which was only cut short by death; for little could Elgar have guessed when holding the emaciated Delius's hands on that summer afternoon and looking forward to the following evening's reception where he would sit at the side of the President of the French Republic, that it would be he and not Delius who would be the first to depart this life. Within six months Delius had followed him.

A week later (the date on the letter is 8th June) Elgar wrote again, this time from *Marl Bank*:

> I wish you would think out (I tremble in making any suggestion) some small composition suitable, as regards difficulty, for small orchestra — your *Cuckoo in Spring* is naturally very much loved, and is within the capacity of some of the minor organizations. We did it in Worcester which, apart from the Festival, boasts no great equipment. I want three movements — any poetic basis you like: Fontainebleau, Grez, your own surroundings. You cannot help being a poet in sound and I say no more on the matter. Something, or things such as I have had the temerity to name, would bring your

wonderful art among the devoted people who mean (and do) well in small things and cannot aspire to perform your large works. Do not be angry.

Delius promised to consider the idea and sent him the score of *A Song Before Sunrise*, which Elgar found 'delightful'. When Elgar became ill and had to enter a nursing-home in October, Delius quickly sent him a telegram of good wishes. In acknowledging it on 13th Elgar wrote:

> . . . it gave me great joy to know that you thought of me in this distressful time. I am supposed to be improving and want to share a few more years with you and hear your 'brave translunary things' and to see and talk once more with the poet's mind in the poet's body — you in fact.

In the following months Delius was informed that Gaisberg would be arranging for some records of Elgar's music to be sent to him. He replied with eager anticipation:

> I wonder whether Falstaff will be among them, as this is a work which I especially love and admire.

In return the Deliuses sent Elgar several boxes of the celebrated *Sucre d'Orge* from the nearby nunnery at Moret-sur-Loing as a dietary aid (they did not hold with conventional medicine). After being operated on, Elgar received a couple of visits from Granville Bantock and reported in his letter of 4th December:

> We have talked much of you and made the old days live again with joy.

Delius replied on 10th December in the following terms:

> Your beautiful letter gave me the greatest pleasure and I treasure it. Also it made me assured that you are feeling better and are gradually conquering your illness. . . .
> I have derived great pleasure from hearing your works on the gramophone. Introduction and Allegro has always been a special favourite of mine and yesterday we had Falstaff. What a magnificent work it is, so greatly conceived, so full of life and in its changing moods so human, vigorous and natural. It is the outcome of a rich nature.

Elgar's final letter was, not inappropriately, dictated on Christmas Day. After the opening pleasantries he continued:

> I am keenly interested in your coming visit to London and scarcely dare hope that I shall be strong enough to be amongst those who will welcome you. I do not know the scheme of the concerts but I wish Sir

Thomas would give us *Paris* and *The Mass of Life* again. It has been a matter of no small amusement to me that, as my name is somewhat unfortunately indissolubly connected with 'sacred' music some of your friends and mine have tried to make me believe that I am ill disposed to the trend and sympathy of your great work. Nothing could be farther from the real state of the case. I admire your work intensely and salute the genius displayed in it. . .

I do not propose to look back on the past year with any great satisfaction but a few events stand out far apart. My visit to you is still a vivid thing in my memory and is one of the things that will endure. The kindness of Mrs. Delius and you to me lifts 1933 out of the ordinary Anno Dominis.

The proposed visit of Delius to London to which Elgar refers was to see his opera *Koanga*, which Beecham was planning to mount at Covent Garden for the first time in this country. Sadly, the performances had to be postponed and eventually took place in 1935 as an act of homage to the dead composer. Sadly, too, Delius's reply to that letter, dictated on 4th January 1934, is the last item in the correspondence, for on 23rd February Elgar died at *Marl Bank*:

It gave me the greatest pleasure today to read in the *Daily Mail* that you are so much better and that you have left the Nursing Home and returned to your own house. This was really splendid news. . .

We often play the records of your works which Mr. Gaisberg sent us. The *Nursery Suite* I did not know. It is charming: the Aubade is a gem. Introduction and Allegro I knew well and love it.

So ended the belated friendship between the two greatest British composers of their time. Perhaps its most appropriate epitaph would be a passage from the letter Delius wrote to his old friend from the days of Musical League, Ernest Newman, on 13th December 1933:

It was very kind indeed of you to write to me and tell me all about our dear friend Elgar. His visit to me here when he spent an afternoon with me was quite an event in my life. It was the first time that the real Elgar was revealed to me and that I could talk intimately with him and that I had the opportunity of appreciating his fine intellect and affectionate nature.

How I now regret that we were not brought together earlier! . . .

Elgar and Mahler
by Sir Neville Cardus

Sir Neville Cardus (1889-1975) wrote extensively on Elgar in his books Ten Composers *(1945) and* A Composers' Eleven *(1958). The following excerpt from a* Radio Times *article is interesting for the unusual comparison it draws between Elgar and his European contemporary, Gustav Mahler.*

Not long ago I asked a distinguished Austrian musician, 'When are they going to understand and take to Elgar's music in Vienna?' His reply was very much to the point: 'As soon as you in England take to and understand Mahler.' The answer went rather deep. For it is the fact, despite all the easy platitudes about the 'universality' of great art, that there are certain sorts of genius which reveal their secrets wholly to none but the people of a like racial psychology, to none but those of a like soil and air and habit of thought and tradition.

You cannot translate Robert Burns into German, and the difficulty is not a mere external matter of finding dialect equivalents in an alien tongue. This particular problem of translation involves a way of thought and life, a *spiritual* accent, not possible to anybody but a Scot — and a Scot of a certain period. So with Heine; to get his essence into English would mean much more than translation in language; the job calls almost for an operation in blood transfusion! Even in the art of music, where we have a language more or less common to all places and countries, there has happened from time to time the phenomenon of a composer whose essential spirit reveals itself but slowly and reluctantly to foreign sensibilities.

Elgar and Mahler are poles apart as makers of music, but they are both in that indefinable category of artists of whom it is possible to say that they are not only national, but, what is more, they 'belong' — as the Americans say — to a particular region of their own land and a particular period in their land's social, intellectual, and æsthetic development. Elgar is an Edwardian — and it would be difficult indeed to explain what is an Edwardian to a Viennese. For we are dealing with subtler matters than ideas, epochs, and national points of view; we are dealing with an *attitude*. And just as the Edwardian secret must always baffle the man born by the Danube, so must the naïve romanticism of Mahler leave Englishmen a little at a distance.

I despair at ever being able to get on to paper even a remote notion of Mahler's finely-shaded compound of a simple domestic sentiment and a cultivated romantic technique of expression. The one was the result of environment; the other came from his study and practice in a city where the world's music is constantly in the air. A few weeks ago Gerhardt sang Mahler's *Kindertoten-lieder* in London. Some of the critics completely misunderstood the point of them. They thought it was 'hitting below the belt' for a composer to exploit anything so intimate and private as the death of children. The objection might have been valid if Mahler really had 'exploited' his very tender subject. But the songs are entirely remote in expression; Mahler puts his painful theme behind a kind of veiled sentiment, cool and implicit. He is a composer of naïve, heartfelt themes — and of very fastidious diction. Elgar is the opposite; a writer almost fulsome in his mode of expression, yet thoroughly English in his choice of those very emotions which make for decent presentation in public places. Elgar's music often goes into great deeps of feeling, but he endows it with a ceremonial gait and stature in which we can share without embarrassment to our British dislike of making ourselves too individual in our displays of sensibility. Elgar's music is always praising England or seeking God — in places like Whitehall or Worcester Cathedral, where there is no danger of anything but a ceremonial exhibition of what lies in our hearts. You can't give yourself away in the presence of a poised and collective or public nobility. At a State funeral it is sometimes hard even to find the corpse, let alone the chief mourner. No need for reticence in the kneeling group or slow-moving procession! I feel that Elgar's music is usually either opening something or closing something institutional; we have in Elgar the Laureate rather than the poet (I need hardly say that all this is not intended as a belittlement of the greatest living composer; I am merely trying to classify style).

Mahler lives a more personal existence in his music than Elgar in his; for that reason his emotional content is less sophisticated. Elgar's music is his own in technique and general style, but, as I say, we can most of us pray with him and march with him, if we are men of England. Mahler had democratic ideals; he wished to establish a species of symphonic music which would appeal to all sorts and conditions of the musically faithful. In his Eighth Symphony he used a gigantic apparatus — a very full orchestra, two mixed choruses, a boys' choir, and seven soloists. But all these many voices sing with Mahler's voice; the discourse aims at a cosmic comprehensiveness, but the accent is domestic and simple. Mahler's music is most times homely, of his particular soil. The dress of culture is — a dress.

Radio Times
1st May, 1931

Elgar and Strauss
by George Sampson

A few weeks ago I heard Elgar's new 'Cello Concerto at the Queen's Hall. The solo was played most admirably by Miss Beatrice Harrison, whom I pause to salute as a player of genius, with the touch of personality that labour can develop but never bestow. No quantity of pains that you take (or inflict) will make you a genius on viol, lute or shawm. Labour will make you technically dexterous, but it will not give you the mysterious something that distinguishes genius from talent, the interpreter from the recorder. Immediately after the Elgar Concerto came Strauss's *Tod und Verklärung*, which I had heard and liked at its first performance here in 1897, and have heard and liked many times since. As I wended homewards, reflecting on the music, it seemed to me that these two pieces were engaged in a kind of conflict. They took at last the shape of two antagonistic forms of art, the art that is thought out, and the art that is felt out. The contest seems worth following, as it may give us a general view of Elgar and what he represents. A general view is certainly all I propose to attempt at the moment.

I am not going to deny that in the art that is thought out there may be a good deal of feeling, and that in the art that is felt out there may be a good deal of thought. The vital difference is that in the one the inspiration is mainly artistic, and in the other mainly intellectual. Now it seemed to me that, however faulty Elgar's concerto may prove when tested by familiarity, it was genuinely felt out, that its inspiration was purely artistic, and that Strauss's tone-poem, with all its camouflage of technical effectiveness, was something elaborately thought out, that its inspiration was mainly intellectual. I believe, in fact, that Strauss thinks in the terms of one art and writes in the terms of another. He is like Berlioz, to whose *Symphonie Fantastique* Strauss's *Tod und Verklärung* is almost exactly parallel. Berlioz was an immensely clever man with a great knowledge of technique; but Berlioz scarcely exists to-day as a musician, because he was a man of letters who tried to express himself in music. Strauss, I feel, is that kind of composer. What captures one at first in his music is its air of literary distinction, and, as this is undeniable and even genuine, one goes on liking him until (as is always the case) the surface wears off, and the nature of the substance exhibits itself. I do not merely mean that Strauss's orchestral pieces are what is called 'programme music.' That does not matter. A great deal of undescribed music is programme music, and the tendency of time is to wear out the programme, and leave the music — if there is any. Elgar's *Enigma Variations* are programme music of which we do not know the programme. Beethoven's great *Leonora* Overture is programme music of which the programme is immaterial; it would remain a superb composition if every other trace of *Fidelio* were lost. The point I make about Strauss is that his compositions are conceived and carried out in the spirit of literature and not in the spirit of music; and what seems to me significant is that he has tended to become more literary and less musical. Consider all his tone-poems from *Don Juan* to *The Domestic Symphony*, and you will, I think, admit the truth of this. *Don Quixote* (another 'cello concerto!) is a specially good example, for here he has jumbled his planes, even though in certain passages he has perhaps touched the height of his purely musical achievement. In trying to occupy the desk-chair and the music-stool at once he has come heavily to the ground.

Long before this the patient reader will have been wanting to remark that he had supposed this article was to be about Elgar, and it seems to be about Strauss. I have not forgotten Elgar. In fact, I have been describing him all the time; for the conclusion of my homeward reflections on that conflict of artistic principles was that Elgar's great merit consists in his being just what Richard Strauss is not — or, if you prefer it, in his not being just what Richard Strauss is. There are places in his work where he stumbles; there are places where he is clearly below his best; there are places where he becomes elaborate merely because he is concealing a thin patch of invention with technical display; but I think there is no place in all the work of his I know where he ceases to be a genuine musician, moved by the spirit of music. Where he succeeds, he succeeds as a musician; where he fails, he fails as Beethoven and Brahms sometimes failed, he fails as a musician, without trying for success of an alien order. Elgar is a man of serious and cultivated taste in literature, but he never writes the music of a man of letters.

That he is a genuine musician is the major proposition to be asserted of him; and I think the next is that he is a genuinely English musician. Some time ago, the art-for-art's-sake people used to maintain that art was universal, not national, and that to talk about British art was as ridiculous as to talk about British mathematics. (Personally I would not talk about either. I know what English is; I do not know what British is.) The fallacy of the contention is obvious. Art is not mathematics. Art is the embodiment of a personality; mathematics is not. The desire for unnational art comes strangely from the countrymen of Shakespeare, for Shakespeare is richly, almost rankly, English. He could not conceivably have been Irish, or Scottish, or Welsh, or French, or Italian or Spanish; and certainly not German. There is the smell of English earth, the touch of English weather, the breadth of English humour, the soul of English character in all that he wrote. Shakespeare is English; Milton might have been translated from the Latin. Elgar's music has an unmistakably English quality. There is nothing of his that could have been written by anyone not English — like Shakespeare, by the way, he is a west-midlander. Whether he writes of Alassio or Spain or Bavaria, he writes as an Englishman. Even when he drops into a sentimental piece like *Salut d'Amour* or a popular tune like the *Pomp and Circumstance* (or *Land of Hope and Glory*) refrain, it is English sentiment, English commonness that he achieves. And how, it may be asked, is he specially English? Well, he is strong, sincere, wholesome, reserved, a little self-conscious, humorous without being witty, learned without being pedantic, original without being eccentric, emotional and sentimental without losing restraint and a care for the decencies of life. He puts all of a reverent heart into his work, but he never parades it as a spectacle. He is never showy or bedizened, neither is he ever dowdy or sordid. You might call his music moral, and, in the best sense, it is respectable. It is the music of a country in which conduct is (or was) three parts of life. Think of *Gerontius,* the subject of which is the death of a man and the passing of his soul into eternity. How easily a musician with all the resources of a modern orchestra and massed voices could let himself run wild with such a theme! But Elgar is not metaphysical as Brahms would have been, or hysterical as Chaikovsky would have been, or realistic as Strauss would have been, or ecclesiastical as Franck would have been. *Gerontius* is not like the *German Requiem* of Brahms, touched with the dread and fear of death, or like the *Requiem* of Verdi, an outburst of almost romantic emotionalism; it is solemn, sincere and deeply moving, but nobly restrained, and mindful of the power that comes from self-reverence, self-knowledge, self-control. By a significant chance the part of

Gerontius found an ideal exponent in the late Gervase Elwes, himself the embodiment of an English gentleman's deep feeling, restraint and dignity. Elgar's First Symphony is inscribed to a dead king of England; but it is not pompous or abject, and its Funeral March is an elegy, not a shriek. Compare his two symphonies with any two symphonies of Chaikovsky, and you will feel the difference between what is English and what is Russian. Scratch a Russian and you find a Tartar; scratch an Englishman and you find a gentleman. Even in the more impersonal Violin Concerto the national character seems to prevail; it is as English as the last movement of the Brahms Concerto is Hungarian. The grace of Elgar is English, not Latin. He does not glitter, and he does not give us, as Debussy does, with French lucidity, a series of epigrams or *choses vues*. Elgar is, as I said, almost self-consciously English, for his favourite musical direction is *Nobilmente*. It is a good word. That is how Cromwell lived and Milton wrote, and Hampden fought, and King Charles died. It is how Algernon Sidney went to the scaffold, and how Robert Scott perished in the Antarctic. Elgar's nobility is not a caste possession, and has nothing in common with the brute tyranny of the Junker, or the elaborate ceremony of the *ancien régime*. It is the nobility of soul on which he calls, not the pedantry of quarterings — a truly English nobility, the nobility of a people, of a land where a great peer was also the Great Commoner.

Another quality for which he should be praised is that he has never written beyond his means. (In parenthesis I should like to pay a similar tribute to another musician, untimely dead, Samuel Coleridge Taylor, who was not a great composer, but who never tried to delude the public into thinking that he was. He never wrote beyond his means, and his music will endure the longer.) The young English composer of a generation ago set out with an oratorio on the scale of the B minor Mass. The young English composer of a time slightly later began with a mythic trilogy on a scale exceeding *The Ring*. The young English composer of recent date procured a quantity of forty-stave music paper, and, having filled every bar of every stave with noises for all possible combinations of instruments (including some new ones), called the product a Symphonic Poem. What early music of Elgar's never came to performance no one but himself can say; but certainly none of his known works overleaped his capacity. He has never made the mistake of writing his last works first. I heard *King Olaf* and other pieces in the 'nineties; I heard *The Dream of Gerontius* as soon as it came to London; I attended the

Elgar Festival at Covent Garden (and a worse place for hearing his music you could never find); I have heard the first performance of all his later concert works publicly given in London; and I see him through all those years a real musician, developing and expanding as naturally as Beethoven developed from the Septet to the last Quartets.

In that development there are the marks of authentic growth. Elgar has grown out of himself, stage by stage, without any abnormality. Walter Bagehot long ago pointed out that an enduring community is one that has the gift of conservative innovation, of matching new institutions to old. That this is true of art as well as of politics Ruskin knew when he said that men of genius are known by their respect to law and tradition, their work being, not innovation, but a new creation, built upon the foundations laid of old. That is a very important principle. The art of To-day that does not contain a little of Yesterday will not have a To-morrow. We are the heirs of time. The iconoclasts who cry 'Let us have done with the Past; we are the men of the Future,' ignore the simple, supreme and determining fact that we are all (themselves included) creations of the Past, and can neither make nor receive except as the Past has taught us. Indeed, all that we create is part of the Past as soon as it is created, and it is the living Past or dead Past according as we add to, or merely repeat, the Past that was our forefathers'. The original child who decides to be totally unlike its parents and to have two heads and four hands will perish as the freak it is. 'Es klang so alt, und war doch so neu,' exclaimed Hans Sachs, when he thought of the puzzling music he had heard. That is the note that all enduring art must have, the note of a genuine ancestry and of a genuine personal quality. Beethoven took the symphony as Mozart left it, and, destroying nothing, made it a new creation. Brahms took the symphony as Beethoven left it, and, changing little, made it the vehicle of a real contemporary utterance. Elgar has taken, one by one, all the old classical forms, but he has not been mastered by their shapes or intimidated by their great traditions. His Symphonies and Concertos are built upon the foundations which were laid by the masters of old, but the building is his own, not an imitation of theirs. His music, with all its homage to the past, is the expression of a new personality. He does not write, he has never written, the Kappelmeister music into which the merely academic mind so readily drops.

At the risk of an anti-climax I will add that another mark of Elgar's greatness is that he can do little things and do them well.

He has 'magnoperated' with the best, but like the other masters he has known how to unbend, and some of his music has become popular in the best sense. It is not given to many musicians to find a song of theirs become, as *Land of Hope and Glory* has, an accepted unofficial national anthem. I am inclined to think it is a weakness of Elgar that he is afraid of his popular vein — he seems at times to avoid the obvious, and seek the recondite, lest the composer of *The Apostles* should be lured into another *Pomp and Circumstance.* 'Be not afraid of greatness' was the fatal advice to one whom ambition was to betray. 'Be sometimes afraid of greatness' is sound advice even to an acknowledged master. But not all of Elgar's minor compositions can be called popular. His exquisite part songs are small, but they are not least among his works.

Elgar had the good fortune to be the son of a working musician, and to grow up in the atmosphere of his art. His development has thus been natural and wholesome, and not academically distorted. The circumstances that prevented him from going as a student to Leipsic perhaps seemed cruel at the time, but the failure saved his art alive. He has had to work his way through many forms of professional drudgery, writing or adapting the things that had to be used practically and immediately instead of the formal impracticable things that perish in the Conservatoire incinerator. Leipsic might have given him a fatally wrong orientation. As it is, he is the one modern musician of high rank and noble achievement that Englishmen can claim as their own. They can claim him with just pride and admiration.

The Bookman
March 1921

PART VII: ELGAR AND THE THEATRE

The *Spanish Lady*
by Sir Barry Jackson

How long ago Elgar first thought of writing an opera I do not know, nor can I tell when the idea of setting a libretto based on Ben Jonson's *The Devil is an Ass* began to take shape in his mind; but his niece, May Grafton, tells me that his desire for a stage-work dates back many years and failed to materialize only because no subject suggested to him ever tempted him strongly enough. He could only wait, according to Miss Grafton, until he lighted on his own choice—which is precisely what happened eventually, though unhappily too late. It was some time in 1932, I think, that he conceived the idea of asking Bernard Shaw for a libretto, with what results might easily be imagined even if it were not positively known that nothing ever came of it. G.B.S., we all know, is an admirable musician, and readers of *Music & Letters* have good reason to be aware of his being an ardent Elgarian, or will become so if they look up the very first article in the number with which this publication began twenty-three years ago; but his reply, recorded elsewhere,[1] was that his plays 'set themselves to a verbal music of their own which would make a queer sort of counterpoint with Elgar's music'. Elgar then began to discuss operatic plans with me, and it soon transpired that he was particularly engrossed in the plays of Ben Jonson. He was, he told me, fascinated by *The Devil is an Ass*, mainly, I think, because while the musical flavour of the whole was to be English, rather like that of the incomparable *Falstaff* symphonic study, Wittipol's disguise as a Spanish lady gave him a chance to introduce a dash of exotic colour.

As a man of the theatre I knew my Ben Jonson well enough, but I confess that I had never looked to him for an opera. What is more, it struck me as odd that a great composer should do so. However, I cast my eye over him once again with Elgar's intention in mind, only to find that *The Devil is an Ass*, apart from being by no means among the best Jonsonian masterpieces, had

---

[1] *Elgar*, by W. H. Reed. Master Musicians series. (Dent, London, 1939), p. 142.

little to recommend it to a musician, even from the literary point
of view, and, so far as I could see, nothing beyond that Hispanic
motif from the musical. At first sight it seemed to me that *Epicoene,
or The Silent Woman*, which hinges on a definitely aural
subject—Morose's execration of noise—was the work to consider. Indeed I strongly urged Elgar to do so; but although he
spoke of his 'usual ill-luck' when in February 1933 the papers
announced a new opera by Richard Strauss—no other than *Die
schweigsame Frau*, for the libretto of which Stefan Zweig had gone
to this very play—I think he had decided finally for *The Devil is an
Ass*. At any rate, he wrote about long-standing plans for it in a
letter to me several months earlier, on September 23rd 1932:

> My difficulty in trying to plan it years ago was the end—the actual
> wind-up—this you may be able to 'see'. I don't know if clubs were
> 'raided' at the time of B.J.—but that would make a tremendous
> scrambling finale—last ensemble.

It was with problems such as these that he wanted me to help
him, and once I had allowed myself to be persuaded that behind
the play's wordiness and complexity of intrigue lay an excellent
story for an opera that could be made clearer to an audience than
the play itself could ever become even without music, I agreed
with some diffidence but also with much pleasure and enthusiasm
to try my hand at a libretto.

If Elgar had really thought of such an opera years earlier, he
had evidently not imagined that he would need a librettist. It is
plain that he had at first meant to let Ben Jonson himself serve him
as author. There is a copy of the play in the possession of the
composer's daughter, Mrs. Elgar Blake, neatly bound in half-calf
and embossed on the back *The Devil is an Ass*, though the volume
contains another play as well—*The Staple of News*. Its pagination
begins at p. 343, and there is a reference to it in the next letter to
me (September 26th 1932):

> . . . in case you should pursue the other B.J.,[2] I am sending you
> Gifford, a copy I got for a shilling or two to 'cut up'. I do not treat
> books badly as a rule, but this edition is of no great character.[3]

---

[2]This may seem to indicate that he was at that very time still wavering
between *The Devil is an Ass* and *Epicoene*, but judging from similar
cryptograms in other letters 'the other B.J.' simply meant Ben Jonson as
distinct from Barry Jackson.

[3]*The works of Ben Jonson. With a Biographical Memoir by William Gifford.*
New edition in 1 vol.,pp. 819. (Edward Moxon, London, 1858.) This is
evidently a re-issue of an edition of 1838, for both the frontispiece, an

The copy in question is full of notes pencilled in by Elgar himself, except one referring to Cunningham's edition of Ben Jonson's works pointing to some curious 'side notes' (stage directions) not found in the Gifford edition. Against this is set the remark 'not my note, E. E.', though that is quite obvious from the very different handwriting.

If Elgar at first wished to set Jonson's actual text, he knew that he would have to do so with a great many cuts, since musical composition inevitably lengthens a play enormously. He appears to have seen no insuperable difficulty in handling the crammed verbosity of Jonsonian blank verse; nor would a great composer be deterred, I imagine, by the limping, hobbling gait it shows almost without respite where 'big Ben' is not at his best, as he by no means is in this play. It is quite possible, indeed, that the forbidding want of ease and flow in this verse and the curious recalcitrance it shows in the matter of scanning may be a positive advantage to a musician, leaving him free to play with his own rhythmic schemes, whereas Shakespeare's wonderful lines in blank verse would continually fascinate and distract him by that soaring and surging 'verbal music of their own'. Much of *The Dream of Gerontius* is in blank verse, and we all know how flexibly Elgar handled it.

Be all this as it may, the pencil-markings in Elgar's copy certainly show that he meant to set Ben Jonson verbatim though not at full length. The cuts are extensive and made with considerable discernment, but do not seem to have been carried out quite consistently everywhere. They are probably in the nature of a mere preliminary run-through. Shackles, the keeper of Newgate, for instance, is removed from the list of *Dramatis Personae* because the scene in a Newgate prison-cell in the fifth act is cut, but that character still appears in the final scene of the play, which is left quite untouched by Elgar, who did not even cross out the epilogue, though he is certain to have meant to omit it, as he did the prologue. The pencil notes, in fact, diminish as the play proceeds, no doubt because the task of arranging it became more and more difficult towards the end of the complicated imbroglio.

These preliminary annotations sacrifice the first scene of Act I and with it all later reference to what it contains: the plea of the under-devil Pug to Satan to let him go into the world and do some

---

engraving of Honthorst's portrait of Jonson, and the title-page with a pretty engraving of Hawthornden, bear that date.

new mischief worthy of Hell's purposes and of his own ambitions, and Satan's consent that Pug should have the help of Iniquity, one of those characteristically Jonsonian personifications of abstracts. Elgar's pencil thus removed the following from the *Dramatis Personae*, apart from Shackles: SATAN, the great Devil; PUG, the less Devil; INIQUITY, the Vice. Pug, however, does appear in the play as arranged by him, Elgar, but simply in the character of Fitzdottrel's personal servant, an expedient in which I afterwards followed him. I find that he wrote to me on October 2nd 1932:

> ... p. 345 gives FitzD's 'Servant', who was to be replaced by Pug; he ought to be about more than a little, I think, as FitzD. says 'he helped to watch my ward'.

(Fitzdottrel's wife has by this time become his ward, for reasons to be explained presently.)

In Elgar's copy the list of characters, then, is left standing as follows:

FABIAN FITZDOTTREL, a Squire of Norfolk (Bass)
MEERCRAFT, a Projector (Baritone)
EVERILL, his Champion (Basso-cant.)
WITTIPOL, a young Gallant (Contralto)
EUSTACE MANLY, his Friend (Tenor)
ENGINE, a Broker (Bass)
TRAINS, the Projector's Man (Tenor)
THOMAS GILTHEAD, a Goldsmith (Bass)
PLUTARCHUS, his Son (Tenor)
?{ SIR PAUL EITHERSIDE, a Lawyer, and Justice
   AMBLER, Gentleman-Usher to Lady Tailbush
   SLEDGE, a Smith, the Constable
MRS. FRANCES FITZDOTTREL (Soprano)
LADY EITHERSIDE (Mezzo-sop.)
LADY TAILBUSH (High Soprano)
PITFALL, her Woman
   SERVANTS, UNDERKEEPERS, &c.
      SCENE—London.

The voices shown in brackets are, of course, added by Elgar, who however had not definitely made up his mind about their allocation. Whether the three characters bracketed together with a query still had to be 'voiced' or whether it was a question of omitting them altogether I am unable to say, though I think the latter is far more probable. Two of the principal male characters might later have exchanged their voices, for we find the following note against them: 'or Dotterel [*sic*] (Beckmesser-Baritone), Meercraft (Bass)'. More interesting still is this: '?Wittipol—

Contralto? played by a woman as in Rosecavalier'. There are two references to these matters in the letters addressed to me:

> I do not see any real fault in the characters pairing off as you feel they will do. Meercraft (good Bass) Dotterel (Beckmesser Baritone) appeal to me to 'characterize' musically . . . do not give yourself too much trouble over it; just think of it occasionally. [23.IX.32.]

> I had suggested to myself long ago that Wittipol might be a woman (Contralto as in Rosen Kavalier).[4] This might upset the disguise, however; of course the contralto business gives a lovely air of unreality (in the best sense) to anything, *e.g.* Handel's operas, &c. [26.IX.32]

The opera, then, was to open with Jonson's second scene, 'The Street before Fitzdottrel's House', the word 'Street' being altered to 'Green' by Elgar. At the top of the title-page there is a little pencilled sketch of the '1st Scene—see p. 346', showing a row of footlights, above which the centre of the floor is occupied by the word 'Green'. Left and right are very rough drafts of houses, marked XXX (l) 'FitzD.'s House' and (r) 'refreshment House— tables'. In the centre, upstage, is what appears to be a pond and a gap between more houses standing farther back, with the words 'road—other houses—maypole?'

There is a more complete and evidently later scenic sketch, made by Elgar in pencil and afterwards drawn over in ink,[5] where two houses are seen on the left in place of Fitzdottrel's, marked 'Ordinary' and 'Engine's House', and the tables have been moved from the prompt side to the O.P. side, in front of the eating-house Elgar was very anxious to have, as his letter of February 1st 1933 shows:

> . . . Don't think of this for a moment if you are too much occupied, but in case you have any 'designing' moment and want a change I send my idea of the 'lay-out' for Act I. I think it is the same as your existing sketch; I want the Tavern—the Ordinary was such a feature of the time and we can get, with reason, a lot of (chorus) people in front.

To finish with that first page (343) of *The Devil is an Ass* in the Gifford edition, there is a note, 'p. 619, good', between the prologue and the cancelled first scene of Act I. This refers to a later page of this one-volume edition, the second occupied by *A Masque of the Metamorphosed Gipsies*. What it was he thought

---

[4]Strauss's Octavian, to whom this refers, is of course a mezzo-soprano.

[5]Reproduced in Reed, *op.cit.*, p. 143.

particularly good there it is hard to tell, but he evidently had some bustling opening scene in mind for which the gypsies provided material. Perhaps some verses (certainly not all!) of Jack's song suited his purpose, such as:

> Be not frightened with our fashion,
> Though we seem a tatter'd nation;
> We account our rags our riches,
> So our tricks exceed our stitches.

It is certain that Elgar intended to interpolate separate poems by Ben Jonson, found in other plays, in his version of *The Devil is an Ass*. Several other references to later pages of the Gifford volume are pencilled into his 'cut up' copy. In the course of the first scene (*his* first scene), for instance, we find the remark 'Song, &c., p. 426, Trio T.B.B.' (tenor and two basses). This points to the song in Act IV, Scene iii, of *The New Inn*.

> It was a beauty that I saw,
> So pure, so perfect, as the frame
> Of all the universe was lame,
> To that one figure, could I draw,
> Or give least line of it a law!
>
> A skein of silk without a knot,
> A fair march made without a halt,
> A curious form without a fault,
> A printed book without a blot,
> All beauty, and without a spot!

Two pages later we come across 'W's [Wittipol's] song to Mrs. FitzD. p. 550, 556'. The former reference is to *The Masque of Beauty*, but the page in question is almost a little operatic libretto in itself, so that at first sight it is difficult to tell what portion of it Elgar had in mind. His musical sketches show, however, that it was 'this full song, iterated . . . by two Elves', beginning:

> When Love at first did move
> From out of Chaos . . .

It would have been a charming thing, with two of the three voices as echoes, and in no need of Jonson's usual learned footnotes, of which he provides no fewer than three for this short poem of less than a dozen lines!

'P. 556 refers to *The Masque of Hymen* (*Hymenaei*), where two possible poems occur on that page, the more probable being the one beginning with the lines:

> O know to end, as to begin:
> A minute's loss in love is sin.

and ending, rondel-like, with almost the same couplet. At the end of *Hymenaei* is a lengthy Epithalamium: it is possible that Elgar had a setting of this in view, or at least a portion of it, since it is hardly in accord with modern notions of propriety throughout. At any rate it seems to be this which gave him the idea of some such nuptial song, an idea he kept to the last and with which I afterwards fell in.

There is only one song in *The Devil is an Ass* itself, the most famous of all Ben Jonson's poems apart from *Drink to me only with thine eyes*; or rather part of it is famous, for it is only the second half, beginning with the line 'Have you seen but a bright lily grow', that is generally known, the earlier and admittedly inferior lines being unfamiliar to any but literary specialists, so much so that they had better be quoted here as the text of an Elgar song unfortunately lost to us:

> Do but look on her eyes, they do light
>   All that love's world compriseth,
> Do but look on her hair, it is bright
>   As love's star when it riseth!
> Do but mark, her forehead smoother
>   Than words that soothe her!
> And from her arched brows, such a grace
>   Sheds itself through the face;
> As alone, there triumphs to the life,
>   All the gain, all the good, of the elements' strife!

There are one or two other marginal notes referring to the composer's musical intentions. The most promising is one connected with the scene where Meercraft tells Fitzdottrel of

> An English widow, who hath lately travell'd,
> But she is call'd the Spaniard, 'cause she came
> Latest from thence, and keeps the Spanish habit.

This lady is to teach deportment to Mrs. Fitzdottrel, who according to her husband is

> Such an untoward thing, she'll never learn
> How to comport with it:

and presently the plot begins to turn on Wittipol's introduction to Mrs. Fitzdottrel, with whom he is in love, in the guise of a Spanish lady. For the moment, however, Meercraft only advises that she should be taught, and Fitzdottrel asks:

> Where! are there any schools for ladies? is there
> An academy for women? I do know
> For men there was; I learn'd in it myself,
> To make my legs, and do my postures.

Elgar cut the last line, but added after 'I learn'd in it myself' the stage direction '(dances) Spanish'; and it was here, no doubt, that he intended to use one of the Spanish dance-pieces he had sketched and later on actually completed up to a point at which someone will, one hopes, be able to take them up and arrange them in some form as finished compositions.[6]

Some passages in the Gifford edition are underlined by Elgar, probably because he thought them important and wished to secure them from possible excision later on, unless he marked them out for some special musical treatment, which is quite possible. Engine's reference to Wittipol:

> Now, he has been
> In Spain, and knows the fashions there;

for instance, may very well have been singled out as an opportunity for some thematic reference, perhaps by means of some Spanish *Leitmotiv*.

That Elgar had very definite ideas of what he wanted to see on the stage I know, for he loved to discuss such matters in great detail. There is some evidence, moreover, in that annotated copy, such as the stage direction 'FitzD. "preens" himself before Manly (and others, supers, &c.)'; and towards the end of Act I he altered the stage situation simply by letting Fitzdottrel say to his wife 'Go, let's in' instead of 'Go, get you up'. Jonson's Act I, that is, for Elgar's own goes as far as the end of the original third, the scenes being ingeniously drawn together to take place in one and the same set, and the action between the original first and second acts being continued by the substitution of '(Fetches in Meercraft)' for '(Exeunt)'.

The opening of Jonson's fourth act as Elgar's second was intended to be turned into a truly operatic scene in the grand manner. Instead of a mere 'Enter Lady Tailbush and Meercraft' the composer intended 'A great assembly, servants, musicians, (?) friends[7]; gorgeous guests arrive'. He saw Lady Tailbush as 'faded and painted' (if I read the third word aright) and Lady

---

[6]According to information received from Mrs. Elgar Blake, these dances were to be published by Messrs. Keith Prowse in fulfilment of a contract signed by the composer some time before his death. I understand that the late Dr. W. H. Reed was entrusted with the editing of the pieces, a task for which he was ideally fitted both by his musicianship and by his personal recollection of Elgar's intentions. Unhappily he was not spared to carry it out.

[7]The word is illegible.

Eitherside as 'young, smart, covetous'; and a little later he interprets the disguised Wittipol's lines:

> Pray you, say to her ladyship
> It is the manner of Spain to embrace only,
> Never to kiss. She will excuse the custom.

by adding in brackets 'finds Lady T. repellent'. Hereabouts there is also another of those references to later pages: 'p. 583, Chorus or Song addressed to the Spanish lady'. The source here is *Oberon, the Fairy Prince*. Neither of the two songs on that page seems suitable, but perhaps the composer's choice fell on the second verse of the later one, a fulsome eulogy of James I which might have done if masculine pronouns had been replaced by feminine. On the other hand I found a passage on the same page, a catch sung by Satyrs, which served me for the girls in the choral opening scene of my own version:

> Buz, quoth the blue fly,
>   Hum, quoth the bee:
> Buz and hum they cry,
>   And so do we.

Finally, at the point where Wittipol gives the ring to Mrs. Fitzdottrel and she comes near to recognizing him ('Sure I have heard this tongue'), there is the note 'this is the great moment and more business must be introduced before FitzD. takes Mrs. aside'.

I have made references to *The Devil is an Ass* without outlining Ben Jonson's plot, or rather his bewildering agglomeration of plots, for the reader, who may easily study the matter further, if he is so inclined, by looking at the play in conjunction with this article. But he will find it a laborious business, just as I know Elgar eventually found it to reduce the Jonsonian cataract of words and maze of situations to a libretto. His fine literary discernment urged him, no doubt, to explore every aspect of the text until he had penetrated it entirely, very much as he had done when he wrote *Falstaff*; but the case was different because this time he had to deal with the actual material of the poet's words, and they were too much for him—more particularly because they were Jonson's who is so explicit as to leave nothing more to be said about his characters. For a composer wants a great deal left to his own imagination—the more the better—and that is why it eventually turned out that the librettist to handle *The Devil is an Ass* (by that time destined to be called *The Spanish Lady*) to Elgar's satisfaction was to be no such 'rare' being as Ben Jonson, but a man of the theatre who claimed to be no poet but could find out by close and continuous personal contact exactly what the composer wanted. I may at least say that I always encouraged him to air his views and to declare his wishes. We saw much of each other in the latter part of 1932 and off and on during the whole of 1933. If we had lived less close together and met less often, I feel sure that a voluminous correspondence would have developed between us comparable, on his side at any rate, to that between Strauss and Hofmannsthal,[8] in which the composer contributed not a little to the literary shaping of his operas. As it was, we were both at Malvern, and most of our discussions took place verbally. Even so a handful of letters remain, from extracts of which it may be gathered how keenly Elgar was intent on details and how great a sense of the operatic stage he possessed.

About the opulence of that stage he had his own ideas, upheld, of course, by the standards he set himself as a composer, which he would not let fall behind those of Wagner or Strauss. My own experience of the stage being that of the sponsor of a repertory theatre in a provincial city, I am afraid that I urged him repeatedly to keep in mind resources within the reach of organizations less magnificently endowed than the Berlin State Opera or the Milan Scala. But he would have none of this. 'If I write an opera', he said, 'it is going to be a grand affair'. He was justified, needless to say: he was a grand composer. From the practical point of view, it will be conceded, I was right, but he could not fail to hold, though nothing would have induced him to express it in so many words, that if this country had no means of producing the grandest of operas written by a composer of his eminence, then it was time we set about finding those means. Unhappily, that work having failed to come to maturity, we now have yet another excuse for not doing so.

The first two letters I had from Elgar concerning our collaboration have already been quoted from above. Here is another portion of that dated September 23rd 1932:

> ... I did not refer to the *other* B. J. because I thought the idea did not appeal to you at all. My feeling has always been that the Elizabethan (for short) dialogue is splendid for recitative. I never thought of Pug remaining at all. It seemed to me that first-act scene (exactly as you say) might be made. I am not sure if anything could be made of the 'cloak affair'; but the projectors (Stock Exchange) might be very

[8]*Correspondence between Richard Strauss and Hugo von Hofmannsthal, 1907-1918*. Translated by Paul England. (Secker, London, 1927.)

evident; all these and the 'title scramble' are of all times; for lyrical moments I have marked out several things from the masques, but I cannot at the moment find my 'cut up' copy of Gifford's edition. I had adumbrated two acts exactly as you say; the first act would grow easily, I think, if the chorus might be *plausibly* introduced for any effect of movement, not, as you will feel, static. A small chorus — not a huge crowd. The period dress appeals to me for opera and padded out as you could do it might make a 'warm and full' thing.

There were three messages, two on postcards, of various dates in the following October, hardly worth quoting; then another undated card written probably towards the end of 1932:

... thank you for the marvellous typed copy .... I like it all, but we must start with more bustling movement, I feel.

In December came some further suggestions:

... We can get rid of the swindlers thus: see p. 13, Act II, cue 'Call in the Constable'. Meercraft shows signs of alarm (Lady T. might also)
    FitzD. tears off the cloak and sword. Meercraft gathers them up and later puts them on and passes the constable with glaring impudence, without question in the confusion — an old trick, but will do here. Everill claws at everything he can and slinks out. I have an affection for Pug and Engine drunk and maudlin — they can remain, of course not prominent.
    Then we can sing the Epithalamium or whatever it really is.

On January 6th 1933 there is a peep into the operatic carpentry-shop: 'Thank you for the verses which I have temporarily tacked into a vacant spot in Act I.'

January 23rd shows him taking fire, for he begins to care about the reactions of others to his music, while he remains, as always considerate to his librettist:

... It quite cheered me to see you and Scott[9] on Saturday and to know that you liked my new tunes — a little anyway. I feel somewhat shy of writing at my age, but on listening to it I fail to notice any marked senility. Do not think for a moment about B. J. in the midst of your vast undertakings. I have plenty to go on with.

By February 10th the flame was well ablaze:

... I longed for you last Sunday; Reed was here and we fiddled fragments of B. J. and the Sym. III with much exhilaration. However, we wanted audience and collaborator.

But an ominous note creeps in here: the third Symphony! It is repeated on March 15th, when he says 'I have to leave B. J. for the

---

[9]Scott Sunderland, with whom he often played piano duets at my house or at Marl Bank, his own.

Symphony for a space'. This had been commissioned by the British Broadcasting Corporation, and Elgar was in honour bound to proceed with it, the more so because he felt far from strong and must have doubted more than once whether he would ever be able, at his age, to carry two of the largest and most difficult works he had ever undertaken to a successful conclusion. But there is no doubt that *The Spanish Lady* again and again tempted him away from the Symphony, so that sketches for both works accumulated side by side in rich profusion if also, unfortunately, in great confusion. He himself knew, of course, what every scrap of music was intended for and how the pieces of his two great jigsaw puzzles would eventually fit together; but they will for ever baffle posterity, not only because they are often scarcely intelligible, but also because they have after all remained woefully incomplete, apart from the one or two more or less finished dances for the opera.

That Elgar did his utmost to satisfy both the B.B.C. and his own conscience with as much work as poor health and advancing age would allow him to put into the Symphony is beyond dispute, nor can it be questioned that he was passionately absorbed in that work; but he was an artist who could not be tied down to one particular task either by any agreement or by mere determination to satisfy an obligation; an artist also, as it happened, capable of carrying out two great creative projects at once. Thus, although the Symphony was uppermost in his mind, he did continue to think about the opera.

To make this record as complete as possible and as useful as it can be made for future generations who may wish to know all they can about a great composer's plans for a major work of which they are in great danger of losing sight altogether, I must now, I suppose, briefly discuss my own libretto, so far as it goes, which was never beyond a kind of fairly elaborate sketch to be discussed and worked up further with the composer. To make matters worse, I seem to have lost the copy of the first scene of the second act, only Act I and the remainder of Act II being now in my possession. However, I remember pretty clearly how that missing scene was developed and shall thus be able presently to give a short outline of the whole scheme as it stood where I last left it. But to begin with, here is the list of characters as we finally devised it:

FITZDOTTREL, a middle-aged fool; vain and stupidly cunning.
MEERCRAFT, a plausible rogue who will take anyone's money.
   Shrewdly cunning.
WITTIPOL, a sprightly young man.

MANLY, a more solid young man; slightly older than Wittipol.

ENGINE, a rogue of lower birth than Meercraft and younger.

PUG, a saucy man-servant.

A WATCHMAN, who is good for nothing else.

TOBIE, a drunken sot.   (Chorus)

COSTARD-MONGER, a simple creature.

PARSON PRELATE, a well-liver and parasite on the great.

A BEAR LEADER ⎫
A PURITAN.   ⎬ (Chorus)

FRANCES, a young lady of great estate and ward to Fitzdottrel,
   who would wed her.

LADY TAILBUSH, a lady of fashion desirous of freedom and
   fortune.

LADY EITHERSIDE, a withered and vinegary copy of Lady
   Tailbrush.

JOAN   ⎫
GRISEL   ⎪
TOBIE'S WIFE ⎬ Townswomen (Chorus)
LAUNDRESS   ⎭

Act I. - SWAGGERERS, APPRENTICES, CITIZENS, GIRLS, CITIZEN'S
WIVES.

Act II. - FOOTMEN, GUESTS AT LADY TAILBUSH'S RECEPTION.

It will be seen that I, like Elgar, retained Pug, not as a devil but
as a servant — and he came in quite as useful in that capacity
without complicating the action by Jonson's hellish sub-plot.
The minor characters of my own invention had no dramatically
vital functions, but they served a musical purpose by offering the
composer opportunities for picturesque treatment. They were
the 'padding' to make the 'warm and full thing' of which he
wrote. The chorus too was to take its share in that, for we were
both anxious to do away with the ordinary, posturing and
perfunctorily made-up operatic crowd and to replace it by a
small group in which every person was to be a real character. This
of course, might have raised awkward musical problems, but I
felt sure that the composer of *Falstaff*, that masterpiece of musical
characterization, would know how to deal with them.

My most drastic interference with the original, so far as the
characters were concerned, was to turn Fitzdottrel's wife into his
ward. Neither Elgar nor I would have minded the 'triangular'
situation, which is not nearly as unsavoury here as in a thousand
other plays, for Wittipol, once his ruse has succeeded, behaves
quite exceptionally well. We should not have minded it, that is to
say, if it had been really essential to the plot. As it was not, we both
felt that the relationship of guardian and ward, with the young
lover anxious to snatch his prey from the amorous Pantaloon, was

at once more pleasing and more plausible, while it certainly made the plot much easier to unravel at the end. Apart from that, it was very much in the operatic tradition, a tradition derived from the *commedia dell'arte,* which is still capable of yielding admirable operatic material. Its Pantaloon has not only his immortal exponents in Italian comic opera, such as Dr. Bartolo in *The Barber of Seville* or the title-part in *Don Pasquale,* but even in Wagner, whose Beckmesser Elgar had in mind at any rate vocally for his portrayal of Fitzdottrel.

Upon my own literary effort I have no wish to expatiate. I need only say that, if only the bare skeleton of the tangled story of *The Devil is an Ass* remained in my version, I did endeavour to keep to something like its spirit and certainly to the atmosphere of the period, though I also tried to leave a good many blanks in order to give the composer as much chance to enlarge to his heart's content on whatever aspect of this or that sense appealed to his imagination. For it *was* the composer's imagination, not my own, which I knew had to be stimulated and satisfied if opera was to be enriched by another great work. But if Elgar had more of his due than 'the other B. J.', I did at least pay some respect to my initials-sake by using his own words where it could conveniently be done. Thus I not only took some of the blank verse from *The Devil is an Ass* itself; I also interpolated as many of his poems gathered elsewhere from his work as would suit my purpose, very much as, we have seen, Elgar himself originally intended to do. I even emulated Jonson in his habit of plagiarizing. The following, sung by a group of apprentices soon after the first rise of the curtain:

> His face is all bowsy,
> Droopy and drowsy,
> Scurvy and lousy,
> Comely and crinkled,
> Wondrously wrinkled,
> Like a roast pig's ear
> Bristled with hair!

sounds doubtless like a direct imitation of Skelton: it is a copy, more or less, of Jonson's flagrant imitation of the Skeltonian manner:

> And in the meantime, to be greasy, and bouzy,
> And nasty, and filthy, and ragged, and lousy,

and so on.

And now here is a synopsis of the plot:

Act I:

A Street in London. Fitzdottrel's house; Engine's house, where Meercraft lodges.

The act opens with scenes of crowd life. After these Lady Tailbush, followed by her suitor, Manly, comes to visit Meercraft, to whom she serves as patron and dupe. The business between her and the charlatan is 'beauty preparations'. After this episode the main imbroglio develops. Fitzdottrel intends to marry his ward, Frances, who is beloved of Wittipol. The latter plays upon her guardian's vanity by presenting him with an extremely gaudy cloak purchased from the second-hand clothes-dealer, Engine. In return for this gift he is to enjoy ten minutes' conversation with Frances. Fitzdottrel is to stand by, while Manly, Wittipol's friend, is to see fair play. After Wittipol's departure Engine introduces Fitzdottrel to Meercraft, who, among other rogueries, is a bogus company-promoter. The foolish guardian falls an easy prey to him and in return for a hundred pounds, a ring and a promise of a possible elevation to the peerage enters into a scheme for the reclaiming of the fenlands by means of windmills. The finale entwines the last two episodes, showing the rogues and the guardian drinking to the success of their schemes while unseen to them Wittipol serenades Frances at her window.

Act II, Scene I:

A front scene depicting Engine's backyard.

News has been spread about that a Spanish lady has arrived in town with details of new fashions and behaviour from foreign courts. Fitzdottrel determines that his ward shall become her pupil in order that she may be a credit to him when he has been created a duke. Meercraft promises to convey a ring on his behalf in order to obtain the stranger's good graces. This Spanish lady is something of a myth, but as she is due to appear at Lady Tailbush's—the rendezvous of a ladies' club—something has to be manoeuvred. Engine produces a Spanish dress for Wittipol from his shop and equips himself as duenna. The two, shepherded by Meercraft, who has also been dressed in some of Engine's second-hand finery, start off for the party at the club.

Act II, Scene II:

The Reception at Lady Tailbush's.

Diversified crowd movement culminating in the arrival of the Spanish lady and her duenna. 'She' creates a great impression and Fitzdottrel has no qualms in leaving his ward in 'her' hands for instruction. To the astonishment of Frances Wittipol discards the Spanish dress, and it is not long before Manly appears with a priest. By the time the company has reassembled and danced a saraband the ceremony is complete. Fitzdottrel raises great confusion on failing to find his ward. He calls for the Spanish lady, but is presented with the discarded dress. The lovers, now united, return, and all join in the Epithalamium.

It remains for me to deal with Elgar's musical sketches. Not being a practising musician, I can only do it briefly and rather superficially; but with the kind permission of Mrs. Blake and the late Sir Edward Elgar's Trustees, as well as the help of the Editor of *Music & Letters*, I may at least give the reader an idea of what Elgar's 'grand affair' of an opera would have been like.

There is an enormous portfolio full of sketches, marked 'B. J.'. Some are mere outlines of themes of not more than two or three bars, some a bare tune with or without a bass and a dash of harmony here and there. Others take up a stave or two, or even a page. They may or may not be fully elaborated, and there are often many versions of the same thing in various stages of development. Two complete sections of vocal score cover a dozen pages or so, and two fragments of finished score start grandly in full orchestral panoply, but trail away into mere outlines after a page or so. Looking through all these loose sheets one gains the impression of ideas crowding into the artist's mind so fast that he could hardly find time to capture one of them before others came tumbling after; and it must always be remembered that Elgar was busy with the third Symphony at the same time.

A great many of the sketches are now impossible to correlate with the libretto, unfortunately; but others—perhaps half of the collection—bear more or less intelligible indications of where and how the composer intended to use them. Names of characters, opening words of songs, references to scenes, and so on, frequently appear at the top of these loose sheets. There are things in the nature of *Leitmotivs* for some of the characters, such as the scrap marked 'FitzD.'s Entry, Act II, 2':

13   Yehudi Menuhin with Elgar at the time that they recorded the
Violin Concerto.

14   George Bernard Shaw with Elgar at Maidenhead.

or this characteristic *fugato*, labelled 'Meercraft':

The following, not in the portfolio, but found as a casual musical note among the typewritten libretto material, shows how carefully small details are sometimes outlined, even in the first sketch:

Trains, a servant, who has no special function in the play, is given a kind of official, non-committal fanfare; Everill, one of the rogues who do affect the action, has the same with a difference: a sharper rhythm and a shrill whole-tone-scale ending with a crude *crescendo* on the last note. It will be noticed, by the way, that these two characters do not appear in my version, which shows that musical sketches already existed before I came on the scene.

Among the scraps that bear a clear indication of where they were to be used is the following, headed 'Tavern music, also Overture':

which is interesting because it hints that the overture was to have been based on later thematic material. The actual place for the tavern music was at the end of Act I, where obviously we should have had a staggering piece of polyphonic workmanship, for a note in the typescript of the libretto shows that Elgar intended to let music heard from the tavern and from Fitzdottrel's house combine with the orchestra in front and with the voices on the stage, Frances singing on the balcony and Wittipol serenading her below. On top of all this he was going to introduce a 'Curfew', a brief sketch for which, in A minor, is among the material left.

The most extended portions among the mass of fragmentary MSS., apart from the few pages of vocal score which appear to have been done as specimens, and perhaps as studies in declamation and recitative, are the four dances: a Saraband, a Bolero, a Country Dance and an 'España burlesca'. This last is not, perhaps, particularly Spanish; but then, neither was the play, or even, when all is said, the disguised 'lady'. The Bolero has the traditional rhythm, and the portions of full score of the opening and the trio section show clearly that it was to have been a lavishly scored piece brilliantly exploiting orchestral virtuosity. It is an amply planned composition with a spacious introduction and coda. The Saraband, on the other hand, is short, being in the traditional binary form, each section being repeated. Its rhythm, too, is the conventional one of ♩ ♩. ♩ | ♩ ♩ , and the harmony keeps more or less closely to plain C major. Nevertheless, like all that Elgar wrote, it has a strong individuality, and it is a fine, stately piece that would sound magnificent even if scored for strings alone, as indeed it was meant to be. The Country Dance would no doubt have been original and graceful:

I have said that 'do but look on her eyes' is an Elgar song lost to us. Among these sketches are two or three Elgar songs almost saved for us. Of the *Echo Song* mentioned above enough is preserved to show that it would have been a beautiful, sensitive thing. It was to have been sung by Wittipol in the first act, with Manly and Engine upstage throwing in the echoing phrases: not a trio so much as a song with vocal refrains merged into the accompaniment, not unlike Elvira's aria, 'Ah chi mi dice mai', in *Don Giovanni*, where Don Juan and Leporello comment on it behind her back. There is the beginning of a charming setting of 'Still to be neat, still to be drest', and a more extended draft of music for the following, which was to go in somewhere, sung by Engine with choral refrains:

Wise men I hold these rakes of old
    Who as we read in antique story,
When lyres were struck and wine was poured,
Set the white Death's Head on the board—
        Memento mori.

Stop not to pluck the leaves of bay
    That greenly deck the path of glory,
The wreath will wither if you stay,
So pass along your earnest way—
        Memento mori.

When old age comes with muffled drums,
    That beat to sleep our tired life's story,
On thoughts of dying (Rest if good!)
Like old snakes coiled i' the sun, we brood—
        Memento mori.

According to a letter from Miss Mary Clifford, Elgar's devoted secretary, this was written on his return from her father's funeral; but it is a fantastic, rather caustic, quite unsentimental piece in quick 3-4 time, in keeping with the tone of the opera, not expressive of any personal feelings connected with the occasion that set it going in the composer's mind. We may take it to be an example of a great creative artist's power of detachment.

Not all the songs were to have drawn their words from Ben Jonson. Among the MSS. are several drafts of a duet for Frances and Wittipol, written first in G major and then turned into Gb major, a note on one of which shows that Elgar was attracted by the metrical scheme of a poem by Dora Wilcox in the *Oxford Book of Australasian Verse*, a shape on which he modelled this duet, though we may be quite sure that he did not intend to use Miss Wilcox's words, but meant either to write his own or to ask me to provide something fitting both the metre and the stage situation. This piece was evidently to occur near the end of the opera, for it bears the remark: 'NB. During this duet WITTIPOL removes his mask and later the lady's dress', which of course means, quite harmlessly, that he divests himself of the costume he had been wearing when he appeared as a Spanish lady at Lady Tailbush's party. Here is an exquisite passage from the duet:

It is tempting to quote more—much more— but one more example must suffice. It comes from a fairly extended sketch for a song marked '?"This is she"' and is a transitional passage leading back to the opening theme (last bar of this quotation):

The characteristic Elgarian sequence will be noticed, but it should be said that, so far as the *Spanish Lady* sketches go, this 'fingerprint' is to be found remarkably rarely. Even so, the stamp of Elgar's genius is unmistakable. There may not be anything particularly new about this work, so far as either he or contemporary music is concerned. The last extract quoted, for instance, is not at all unlike the charming *Shepherd's Song* of 1895. But there are also some new departures and audacities, such as a fine strident, acid passage in consecutive triads. Of course all this is neither here nor there: it does not matter whether a great work of art is traditional or subversive. Only small art relies either on convention or on sensation. Elgar's work is to be viewed *sub specie aeternitatis*, and so posterity will view the music of *The Spanish Lady*—what there is of it. It is perhaps not more than there was of Verdi's *King Lear*, to mention another operatic work of the first importance which is lost to us for ever. But of the music for Verdi's fourth Shakespearean opera even the sketches have disappeared, whereas we have at least that large *dossier* of material for Elgar's Ben Jonson opera, a work which, had it been completed in the composer's old age, after many years of almost complete creative inactivity, would have been a case strikingly similar to that of the Italian veteran's *Falstaff* and, we may be sure, a musical masterpiece comparable to it. Which is as much as to say that it would have been among the half-dozen of the world's greatest comedy-operas.

Music & Letters, January 1943

The Starlight Express
by A. E. Keeton

1.—THE SCORE

Elgar was a genuine theatre composer; had he been born in an operatic country, indubitably he would have turned to opera.[1]

This remark is pertinent; nevertheless, one of Elgar's very few contributions to the stage, *The Starlight Express*, was not composed until he was fifty-one. It was first given at the Kingsway Theatre during the winter of 1915-16, had but a short run of some six weeks and has never been revived. From the outset this score seemed dogged by disaster. The Zeppelins of the last war were becoming more and more persistent over London that Christmas, making anxious going for a large theatre crowded with children both on and off the stage. Elgar himself is said to have been far more preoccupied about ensuring all possible safety for the children, organizing A.R.P. drills and shelters, and so on, than with the actual rehearsals. Basil Dean was to have been producer and had already begun his work when he was suddenly called up to serve in France. Lena Ashwell replaced him. It was her first experience in this kind of theatre work, and her whole style, stagecraft and general tradition—whatever their individual merits—were certainly singularly remote from juvenile mystical phantasy and music such as Elgar's. Finally the Kingsway Theatre was burned to the ground and with it went all the *Starlight Express* stage properties, settings, band-parts and conductor's score. What was not destroyed, however, was Elgar's precious manuscript full score with his own emendations, his own ideas as to the exact interpretation he wanted and various improvements on his first draft score, doubtless copied in by his intrepid music scribe, Lady Elgar. The score is signed 'Edward Elgar, Finis,' with underneath, presumably, his wife's initials, 'A.E., December 1915'. It has remained safely in the hands of its publishers, Messrs. Elkin & Co. In 1933 the conductor Joseph

---

[1] *Elgar: his Life and Works*, by Basil Maine, 2 vols. (G. Bell & Sons, Ltd., London, 1933)

Lewis, an Elgar enthusiast, borrowed the full score and constructed from it a selection for broadcasting of about forty minutes' duration. From that year on down to 1940 the B.B.C., under Mr. Lewis's direction, gave this broadcast annually on February 24th, the anniversary of Elgar's death—a meagre enough presentation of a three-act work of some two and a half to three hours' duration. Still, it was at least a slight memento. In 1940, however, this broadcasting score was also, alas, destroyed by enemy action and went up in smoke with quantities of other valuable material in the hands of the B.B.C.

The Music Makers, Op.69, has been cited as the score in which Elgar gave the freest rein to his love of self-quotation. I should say, though, that *The Starlight Express*, in proportion to its length, is even fuller of self-reminiscences. I have found it a really engrossing study to unearth these from one source and another. The first germ can be traced back to 1871, when Elgar, aged fourteen, composed the libretto and score of a musical play for children, *The Wand of Youth*. It was performed in the home circle, and the story goes that the composer, needing an unobtainable double bass for certain special effects, in the forthright manner characteristic of him his whole life long simply made one for himself. All that remains of this early effort is its title and a handful of pieces which Elgar arranged thirty-six years later in his two orchestral suites, Op. 1 (a and b), with the sub-title *Music for a Child's Play*. The 'Little Bells' tune from the second suite is a leading theme throughout the whole of *The Starlight Express*, merging in the finale of the last act into the old carol *The First Nowell*, out of which Elgar created a gem of polyphony, and one wholly native in its provenance.

In other parts of the score there are distinct echoes from the Spanish serenade, *Stars of the Summer Night*, Op. 23; from *Caractacus*, Op. 35; and from Op 42, the incidental music to George Moore and W. B. Yeats's play *Grania and Diarmid*. There are also decided flashes from two of Elgar's finest groups of unaccompanied part-songs, Opp. 45 and 53.

In the shimmering 'landscape' music of the second act of *The Starlight Express* I was rather surprised to find no quotations either from the *Bavarian Highlands* score or the overture *In the South*, but there are clear suggestions of the *Falstaff* dream interlude music, Op.68.[2] Still closer than any of these reminiscences is the lovely

──────────────
[2]   I have to thank Messrs. Novello, Boosey & Hawkes, Schott and Keith Prowse for most kindly lending me so many of their Elgar publications for

Dream Children suite. Pondering over this particular score I have wondered whether Elgar, reading Lamb's essay, asked himself whether here was a possible libretto for the theatre music that perpetually haunted him. Perhaps it was the pervading sadness of Lamb's sketch that made him reject the idea.

With all this *The Starlight Express* is thoroughly homogeneous in its fabric, terse and pellucid. The main exposition rests throughout with the orchestra, which Elgar kept to small Mozartian proportions. As always when he felt and enjoyed his own music most intensely, he links it here in tender intimacy with his life and friendships; for I find this intimacy as much in *The Starlight Express* score as in the *Enigma Variations* and in the only too few works for solo string instruments he left us. He uses no chorus, but of the two vocal parts for baritone and soprano, the baritone is really the prolocutor—a sort of Greek chorus throughout—a hurdy-gurdy man adored by the children. Elgar gave his hurdy-gurdy man plenty to do both as singer and actor. The part was beautifully interpreted by a promising young baritone, Charles Mott, lent to Elgar by Beecham. Shortly after his appearance in *The Starlight Express* Mott was killed on the Flanders front. The soprano part flits through the score like a spirit of laughter, half sylph, half human, a truly Shelleyan phantom—with short strophes of song that an Agnes Nicholls in her day or a Maggie Teyte might have well loved to sing. Neither fine incidental music nor music to attract children, of whatever nationality, has ever overcrowded the world's repertory. In the latter category I can recall little in opera, ballet and what not beyond Humperdinck's *Hänsel und Gretel*, Stravinsky's *Petrushka*, Tchaikovsky's two fairy-tale ballets *Nutcracker* and *Sleeping Beauty*, Rimsky-Korsakov's *Snegurotchka* or Ravel's *Ma Mère l'Oye*. In the former I should like to mention the much slighter yet of its kind first-rate incidental music composed round Maeterlinck's *Blue Bird* or Barrie's *Mary Rose* by Norman O'Neill and *Where the Rainbow Ends*, which has stood a perennial test of over thirty years' popularity with Roger Quilter's delightful score. As far as its music is concerned *The Starlight Express* deserves full prestige and prominence amongst the best incidental *and* children's music.

---

comparison. But first and foremost I have to thank Messrs. Elkin & Co. for entrusting an irreplaceable manuscript to my keeping for some weeks.

II.—THE SCRIPT

May runs laughing into June—the scene is set in mountain, forest,
lake.... Night slowly brings her mystery and beauty to the world....
Filmy patterns of lines spinning through the air stretch from the
summits of the distant Alps and knot themselves to the crests of pine
trees far below.... There is a tautness in each of these lines. They will
twang with delicate music if the winds sweep across them.... They
link up with cables of thick, elastic darkness—the rails of the
'Starlight Express' packed with children and initiate grown-ups
scattering magic stardust on a peacefully sleeping world.[3]

Librettos that grow root, stem and flower from the same kind of
soil as a composer's music can be counted on one's ten fingers. It
would be hard, I think, to find a type of fantasy with an approach
to life and childhood as peculiarly akin in all its essentials to
Elgar's musical vision as in Algernon Blackwood's *Prisoner in
Fairyland*. First published in the spring of 1913, this book at once
made its author's name. Messrs. Macmillan, his publishers,
consider it Blackwood's most outstandingly characteristic work.
It is still in demand. By an odd coincidence Blackwood's
fundamental moral is practically identical with the germ idea
evolved by the fourteen-year-old Elgar for the book of his juvenile
musical play composed when Blackwood cannot have been more
than three years old. The pity of it is that an overloaded, over-
symbolized stage script concocted from *Prisoner in Fairyland*
inevitably swamped Elgar's music, and that what should have
been an epoch-making success proved a wretched fiasco. Written
a year or more before the holocaust of 1914-18 and re-read to-day
in a bomb-riven world of shattered humanity, Blackwood's book
can hold the imagination in far firmer grip by its prophetic
conception even than in 1913. The author's main thesis is that our
planet is more and more sadly deflecting from its star-born origin
as an integral unit in the federation of an infinite universe. He
covers more than five hundred closely written pages spread over a
huge panorama crowded with a cosmogony of children, grown-
ups, animals, birds, trees, flowers—all portrayed with a mysterious aura of their own and held together with a most arresting
anthology of excerpts from star prose and poetry collected from
many nations. Here I think Mr. Blackwood had best take up the
tale himself:

> I am no playwright; I possess none of the necessary talents. I have
> never started a play on my own initiative. One or two small stage

---

[3] From Algernon Blackwood's *Prisoner in Fairyland*.

productions of my work have always been the outcome of requests by others to dramatize some story or it might be simply the flash of an idea in one of my books. Thus the little play *Going through the Crack* was developed for me out of my novel *The Education of Uncle Paul* meaning the tiny opening perceptible between Yesterday and To-morrow. In 1915 when *A Prisoner in Fairyland* was at its high peak of circulation a Miss Violet Pearn obtained my permission to adapt it as a play for children. Music only emerged as quite an afterthought. Elgar's name cropped up—I had never met him and knew next to nothing of his music. However, various people, myself amongst them, were bold enough to approach the great man. He at once fell in with the proposal.

How Elgar could possibly have accepted the involved farrago of Miss Pearn's script of muddled, or what the grown-ups in Blackwood's book call 'wumbled', mysticism is inexplicable.[4] I can only imagine that Elgar was so delighted with the main theme of Algernon Blackwood's airborne night express, driven and manned by the march of youth, that he hardly glanced at the script, leaving the producer to fit it into the music. The charm and fascination of Blackwood's style is his power of elaboration and embroidery in his own medium of words which he crowds like flights of birds, tender and gay in their plumage, and full of verbal music. Elgar, on the other hand had a wonderful faculty for terse condensation. Compare for instance his manipulation of Newman's *Dream of Gerontius* (which takes far less time to perform as an oratorio than to read as a poem) with Gustav Holst's treatment of the opening description of *Egdon Heath* in Hardy's *Return of the Native*, one of the most unforgettable examples in our language of words piled up with irresistible force and light in each expressive facet, read in a flash of time, whereas Holst's setting, of which one would not wish to eliminate a note, takes quite a quarter of an hour to perform. For artists of the temperament of Blackwood and Elgar, if only we have eyes to perceive, a star is reflected in every one of life's puddles. In their analogous philosophy a miracle can be lurking round the corner of most human existences. And miraculously there happens to be alive

---

[4] O. B. Clarence, who played the one adult spoken part of the 'wumbled Daddie', has written to me: 'It is all so long ago now and I've played so many parts since that a good deal of my experience in *The Starlight Express* has faded from my memory. I do remember, though, that it was one of the strangest and most moving parts I've ever had. The music was haunting in its beauty—I was proud to be associated with it—at the same time I felt there was something wholly wrong in the script'.

now, and in the full flush of his artistic career, one with much the same kind of imagination as Elgar and Blackwood, who, I believe, could, if he would, distil a script from *A Prisoner in Fairyland* to fit Elgar's score perfectly. I am thinking of J. B. Priestley, who has the same insight into the child mind, the same brand of what one may term true mystic clear-sightedness. He is, besides, musically equipped for the task, and above all completely at home in theatre or film world—and what a magnificent film, provided of course that Elgar's music be jealously respected, this Blackwood-Elgar *Starlight Express* combination conjures up. Is there no one to put the proposition before Mr. Priestley? In any remodelling, though, Blackwood's lyrics should certainly be retained exactly as he wrote them. Elgar's settings of these are amongst his most beautifully conceived vocal work.

Music & Letters,
January 1945

PART VIII: ELGAR'S ART EXAMINED

The Apostles and Elgar's Future
by E. A. Baughan

---

*This is the most substantial of the three contributions made by E. A.
Baughan to this volume, and is taken from his book* Music and
Musicians, *published in 1906. It is a percipient summary of the
composer's career up to the date at which it was written.*

In estimating the progress a composer has made, we must, I think,
distinguish between his gradual mastery of his means of
expression and the thing he expresses. It is true that the two
develop to a great extent, for the desire to say more, prompted by
a real psychic growth, results in an advance of technique. With
Sir Edward Elgar this harmonious development is clearly to be
traced from the early choral works to *The Dream of Gerontius*. In his
orchestral compositions the advance has continued from the
Enigma variations to the Introduction and Allegro for strings.
The first performance of *The Apostles* three years ago did not,
however, carry out the promise of *The Dream of Gerontius*. True,
the later work is an advance in technique; it is an advance in
homogeneity of style; it is an advance in individuality. At the
same time, I left the concert-room after that first performance
with very mixed feelings. For some two hours and a half I had
been listening to music in which a modern composer had
employed every resource of modern art, every daring boldness of
harmony, every imaginable colour on the orchestral palette, and
yet the whole left me unsatisfied. I was conscious of a want of
central grip, of a comparative failure of emotional inspiration as
distinguished from imagination. It was as if the picture Dr. Elgar
has painted astonished me by its rich conceit of detail, by the
polychromatic hues of its background, while the design itself, the
very reason for this particular kind of picture, was too crowded
and ineffective. The work is not one picture, but a series, and the
mind wanders from one to the other until the impression created
by one cancels the impression created by another. The point of
view shifts and changes. At one moment Judas claims our
sympathy; then one's heart goes out to Mary Magdalene; again
one is bidden to feel the mystic thrill of the Ascension. Realism

treads on the heel of mysticism.

The composer, in a note to the published score, tells us that it has long been his wish to compose an oratorio which should embody the Calling of the Apostles, their Teaching (schooling), and their Mission, culminating in the establishment of the Church among the Gentiles. *The Apostles* carries out the first portion of this scheme; the second remains for production on some future occasion. It may be that Elgar will gather up all the threads of the first and second parts, and give the world a work which will at once be an explanation of, and be explained by, the music we already know. All that now sounds scrappy and disconnected may then fall into its proper place as an introduction. But the scrappiness is certainly present in *The Apostles*. The libretto is a patchwork of lines from the Scriptures and from the Apocrypha joined together so that seven distinct pictures (some of them are sub-divided into panels) are the result. The work opens with a choral prologue, 'The Spirit of the Lord is upon Me.'

Then we have the Calling of the Apostles, conceived somewhat in the vein of an old miracle play, with its combination of naïve realism and mystery. 'By the Wayside' is practically made up of the Beatitudes, with interjectory comments by the Virgin Mary, Judas, Peter and John, and the people. That is quite in the style of a mystery-play, and, musically, there is a simplicity, and yet a fresh invention, which makes this section, to my mind, the most successful of the whole oratorio. The third picture has the Sea of Galilee as its background. The wind lashing the waves into foaming billows which threaten His Disciples, labouring at their oars, is described with wonderful orchestral realism, and against this background we have the pathetic figure of Mary Magdalene, symbolical of the sinners who repent of their sins in deep anguish of soul, and cry aloud for mercy and peace. The chorus punctuate her agony with Bacchanalian praise of 'costly wine and ointments.'

The combination of this fanciful, voluptuous music, having the suffocating scent of flowers, so fresh and original is it, with the long-drawn declamation of the troubled Magdalene, makes a picture at once bold in its realism and pathetic in its humanity. But, it will be seen, this third picture is hardly the natural sequence of those that have preceded it. A second panel takes us to Cæsarea Philippi, where Jesus and His Disciples discourse of His Godship. A scene, 'In Capernaum,' describing the forgiveness of Mary Magdalene, to the accompaniment of a singularly happy chorus of women shocked by His tender leniency, completes the triptych, and the whole is rounded off by a final chorus, 'Turn you to the Stronghold,' which has no real place as a natural sequence of the three pictures. From realism and reflection, mixed with unconventional *naïveté*, we are here carried into the realm of reflection, to the domain of the abstract. The fourth section changes the point of view once again. It opens with Christ teaching His Apostles, and then the scene shifts to the Betrayal of Judas, the Denial of Peter, and the Repentance of Judas — again, a sudden change from mysticism to dramatic realism. 'Golgotha,' the fifth picture, describes the lamentations of Mary and John before the Cross, the sixth presents the scene at the sepulchre, and the last of all the Ascension, the whole ending with a mystic chorus interpolated with the utterances of the Apostles and the Holy Women.

Such a combination of abstract and concrete ideas does not give music full scope for the expression of its highest qualities. In painting it is different. We all know what sublime suggestiveness is created by the realistic manner of the old painters. In their case the spiritual is symbolized by the material, and from the latter our thoughts are lifted, insensibly and unconsciously, to higher issues than the outside presentment of them. Music, however, is not visible. We hear it, and it is gone. The impression it makes is momentary, obliterated by the next impression. To the composer himself this is not so, of course, and it may be that when one knows *The Apostles* by heart, as one knows the *Messiah*, the mind will retain the different impressions as rigidly as the eye can rest on a picture, and so the realism and the spiritualism may fall into their proper places, and a whole and abiding impression may be created. It may also be, as I have said, that the third part of the oratorio, when it is produced, will form a natural climax which will throw light on the music we have already heard. But, taking *The Apostles* as it stands, its shifting pictures convey an impression of vague illusiveness. The central idea is not clear; the composer does not knock imperatively at the door of the inner chamber of the soul.

I have spoken of the advance in the technique of his art which Elgar has shown in this latest work of his. In the first place, he has employed the *leitmotif* system with a persistency which has been equalled by no composer since Wagner. To my mind, there can be no question of the logical need of this use of the representative theme, but I must admit that it is apt to be illuminative on paper more than in hearing (which is the proper standpoint for the judgment of music, though it is a standpoint which is apt to be ignored nowadays), unless the invention of themes is distinctive. They must have unmistakable character- they must be inspirations, or else they conjure up no definite ideas, and their constant recurrence either passes unnoticed in the swirl of the orchestral current, or it serves to produce a feeling of irritation. One has the feeling of chasing shadows instead of realities, of watching faint outlines which should develop clearly but do not. Elgar has invented some characteristic themes, and, especially, some characteristic harmonies, which serve to give connection to the music, but as a whole his specific musical invention has not been equal to his imagination, and his themes are used too much as disconnected labels, and sometimes mar the flow of the work.

The atmosphere of his music is fascinating; one feels that it is the right background. But too many of the themes do not stand out with sufficient clearness. They are adumbrations of ideas rather than a realistic musical picture of them. And in too many cases these themes are not developed with much strength, and are introduced scrappily. This lack of strong musical development which would build up a climax naturally is a fault of the work. Climaxes of noise there are. Elgar knows how to heap up his material so that the total effect is monumental in its own way, but it is too much the climax of large forces. Again, the essential poverty of the themes, or of most of them, robs the restless polyphony of its power. There seems to be a fixed idea among modern composers that polyphony has a fine effect because it is polyphony. Provided the writing is ingenious on paper, it is assumed that it must sound well. I am afraid that a good deal of Elgar's orchestral polyphony does not make a clear impression. Again, as in *The Dream of Gerontius,* the choral part-writing is more ingenious on paper than effective in performance. As an instance I may mention the scene in 'The Calling of the Apostles,' in which the three Apostles, the angel's voice, and the chorus are woven up into an ingenious whole, and also the finale, in which the semi-chorus, the chorus, and the soloists are combined with great skill. The effect, however, is not clear, but a maze of moving parts which results in an extraordinary texture of sound that confuses rather than thrills the mind.

On the whole the composer has been most successful in his orchestral comments, which really amount to a symphonic poem of stupendous proportions. His vocal writing shows a great advance in ease of declamation, but none of the vocal music has any very striking qualities. To this is due, perhaps, the impression that the imaginative atmosphere of *The Apostles* is more distinct than is actual inspiration or invention, and also the lack of vocal interest may rob the work of its human appeal. To my ears there certainly is wanting a clear voice in the music, as if the composer had detached himself too much from his subject and viewed it from the outside. *The Dream of Gerontius* was very different in that respect. Less ambitious as music, less grandiose, and less complicated in its general woof and web, with the exception of the choral writing, there is a real voice running through it, something which we recognise as the expression of the composer, something which a real human being is saying to us in all sincerity from his soul. In *The Apostles* the subject itself forbids that psychological expression. The realistic presentment of the greatest drama of all ages places the composer outside it, as a spectator, as a deeply impressed spectator, if you will. Some great geniuses can take that attitude, and from the very amplitude of their temperament and mind so saturate their objective musical picture that it contains all that they wish to illustrate and something more — themselves. I am thinking of Bach, of Wagner, and of Handel. But I do not fancy Elgar has that amplitude of temperament. His is a genuine musical nature, and he has sensitive imagination and keen poetic feeling. He is essentially a lyrical composer, and, on the othe side, he has power of realistic description, but he is not of the men who can take such a subject as *The Apostles* and make it at once a monument to the world-drama and an expression of themselves.

Many orchestral and choral passages of singular beauty make *The Apostles* a notable achievement in the annals of British music. But, after all, a composer who takes in hand such a subject must be measured by it, and however ingenious, picturesque, imaginative, and beautiful his music may be here and there, unless it rises to the height of its theme, and impresses one as its illustration, the work as a whole must be considered a comparative failure. And in that sense *The Apostles* is a failure — a glorious failure.

* * *

The Apostles, then, seems to me a glorious failure. In workmanship and in individuality it is, no doubt, an advance on *The Dream of Gerontius*. In the earlier work there is no such finely conceived and worked-out climax as that of the Ascension in *The Apostles*. Nor is there anything to equal the Judas music and the strangely poetical Beatitudes. Indeed, one could point to passage after passage that marks a real advance in the composer's technical mastery and conception. The work is a glorious failure, for all that. Perhaps the mingling of realism and abstract religious enthusiasm is intentional, and the composer in some details may have taken Wolfram's *A Christmas Mystery* as his model, if he did not go farther back and learn something from Bach. But he has not got his proportions right. Thus the repentance of Mary Magdalene, which really has nothing to do with the Apostles, is made the subject of lengthy treatment. It is merely an unessential detail. Too much space, also, is taken up by the description of the calling of the Apostles in its realistic aspect — I have almost written, in its theatrical aspect. For some reason or other the figure of Christ is shrouded in the background; His death is passed over and His utterances are not the most musically impressive part of the work. Then the Apostles themselves are not very important figures. They are merged in the realistic background. The total impression of the composer's scrappy treatment is that the oratorio has no central idea — nothing which rises to a natural climax, as the story of the anguish of the soul of Gerontius rises. *The Apostles* is a series of musical pictures, but not a series that originally illustrates one idea, or a set of closely related ideas. In proof of this assertion, it may be said that several sections of the oratorio could be omitted without harming the work as a whole. To add to the disconnected nature of *The Apostles,* the music which illustrates the background in which this story of the beginnings of Christianity is set, is much more successful than that which expresses the religious ideas.

Frankly, I have but little sympathy with Sir Edward Elgar's attitude towards religion. It is too mediæval; too much of the Church of Rome. In *The Dream of Gerontius* there was an expression of the same attitude of mind, but in that work the music has such a personal note that it is affecting and interesting as a psychological drama. The sentiment of Elgar's music in both oratorios is almost grovelling in its anguish of remorse, and it has the peculiar sentimentality that is characteristic of the later Roman Catholic Church. No doubt it appeals to many, but I must confess I prefer the human tenderness of Brahms, in his Requiem, the massive manliness of Handel at his best, and the aloofness of Bach and Palestrina. In the works of these masters, Man expresses his reverence for his Maker, without losing his manliness. In Elgar's music I detect the hysterical prostration of the confessional. It is too much a repentance of nerves. This frame of mind no doubt appeals to many, especially to those who share the composer's religious views. At any rate, it has always been an expression of the composer from the days of *The Light of the World*. But I remember that there have been two Elgars: he who has written *King Olaf, Caractacus,* the Military marches, the Coronation Ode, the *Enigma Variations,* and, especially, the *In the South* overture, and the composer of *The Light of the World, The Dream of Gerontius,* and *The Apostles*. One Elgar dwells in the sunshine and air; the other lives in an atmosphere of religious sentimentality and highly coloured mysticism. To prefer one of these men to the other is, of course, a matter of taste, but it certainly seems to me that the composer's secular work has more vitality and originality. Indeed, I am inclined to place his *In the South* and the Introduction and Allegro overtures far above either *The Dream of Gerontius* or *The Apostles* in completeness of achievement. For one thing, he has always been at heart an instrumental composer. In his earlier works his treatment of the voice was really instrumental, and even now his vocal writing is not equal to his mastery of the orchestra. For these reasons I hope the religious phase of his creative career will pass.

The enthusiastic admirers of the composer — I mean the writers who refuse to criticize his latest works at all, for all of us are enthusiastic admirers to a certain extent — hail *The Apostles* as a climax of Elgar's career as a creative artist. What an advance is shown from *King Olaf* to that latest masterpiece! — an advance not only in technique, but also in soul-life. Is that estimate right? Has the composer really advanced in the same way that the Wagner of *Tannhäuser* is not the Wagner of *Tristan?* His out-and-out admirers will tell you that the Elgar of the early compositions is not the Elgar of the later — in which they are right enough; but they do not try to reconcile the two, and it seems to me they take any advance of technical equipment as equivalent to an advance in actual creation.

I cannot subscribe to that view of the composer. So far from Elgar having arrived at the true expression of his genius in *The Dream of Gerontius* and *The Apostles,* it appears to me that he has only reached a point in his career from which will spring a new phase of his creative life. I am not at all sure, for instance, that in writing for orchestra and voices he has really found the true expression of himself. When once Wagner had thrown over his ambition to shine as a dramatist, all his efforts were concentrated on music-drama. Apart from the overtures and preludes to his operas, he composed only one work of absolute music, the *Faust* overture. Orchestral music alone did not give him the scope he required. Now with Elgar, on the other hand, it was to orchestral music that he was first attracted, and his compositions in this *genre* show a decidedly more mature artistry than his choral works. The *Froissart* overture, composed some six years before either *King Olaf* or *Lux Christi,* is even more successful than the choral works that came from his pen several years later. The orchestral 'Meditation' to the *Lux Christi,* indeed, is of more value to my ears than the whole of that choral composition. Again, the popular *Enigma Variations,* the *Cockaigne* overture, and *In the South* are, in their several kinds, more completely successful than the oratorios.

A composer of music, no more than a painter or a literary man, can expect to shine in all branches of his art. There are exceptions, of course. Millais was a great portrait painter, and he was equally successful in subject-pictures and landscape. But as a rule you will find that the painter who has made the most enduring fame has chosen one branch of his art, and has never been long seduced into trying his hand at other branches. A very few novelists have been equally successful as dramatists; but it is the exception, and not the rule, although the novel and the play are not so far apart as orchestral and choral composition of music. Almost all the great composers have written both orchestral and vocal music, but they have shone in one of the two forms of art, and not in both. Elgar is neither a composer of oratorio, who occasionally writes a work for orchestra, nor is he a composer of orchestral music who now and then attempts to win laurels in oratorio. He is trying, it seems to me, to turn his attention to both branches of the art equally. I do not think that success lies that way; and, when we consider the drift of his genius, it is not at all clear that he has the natural gift of song. From *King Olaf* onwards his writing for the voice is uninteresting, and in his earlier works is much too instrumental in shape — that is to say, the melodies that come to him as expressing the words do not seem to be the natural outcome of them. The melody is either too short or too long, and its phraseology is not conditioned by the sense and the emotional meaning of the verse.

In *The Dream of Gerontius* and *The Apostles* there is a decided advance on the earlier works in this respect, but the declamation has not the well-marked outlines of the born musical dramatist: it is too level and monotonous. His writing for chorus, on the other hand is often well calculated for choral effect. This is especially noticeable in *King Olaf*. In the later works there is a disposition to treat the choir as an orchestra, with which, indeed, it is woven up as if it were a second instrumental force. Take away the orchestra from *The Apostles* and there is not much of interest remaining. On the whole, I am inclined to think that the advance of Elgar's technique is an orchestral advance. He has found that the choir, as a reinforcement of the orchestra, gives him an enormously large palette for polyphonic colour; but that means he has not really understood, or, understanding, has waived, the true function of the voice in conjunction with the orchestra. He does not conceive his oratorios from the standpoint of human expression. In this he has not really advanced from the early work, *King Olaf*.

Then there is the psychological change to which I have already referred. In *King Olaf*, and again in *Caractacus*, it is surprising how little introspective he was. In the former work, especially, there is a buoyant life and picturesqueness which later on gave way to a very personal religious feeling. I admit that here we are face to face with a question of art which will be answered by each according to his individual temperament. No doubt there are many to whom Elgar's vein of religion appeals very deeply. It is certainly human — that is the charm of *The Dream of Gerontius;* but at the back of it there is a curious weakness, an anæmic sentimentality, as it were, which has conditioned the music. Without having any strong feelings in the matter, I yearn for the breezy faith of a Martin Luther. In *The Dream of Gerontius* the personal note has its own value, from an artistic point of view; but is any one really interested in *The Apostles* as Elgar has presented them in a series of musical cinematagrams?

Edward Elgar
by George Bernard Shaw

It should not be forgotten that George Bernard Shaw (1856-1950) began his literary career as first art critic and later music critic before turning to theatrical criticism and finally to the occupation of playright for which he is most celebrated. He was therefore well-equipped, when the magazine Music & Letters *was launched in 1920, to contribute an appraisal of Elgar's career to its first number. This is reproduced here with all its eccentricities of grammar and spelling. It was perhaps inevitable that the Irish wit should tread on one corn, and the mild rebuke which Elgar penned and which was published in the following number is appended.*

Edward Elgar, the figure head of music in England, is a composer whose rank it is neither prudent nor indeed possible to determine. Either it is one so high that only time and posterity can confer it, or else he is one of the Seven Humbugs of Christendom. Contemporary judgments are sound enough on Second Bests; but when it comes to Bests, they acclaim ephemerals as immortals, and simultaneously denounce immortals as pestilent charlatans.

Elgar has not left us any room to hedge. From the beginning, quite naturally and as a matter of course, he has played the great game and professed the Best. He has taken up the work of a great man so spontaneously that it is impossible to believe that he ever gave any consideration to the enormity of the assumption, or was even conscious of it. But there it is, unmistakeable. To the north countryman who, on hearing of Wordsworth's death, said 'I suppose his son will carry on the business' it would be plain today that Elgar is carrying on Beethoven's business. The names are up on the shop front for everyone to read. ELGAR late BEETHOVEN & CO., Classics and Italian and German Warehousemen. Symphonies, Overtures, Chamber Music, Oratorios, Bagatelles.

This, it will be seen, is a very different challenge from that of, say, Debussy and Stravinsky. You can rave about Stravinsky without the slightest risk of being classed as a lunatic by the next generation. Without really compromising yourself, you can declare the *Après Midi d'un Faune* the most delightful and enchanting orchestral piece ever written. But if you say that Elgar's *Cockaigne* overture combines every classic quality of a concert overture with every lyric and dramatic quality of the overture to *Die Meistersinger* you are either uttering a platitude as safe as a compliment to Handel on the majesty of the *Hallelujah* Chorus or else damning yourself to all critical posterity by a *gaffe* that will make your grandson blush for you.

Personally, I am prepared to take the risk. What do I care about my grandson? give me *Cockaigne*. But my recklessness cannot settle the question. It would be so much easier if *Cockaigne* were *genre* music, with the Westminster chimes, snatches of *Yip-i-addy*, and a march of the costermongers to Covent Garden. Then we should know where we are: the case would be as simple as Gilbert and Sullivan. But there is nothing of the kind: the material of the overture is purely classical. You may hear all sorts of footsteps in it; and it may tell you all sorts of stories; but it is classical music as Beethoven's *Les Adieux* sonata is classical music: it tells you no story external to itself and yourself. Therefore who knows whether it appeals to the temporal or the eternal in us? in other words, whether it will be alive or dead in the twenty-first century?

Certain things one can say without hesitation. For example, that Elgar could turn out Debussy and Stravinsky music by the thousand bars for fun in his spare time. That to him such standbys as the whole-tone-scale of Debussy, the Helmholtzian chords of Scryabin, the exciting modulations of the operatic school, the zylophone and celesta orchestration by which country dances steal into classical concerts, are what farthings are to a millionaire. That his range is so Handelian that he can give the people a universal melody or march with as sure a hand as he can give the Philharmonic Society a symphonic adagio such as has not been given since Beethoven died. That, to come down to technical things, his knowledge of the orchestra is almost uncanny. When *Gerontius* made Elgar widely known, there was a good deal of fine writing about it; but what every genuine connoisseur in orchestration must have said at the first hearing (among other things) was 'What a devil of a fortissimo!' Here was no literary paper instrumentation, no muddle and noise, but an absolutely new energy given to the band by a consummate knowledge of exactly what it could do and how it could do it. We were fed up to the throats at that time with mere piquancies of orchestration: every scorer of ballets could scatter pearls from the *pavillon chinois (alias* Jingling Johnny) over the plush and cotton velvet of his harmonies; but Elgar is no mere effect monger: he takes the whole orchestra in his hand and raises every separate instrument in it to its highest efficiency until its strength is as the strength of ten. One was not surprised to learn he could play them all, and was actually something of a virtuoso on instruments as different as the violin and trombone.

The enormous command of existing resources which this orchestral skill of his exemplifies extends over the whole musical field, and explains the fact that though he has a most active and curious mind, he does not appear in music as an experimenter and explorer, like Scryabin and Schönberg. He took music where Beethoven left it, and where Schumann and Brahms found it. Naturally he did not pick up and put on the shackles that Wagner had knocked off, any more than he wrote his trumpet parts in tonic and dominant *clichés* in the eighteenth century manner, as some of his contemporaries made a point of honor of doing for the sake of being in the classical fashion. But his musical mind was formed before Wagner reached him; and his natural power over the material then before him was so great that he was never driven outside it by lack of means for expressing himself. He was no keyboard composer: music wrote itself on the skies for him, and wrote itself in the language perfected by Beethoven and his great predecessors. With the same inheritance, Schumann, who had less faculty and less knowledge, devotedly tried to be another Beethoven, and failed. Brahms, with a facility as convenient as Elgar's, was a musical sensualist with intellectual affectations, and succeeded only as an incoherent voluptuary, too fundamentally addleheaded to make anything great out of the delicious musical luxuries he produced. Mendelssohn was never really in the running: he was, in his own light, impetuous, and often lovely style, *sui generis,* superficial if you like, but always his own unique self, composing in an idiom invented by himself, neither following a school nor founding one. Elgar, neither an imitator nor a voluptuary, went his own way without bothering to invent a new language, and by sheer personal originality produced symphonies that are really symphonies in the Beethovenian sense, a feat in which neither Schumann, Mendelssohn nor Brahms, often as they tried, ever succeeded convincingly. If I were king, or a Minister of Fine Arts, I would give Elgar an annuity of a thousand a year on condition that he produced a symphony every eighteen months.

It will be noted, I hope, that this way of Elgar's of accepting the language and forms of his art in his time as quite sufficient for anyone with plenty of courage and a masterly natural command of them, is the way of Shakespear, of Bach, of all the greatest artists. The notion that Wagner was a great innovator is now seen to be a delusion that had already done duty for Mozart and Handel: it meant nothing more than that these composers had the courage and common sense not to be pedants. Elgar has certainly never let any pedantry stand in his way. He has indeed not been aware of its academic stumbling blocks; for, like Bach, he has never been taught harmony and counterpoint. A person who had been corrupted by Day's treatise on harmony once tried to describe a phrase of Wagner's to him by a reference to the chord of the supertonic. Elgar opened his eyes wide and, with an awe that was at least very well acted, asked 'What on earth is the chord of the supertonic?' And then, after a pause, 'What *is* the supertonic? I never heard of it.'

This little incident may help to explain the effect produced at first by Elgar on the little clique of musicians who, with the late Hubert Parry as its centre, stood for British music thirty-five years ago. This clique was the London section of the Clara Schumann-Joachim-Brahms clique in Germany; and the relations between the two were almost sacred. Of that international clique the present generation knows nothing, I am afraid, except that when Madame Schumann found that Wagner's *Walküre* fire music was to be played at a concert for which she was engaged, she at once declined to appear in such disgraceful company, and only with great difficulty was induced, after anxious consultation with the clique, to make a supreme effort of condescension, and compromise herself rather than disappoint the people who had bought tickets to hear her. This is too good a joke against the clique to be forgotten; and the result is that poor Clara and Joachim and company are now regarded as a ridiculous little mutual-admiration gang of snobs. I entreat our snorting young lions to reconsider that harsh judgment. If they had heard Clara Schumann at her best they could not think of her in that way. She and her clique were snobs, no doubt; but so are we all, more or less. There are many virtues mixed up with snobbery; and the clique was entirely sincere in its snobbery, and thought it was holding up a noble ideal in the art it loved. Wagner was about as eligible for it as a 450 h.p. aeroplane engine for a perambulator.

It was much the same at first with Elgar and the London branch of the clique. A young man from the west country without a musical degree, proceeding calmly and sweetly on the unconscious assumption that he was by nature and destiny one of

the great composers when as a matter of fact he had never heard of
the supertonic, shocked and irritated the clique very painfully. It
was not, of course, Elgar's fault. He pitied them, and was quite
willing to shew them how a really handy man (they were the
unhandiest of mortals) should write for the trombones, tune the
organ, flyfish, or groom and harness and drive a horse. He could
talk about every unmusical subject on earth, from pigs to
Elizabethan literature. A certain unmistakeably royal pride and
temper were getatable on occasion; but normally a less
pretentious person than Elgar could not be found. To this day
you may meet him and talk to him for a week without suspecting
that he is anything more than a typical English country
gentlemen who does not know a fugue from a fandango. The
landlady in Pickwick whose complaint of her husband was that
'Raddle aint like a man' would have said, if destiny had led her to
the altar with the composer of the great symphony in A flat,
'Elgar aint like a musician.' The clique took Mrs. Raddle's view.
And certainly his music acted very differently from theirs. His
Enigma Variations took away your breath. The respiration
induced by their compositions was pefectly regular, and
occasionally perfectly audible.

That attitude towards him was speedily reduced to absurdity
by the mere sound of his music. But some initial incredulity as to
his genius may be excused when we recollect that England had
waited two hundred years for a great English composer, and
waited in vain. The phenomenon of greatness in music had
vanished from England with Purcell. Musical faculty had
survived abundantly. England had maintained a fair supply of
amazingly dexterous and resourceful orchestral players, brass-
bandsmen, organists, glee singers, and the like. But they lacked
culture, and could not produce a really musical atmosphere for
the local conductors who tried to organize them. And the only
alternatives were the university musicians who made up the
metropolitan cliques, gentlemen amateurs to a man, infatuated
with classical music, and earnestly striving to compose it exactly
as the great composers did. And that, of course, was no use at all.
Elgar had all the dexterities of the bandsmen; sucked libraries dry
as a child sucks its mother's breasts; and gathered inspiration
from the skies. Is it any wonder that we were sceptical of such a
miracle? For my part, I expected nothing from any English
composer; and when the excitement about *Gerontius* began, I said
wearily 'Another Wardour Street festival oratorio!' But when I
heard the *Variations* (which had not attracted me to the concert) I

sat up and said 'Whew!' I knew we had got it at last.

Since then English composers have sprung up like mushrooms: that is, not very plentifully, but conspicuously. The clique is, if not stone dead, toothless; and our Cyril Scotts and Percy Graingers, our Rutland Boughtons and Granville Bantocks and the rest pay not the smallest attention to its standards. The British Musical Society offers to name forty British composers of merit without falling back on Elgar or any member of his generation. But, so far, Elgar is alone for Westminster Abbey.

As I said to begin with, neither I nor any living man can judge with certainty whether these odds and ends which I have been able to relate about Elgar are the stigmata of what we call immortality. But they look to me very like it; and I give them accordingly for what they may prove to be worth.

Music and Letters,
Volume 1 Number 1, 1920

The following issue of Music and Letters *contained a letter from Elgar, dated 7th March 1920. It ran as follows:-*

Dear Sir,

My attention has been called in the last week to a sentence in an article on myself in your first number, which mentions a clique associated with the name of the late Sir Hubert Parry. Cliques have always existed in music and always will exist; they do not matter. All I am concerned with is the mention of Sir Hubert Parry's name, with the implication that he in some way slighted me. This is quite a mistake.

The moment to enumerate the many occasions on which Parry advised me and encouraged me is not now; I hope to make known all I owe to his ungrudging kindness at some future time.

Yours faithfully,
Edward Elgar.

The Athenæum.

The Violin Concerto
by W.H. Reed

Walking down Regent Street one morning in the early months of the year 1910, I met Sir Edward Elgar, who, to my surprise, stopped and asked me if I had any time to spare, as he wanted a little help with something which he was sketching out for the fiddle, and he wished to settle some questions of bowing and certain intricacies of violin technique.

He was staying at a flat in New Cavendish Street at that time, and asked me if I could come there one day as soon as possible. As can easily be imagined, I felt very flattered at being asked to help, and made an appointment for the following day.

On my arrival in the morning I found Sir Edward striding about with a number of loose pieces of MSS. which he was arranging in different parts of the room. Some were already pinned on the backs of chairs, or fixed up on the mantelpiece ready for me to play, so we started without any loss of time. I discovered then that we were playing a sketchy version of what is now the Violin Concerto. The main ideas were written out, and, to use one of his own pet expressions, he had 'japed them up' to make a coherent piece.

I understood him to say that he had started working at a Violin Concerto some time before, and that he had played the first movement with Lady Speyer (Madam von Stosch), but, being dissatisfied with it, he had put it aside for a while.

Now, however, he seemed to see it all in a new light, and he was very excited as he told me how it had to be laid out, he was using some of the same themes, but treating them differently, and, of course, introducing a great deal of new material. It was a unique experience for me to see Elgar as a composer in such an intimate way, and to note his methods and the workings of his mind; also the discussion and analysis of the Concerto as it grew were a great joy, and indeed an education to me, during this and many other visits which followed.

Sir Edward was always very modest and diffident, but he knew very well when anything he had written gave him pleasure; there was no false modesty about his joy on hearing the solo violin boldly entering in the first movement with the concluding half of the principal subject instead of at the beginning, as if answering a question instead of stating a fact.

Several times we played that opening to his great satisfaction at the novelty of the idea.

It will be noted upon analysis that the solo violin does not play these two opening bars anywhere throughout the Concerto. See Figs. **9, 19, 26,** and eight bars before the end of the first movement. Also in the finale at Figs. **101** and **107** (at the beginning and at the end of the cadenza). It is true that the violin takes part with the orchestra in a variant of the theme at Fig. **21,** in the first movement, and again two bars before **40,** but this is only in the nature of a discussion of the thematic material, and not a definite statement.

I have often been asked how, and in what way, a practical violinist or pianist can help a great composer when he is engaged upon a concerto for their respective instruments? It is surely obvious that he can be of valuable assistance in bringing into actual being what has hitherto existed only in the composer's imagination. He can play the same passage in a dozen different ways, with different accentuation, different phrasing (and, in the case of a violinist, different bowings), even different spacing of the intervals in an arpeggio passage, or rearrangement of the notes without necessarily altering in any way the harmonic structure, *e.g.* a violinist would naturally render a close *arpeggio* of the common chord

suitable for the fingers on the pianoforte, as

in most cases this extended spacing of the notes being more effective for the violin. Undoubtedly a passage of this sort can be played in either manner and in a variety of other ways, so the composer naturally listens carefully before deciding which method of expressing the chord of C major fits in best with his mental picture of the conception, or the context which he may have in his mind.

On my arrival at the flat in New Cavendish Street, and later *Plas Gwyn* in Hereford (where the Concerto was eventually completed) I was frequently confronted with a piece of MS. on which might be written, *e.g.*

and a query 'Can this be played in octaves at the tempo?' After trying it, and saying that it was quite possible, this octave passage was adopted (three bars after **21** and the similar one two bars later); also for the repetitions at **40,** and later the octaves were again added as he wished, and that was how it was written when first I played the Concerto. Later on it underwent another change. Alternate octaves were taken out, leaving one on every other note instead of each semiquaver as before, the effect being much the same, and the execution very much simpler, and probably cleaner in performance.

Then on another sheet of MS. would be written

(**21.7**), which (after repeated trials and rearrangements of the notes required for the harmony) resolved itself into the semiquaver passage eventually decided upon and duly recorded in the movement

It is of interest to notice the arrangement of accents in **21.7, 8.** In the first bar the accent is on the first and fourth semiquaver, in the second bar it is on the first and second semiquaver, the alteration of rhythm enhancing the forceful character of this working-up section besides avoiding any possibility of monotony in the musical figuration.

The *Con Fuoco* passage after **42** was originally (after many phases) set out as in

though this ultimately underwent a slight modification, as can be seen by comparing the example with the published version.

Similarly the passage

is seen to be more complicated in some ways than the final form in which it now appears (before and after **44**).

The slow movement always brings very pleasant memories to my mind. Most of it was composed at a house called *The Hut*, belonging to the late Leo Schuster, a very delightful spot at Bray, near Maidenhead. There is a studio standing a little way from the house, and quite close to the Thames which flows past at the edge of the lawn. Whenever I play this *andante,* or hear it played, a mental picture of the studio flashes to my mind. It was a home for all the quaint objects and curios that Mr. Schuster had collected in many parts of the world, and there were also a grand piano and a writing desk, so that Sir Edward could steal away from the house and repair to the studio at any time, where he could work to his heart's content without interruption.

As I saw it, in that early spring, with all the young green on the trees and the swans lazily floating by on the river, so the vision comes to me again with the music that was written there, music that depicts with such fidelity the poetry and beauty of the scene. Many times I went to Bray, and played again the first movement and then the slow movement as it came into being in that quiet spot.

The passage leading up to **47** was played in varying ways until I found what it was Sir Edward really wanted. We tried the last few notes in harmonics, the sound of which pleased him so much that that method of interpretation was instantly adopted, and he at once wrote *armonico* over it.

We had great fun over the *ad lib* passage four bars before **51** with the sudden leap of a twelfth up the G string. The first time we tried it this way instead of going to a more reasonable position on the D string, the effect so electrified him that I remember he called out 'good for you' when I landed safely on the E with a real explosive *sforzando*.

Much work had also to be done with the passages at **52** and **54** shaping these arabesques, and deciding whether they should be demisemiquavers or whether the groups should be written as broken triplets, i.e.,

or

a very subtle, but important distinction.

The finale was begun in the studio at Bray, though as Sir Edward very soon went to his home at *Plas Gwyn*, Hereford, most of it was written there.

Soon he arrived at the point where he had an inspiration for an elaborate cadenza which was to be carried out in a new manner. This would sum up, as it were, all the principal ideas in the Concerto, and it would be accompanied by the orchestra practically throughout.

When I arrived at Hereford I found fragments of MSS, pinned up on the backs of chairs and at any vantage point, just as I did on my first visit to the London flat.

How excited he was about the cadenza! We played each of the passages in every imaginable way, and the lento between **105** and **106** nearly moved him to tears as he repeated it again and yet again, dwelling on certain notes and marking them *tenuto, espress, animato* or *molto accel.* as he realised step by step exactly what he sought to express.

Some alterations have taken place in the last movement since those days when I first played it from the MS. and I have never quite got used to the passage one bar before **71** and its companion one bar before **91**. When I first played it, the passage was as

It was originally printed thus, but in a later edition it appeared as

The other passage before **91** has a similar alteration, see

as was originally printed.

The passages from **76** to **78** and from **90** to **92** were very difficult to mould into their final shape, and it took a considerable amount of time to find suitable bowings to fit these intricacies.

Sir Edward would never pass anything until he was completely

15   Elgar with W. H. Reed (right).

16 Elgar conducting.

satisfied; he would view each bar from every possible angle, and would ask me to repeat it any number of times, shaping and reshaping it until he succeeded at last in crystallising his ideas and getting them down on the score.

Another and most drastic alteration was made in the final coda after the first printed version was 'in proof.' As we first played the Concerto in those days, it ended as in

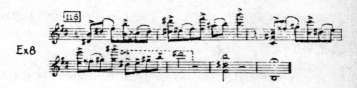

Ex8

instead of the passage which now appears at **116.**

In the summer it was finished, and, in the beginning of September, when I arrived at the house of Herbert Brewer in Gloucester for the Three Choirs Festival rehearsals, I found that Sir Edward had already called in twice to see me, and to tell me that he had invited a few friends and enthusiasts to a little party on the Sunday evening. As the opening service of the festival takes place in the Cathedral in the afternoon, everyone is free for the evening, so Sir Edward asked me to play through the whole Concerto with him. In the house he had taken for the festival was a large room containing a grand piano. The guests were all assembled and the lights lowered, except those over the piano and the music stand. Sir Edward took his seat at the piano, and a tense whisper to me 'You are not going to leave me all alone in the tuttis, are you?' we began.

That evening is a never-to-be-forgotten memory to me, and I always feel, as I think of it, deeply grateful to him for giving me the opportunity of enjoying such an artistic experience. I must confess to a few qualms as I took my violin out of its case that Sunday evening, and realised that probably nearly all the prominent musicians engaged in the Festival were there, besides some of the musical critics and the house party, but my fears vanished at the first note, and I became thrilled by the atmosphere created, the very evident appreciation of the listeners and the magnetic force which flowed from Sir Edward.

The Two Elgars
by Frank Howes

Frank Howes was Chief Music Critic of The Times *from 1943 to 1960. His numerous books include* The English Musical Renaissance, *published in 1966. The present essay dates from 1935.*

Let it be granted that Elgar was a great composer. It will be conceded that he wrote a certain number of things of which his admirers are not proud. The same is true of any other great composer with this difference: when Bach, Beethoven and Schubert wrote bad music it was dull, empty music they wrote; when Elgar writes bad music the badness is of another order — it sounds meretricious. A similar distinction may be observed in the work of that other great modern symphonist, Sibelius. Personally I have never got over my liking for the *Valse Triste*, but a good case can be made out for the existence of a gulf between Sibelius's great and his inferior music. And the inferiority consists in a certain falsity and tawdriness, a kind of artistic insincerity. It is the same thing as most English musicians feel about Liszt. How is the existence side by side in these great composers of the true and the false, the profound and the superficial, the beautiful and the tawdry, to be accounted for?

The old explanation of any phenomenon of this sort, moral or æsthetic, was based on a simple dichotomy: the flesh was at war with the spirit, the body with the mind. Man had a higher and a lower nature which dwelt together in the same personality — the division was, so to speak, horizontal. But without claiming finality for the newer and more subtle psychology it at least seems likely that the division in our minds is more often vertical: body is not at war with mind, but one set of psychophysical (body-mind) characteristics struggles against another set. The temptations of the body are after all of a very simple and rudimentary order. Most of the major moral conflicts are between two sets of psychophysical motives, not between crude desires and weak wills. In a word, two different but complete persons struggle in the breast of the single man for the determination of his conduct. We are all so far dual, if not multiple, personalities. In the case of

Sibelius a gross physical trait may indicate this duality, for it is said that the two sides of his face are not the same. But most people by the time they reach middle life have imposed a harmony on their constituent personalities. Some, on the other hand, conspicuously fail to do so, and even develop distinct and alternating personalities, which are recognised by morbid psychology as a form of mental disintegration. We have just been shown a conspicuous example in our own world of music, the case of Philip Heseltine and Peter Warlock as diagnosed with every probability of correctness by his friends. In his case the secondary personality rose up and ultimately overwhelmed the primary and principal. It is, however, possible in a sane and healthy individual for two personalities to live comfortably side by side and establish a definite relationship with each other. Such a one was Fiona Macleod. Such a one was Lord Curzon — an example I choose deliberately because he had certain affinities with Elgar. Mr. Harold Nicholson has shown in Lord Curzon a certain simplicity and understanding of fundamentals persisting behind a façade of elaborate splendour and pride in vainglorious inessentials. The same combination can be seen in any score of Elgar's.

Here it will be objected that I am deducing a man's character from his music. I am. I do not believe that a man can write anything, least of all music, without revealing himself. It is true that eminent novelists rarely look like the picture we form of them from their books, and it is also true that some executive musicians have been known to play like angels and to behave in the ordinary affairs of life like cads. But no composer ever penned a bar of music without telling any hearer with ears to hear the sort of man he was. Impenitent, therefore, I affirm my belief that composers write their autobiography in their music, and if any reader cannot accept this argument at least for a moment, he should proceed no further with my remarks on Elgar for their foundation will have been undermined. I once met Elgar at tea; beyond that I have no knowledge of the man beyond what is revealed, I think quite plainly, in his music.

The two Elgars may be roughly described as the Elgar who writes for strings and the Elgar who writes for brass, or, somewhat shifting the line of demarcation, the Elgar who wrote sublime works like *Enigma,* the *Introduction and Allegro* and the Violoncello Concerto, and the Elgar who wrote excellent tea-shop music — the *Chansons, Rosemary, Sérénade Lyrique,* etc. But the two Elgars often combined in the same works just as Lord Curzon often allowed his passion for 'unparalleled magnificence' to take over some piece of simply conceived policy. I find the evidence of this in the symphonies not so much by being able to put my finger on any particular passage and say this was written by Elgar A and this by Elgar B, but by an ambivalence that permeates them as wholes. I have risen from my seat in wrath and gone out before the end unable to endure more of what Mr. Turner once called the 'Salvation Army symphony'; I have sat motionless and enthralled to the last note. (I come and go over *Madame Butterfly* in much the same way and probably for a similar reason according to the quality of the performance.) But this hardly proves my case. A more instructive example is *The Music Makers*. This cantata was recently performed alongside the Violoncello Concerto at a commemoration of the composer and the juxtaposition vividly revealed the two Elgars.

Elgar thought well of *The Music Makers* because he admired the poem. But being passionately excited about a poem may even preclude the imagination from getting to grips with it. Dame Ethel Smyth's *The Prison* is a very good example of appreciation of a poem satisfying and soothing a composer's imagination instead of providing the creative itch. She has set but has not composed *The Prison,* just as Elgar has set but not composed *The Music Makers.* The composers appear to have felt so strongly that the truth of the poems completely expressed their own feelings that they have had nothing more to add to them. The self-quotations in *The Music Makers* were deliberately made but they are proof positive of a less than half-stirred imagination. A composer may take an indifferent text and so dwell with it that he digests and absorbs it and makes from it a great work, but he will in that case have created, not borrowed, music for it. The second-hand music in *The Music Makers* is evidence not of simple vanity (as it might be in *Heldenleben*) but of a weak impulse to compose it. Elgar A, having nothing to add to a poem which so adequately expressed his sentiments and convictions, yielded the pen to Elgar B, who added those obvious, meretricious touches about 'trampling a kingdom down' and so on. Even at the point where *Nimrod* is quoted to illumine the passage in which 'one man's word wrought flame in another man's heart,' where one might think the quotation apt and legitimate the case is betrayed by the impossibly gauche fitting of the words to that noble tune — for spiritual lapses often show themselves, as Sir Henry Hadow has said, in some technical flaw:

Music Makers

ELGAR

But on one man's soul it hath bro-ken, A light that doth not de-part......

These things cannot be picked out in this way. They do not occur when the artistic imagination has been fired to a heat sufficient to make a good work. The total effect of *The Music Makers* is of something below Elgar's best, of something with a streak of tawdriness in it.

Now tinsel will not pass for gold, and the existence in Elgar of a vein of tinsel among a rich vein of gold has long been recognised. A good deal of fuss was made a few years ago when so much was openly said. Those who protested against it took exception to the occasion on which it was said, but it was the substance of it that was the real offender. Misrepresentation rarely matters (*magna est veritas et prævalebit*); it is the truth which smarts. But if the truth stings, so do most other antiseptics, and we may as well recognise that Elgar was two men. Elgar A had those direct intuitions of the essentials of things, those subtle perceptions of reality which led to wonderful, finely tempered, whimsical, tolerant, benevolent ruminations on the richness of life — *Nimrod,* the slow movements of the Violoncello Concerto and the String Quartet. Elgar B liked the brave shows of things. There is a place for shows and when Elgar wrote *Pomp and Circumstance* and *Cockaigne* he knew what was what and deceived neither himself nor others. Elgar B also wrote the honest tea-shop music, where also there is little ambiguity. But what is embarrassing is when the two undertook a work jointly, just as it was in diplomacy when the two Curzons combined to execute a single policy. Elgar B often borrowed from Elgar A the word *nobilmente,* which signified a combination of dignity with intensity of expression, when he wished to transmute tinsel into gold. The composer's constant use of the word suggests a subconscious uneasiness on his part that though Elgar A's music was solid right through, Elgar B's music would not always support the weight placed upon it. On the other hand, Elgar A acquired from Elgar B that breadth of effective appeal, that vitality which is implicit in anything to which the epithet 'vulgar' might be applied, so that he achieved with it something bigger than more fastidious composers ever can do. In these days when art has lost the aristocratic reference which it had in the eighteenth century, it must at some point make contact with 'the vulgar,' if it is to speak to the millions of modern democracy. Delius, for instance, can never be a great composer as composers with a more universal appeal are great. Elgar B did this for Elgar, but Elgar A has inevitably paid something for the service so rendered. Thus the two Elgars helped one another, but they never quite became one, even as the many Liszts never became one, but at the end the two Verdis and the two Wagners became one great composer without qualification.

Music & Letters,
January 1935

What have we learnt from Elgar?
by Ralph Vaughan Williams

The January 1935 issue of Music & Letters *was devoted to tributes to Elgar, whose death had occurred almost a year previously. Among them was this one from Vaughan Williams, who prefaced it with the disarming remark, 'This is not an article, really, but a few ideas set down without much method'.*

Of course, orchestration. There is no need to labour that point, but it is extraordinary that people writing in admiration of his orchestration have taken it for granted that he was not also a great choral writer. Such people should be taken to hear a pianoforte rehearsal of *Gerontius;* they would then soon change their minds.

Elgar understood how to use the voice just as well as he understood how to use the violin. Perhaps some of the misapprehensions about his choral technique come from the fact that it developed out of his orchestral technique. He will, for instance, at a particular place add the altos to the tenors to reinforce the tone and enrich the colour just as he might add the violas to the 'cellos; *e.g., Gerontius* vocal score, p. 16, second and third bars of figure **35.**

After the first performance of *The Kingdom* a distinguished musical amateur, one of those who have not got beyond worshipping orthodox technique for its own sake, complained to me that the double choruses in that work were not really in eight parts at all. I think he somehow felt that he had been cheated and was inclined to ask for his money back. If he had known a little more he would have remembered that Bach in the *Matthew Passion* owed him just as much hard cash as Elgar. Take, for example, pp. 104 and 105 from *Gerontius,* figure **69.** I am aware that this passage is for full and semi-chorus, but the principle is the same.

This kind of choral technique has been used before to a certain extent by Wagner and even by Handel, from whom avowedly Elgar learnt so much, but it had never, I think, been used so consistently or so successfully. But to return to the orchestra. I would like to mention two points: (1) Orchestral daring, the

outcome of an absolutely sure touch. For example, the counter-melody for one muted horn at the beginning of the A flat symphony (miniature score, p. 4, starting at the second bar of figure **1**). I feel pretty certain that if a student had brought this passage to his teacher he would have crossed it out and told the student that he did not know the elements of orchestral balance; and yet Elgar has so placed it that it comes through with entire clearness. (2) Orchestral economy. We expect this of Debussy or Ravel, 'the just enough and no more' kind of texture. Elgar's orchestra looks and sounds so full that subtlety is the last thing we expect from it. Now let us take an extreme case, the choral climax, *Praise to the Holiest*, from *Gerontius* (part II, figure **74,** vocal score, p. 111; full score, p. 150). Here one would expect every instrument to blaze away and that orchestral subtlety was out of place and that the composer would be content to let the instruments double the voices with perhaps a little figuration on the strings. Here, however, is the outline of the trumpet and trombone parts in this passage:

For the first four bars the third trombone and tuba double the bass voice, except for a thoughtful rest in the third trombone part. After a blaze for all the brass on the first bar the first and second trombones are silent for two bars, the voices are too high to need the heavy tone of trombones. In the fourth bar the trumpets leave off because the sopranos are high and do not need their support and the trombones are added to give weight to the middle parts. On the last beat of bar four the brass is all silent (except the fag-end of the tuba dotted minim), partly because the chorus is there momentarily less forcible and partly to give breath for another blaze on the sixth bar (note also the stress mark on the *second* beat of the fifth bar but *not* on the third).

Many conductors with limited orchestral resources when dealing with modern works are under the painful necessity of dispensing with the 'extra' instruments; they must either leave them out altogether or write them in for some other instrument. I have lately had to do this both with Wagner and Elgar. I have found that with Wagner the extra instruments could almost always be dispensed with altogether, with a little loss of colour it is true, but with no damage to the texture. But when it came to Elgar the case was quite different. Even in the accompaniments to choral movements there was hardly anything that could be left out without leaving a 'hole' in the texture.

To say that a man is a great orchestrator is not, of course, to say that he is a great composer. What I have said above about Elgar's orchestration is probably equally true of even second rate people like Saint-Saëns and Berlioz. The one question we have to ask is, has Elgar achieved beauty? This is the one thing that is vital. And this is the one question that Elgar commentators seem to shirk. They talk of his irony, his humour, his skill. There seems a general consensus of opinion among this class of critic to praise Elgar's *Falstaff* at the expense of his other works. They try to correlate music with literature. I rather suspect these people of not being very sure of their literary qualifications and therefore anxious to parade them rather than take them for granted. The best composer is surely he who has the most beautiful melodies, the finest harmony, the most vital rhythm and the surest sense of form. There is no other criterion. I lose patience with those people who try to put up Berlioz as a great composer because he interpreted Shakespeare, because he could give literary reasons for his beliefs, and do not see that a composer like Dvorák, a reed shaken by the wind, is far the greater man of the two because the wind was the divine afflatus.

Elgar has the one thing needful, and all his philosophical, literary and technical excellences fall into their proper place: they are a means to an end. But to say that he has beauty is only half the truth: he has that peculiar kind of beauty which gives us, his fellow countrymen, a sense of something familiar — the intimate and personal beauty of our own fields and lanes; not the aloof and unsympathetic beauty of glaciers and coral reefs and tropical forests.

Glinka used to say that he wanted to 'make his own people feel at home.' There are certain pieces of music which are so much a part of our national consciousness that we cease to criticise them. We know they must be good, otherwise they would not occupy the position they do in our hearts. We do not consciously appraise them, but accept them without comment as definitely belonging to us. Such must be the attitude of mind of a German to his best loved chorales, to the Wälsung theme in the *Ring,* to Schubert's *An die Musik.* Such is our feeling towards *Fairest Isle, Lazarus* or *St. Anne,* and during the last thirty years certain pieces by Elgar have come to hold that position for many of us; such things as *Nimrod* and *W. N.,* or *Softly and Gently* have this peculiar quality. When hearing such music as this we are no longer critical or analytical, but passively receptive. It falls to the lot of very few composers, and to them not often, to achieve this bond of unity with their countrymen. Elgar has achieved this more often than most, and be it noted, not when he is being deliberately 'popular,' as in *Land of Hope and Glory* or *Cockaigne,* but at those moments when he seems to have retired into the solitude of his own sanctuary.

I suppose one may say that when one has cribbed from a composer one has learnt from him. Certainly many of my generation and of the next below me have learnt much from Elgar in that way. I am astonished, if I may be allowed a personal explanation, to find on looking back on my own earlier works how much I cribbed from him, probably when I thought I was being most original.

Now a crib is not merely an accidental similarity of outline; thus I do not consider that the opening of my London Symphony is a crib from the beginning of *Gerontius,* part 2; indeed, my friends assure me that it is, as a matter of fact, a compound of Debussy's *La Mer* and Charpentier's *Louise.* Real cribbing takes place when one composer thinks with the mind of another even when there is no mechanical similarity of phrase. When, as often happens, this vicarious thinking does lead to similarity of phrase the offence is, I think, more venial. In that case one is so impressed by a certain passage in another composer that it becomes part of oneself.

Professor Dent points out that Schubert was influenced by Beethoven, not so much generally as from particular examples. He instances the *Death and the Maiden* tune as being influenced by the slow movement of Beethoven's Seventh Symphony.

If I may again be personal, I find that the Elgar phrase which influenced me most was *Thou art Calling me* in *Gerontius* (vocal score, p. 7, fifth bar of figure **22**), not so much perhaps in its original form as when it comes later on in combination with another theme (*e.g.*, p. 19, figure **37**). For proof of this see *Sea Symphony* (vocal score, p. 84, nine bars before letter **B**) and *London Symphony* (full score, p. 16, letter **H**).

I expect that most of my contemporaries, if they were to look into their early works, would have similar confessions to make.

Closely connected with the above is another question: From whom did Elgar himself derive? We can, I think, learn much from this. I need hardly, I suppose, premise that every artist derives from those before him. No composer appears absolutely new out of the welkin; indeed when, like Schönberg, he is said to do so he is to my mind at once suspect. But it is a mistake to suppose that there is an unbroken line of great composers, one handing on the torch to the next; that Mozart comes from Bach, Beethoven from Mozart, Wagner from Beethoven and so on.

There are two influences that affect all artists, great and small — the initial derivations of their music absorbed probably in their youthful and most impressionable years and the external influences that affect them later. It is the first of these which is especially useful to us in learning from Elgar. Small men are influenced by great, great by small. Several of us have been influenced by Elgar. By whom was Elgar himself influenced?

Hubert Parry derived largely from S.S. Wesley, but that influence seems to have passed Elgar by. We must, I believe, look for the germs of the Elgarian idiom to the little group of organists who were writing small but rather charming music when Elgar was a young man, such as Henry Smart and John Goss.

I suppose the opinion that Elgar could possibly have learnt anything from Henry Smart will produce a letter of protest signed by distinguished artists and literary men who know nothing and care less about the subject, followed by vapourings by Philip Page and G.B. Shaw, but anyone who has any knowledge of æsthetics or of musical history will know that this is the way that things happen. Schubert's melodic inspiration can be traced to the popular dance and march composers popular in Vienna in his time, and Wagner's early work is directly attributable to certain completely forgotten opera composers of his early years. Once again, great men learn from small, and small from great.

Elgar's career disposes of two fallacies: (1) that a great composer is great from the first minute that he puts pen to paper; (2) that he is not recognised by his contemporaries but is only discovered years after he was found starving in a garret. The true Elgar only appears with the *Enigma Variations* written when he was nearly forty. Is it surprising that before that, even before *Caractacus* and *King Olaf,* he failed to impress those older than himself with his greatness. The *Enigma Variations* brought him recognition at once. It was Hubert Parry who when he saw the manuscript score left his after-dinner armchair and rushed out in the rain to show it to Richter. It was Stanford who on the strength of the *Variations* offered Elgar the greatest honour it was in his power to give by recommending him for an honorary doctorate of Cambridge University.

We can then dispose once for all of the nonsense written by certain journalists about Elgar being cold-shouldered by the great men they are pleased to call 'academics,' because they happened to be learned as well as musical. I think that this false scent was started in *Music and Letters* by Mr. G.B. Shaw with characteristic disregard of facts and Mr. Shaw received a well-deserved snub in the next number of the paper from Elgar himself.

I hope it is not an impertinence to be curious about the way in which the mind of a great artist works. Certainly if we could know that, or even guess at it we should learn a lot — not that I am under the illusion that by analysing an artist's method one can catch any of his inspiration, but I do think that one composer can, by finding out or guessing how another composer works, review and perhaps correct his own methods.

Only the merest amateur imagines that a composer when he sets out to write a piece of music sits down and deliberately writes out bar one complete, followed by bar two complete and so on; Beethoven's notebooks disprove this, nor does anyone who knows think that ideas invariably spring from a composer's head 'ready for wear,' or that there are never any lucky accidents. There is one passage in *Gerontius* in which I am always much intrigued to know what the composer's method was. Readers will remember that the melody of *Angel's Farewll* appears (126-9) twice simply and the third time accompanied by a counter-melody, namely the music which has already appeared in the chorus *Lord Thou hast been our refuge*. Greatly daring, I suggest that Elgar's mental process was as follows: (1) The original melody occurs to the composer; (2) at the second repetition something additional in the way of a counter-subject seems to be indicated; (3) this counter-subject when invented seems to require the human voice to do it full justice; (4) it must therefore be supplied with words; (5) this counter-melody will not make its full effect unless it has already been heard separately; (6) therefore the episode for chorus (vocal score, p. 165, figure **12**) was written *after* the invention of the *Angel's Farewell*.

I need hardly add that this is purely imaginary and has absolutely no authority.

Music & Letters,
January 1935

Elgar and the Public
by C. W. Orr

The following essay by C. W. Orr (1893 - 1976) is interesting because it reminds us that Elgar's music, even after he attained recognition, was not always accorded the attention it merited in the country of his birth. Orr, himself a minor but nonetheless neglected composer, knew how this could affect a creative artist and he makes us realise that Elgar's self-pity was not entirely without just cause.

The position of Elgar in England has been something of a paradox till within quite recent years. He has been made a knight and remains a very great composer. He has been given the Order of Merit by the King, and the cold shoulder by the public. He is one of the most distinguished of living Englishmen, yet there are plenty of third-rate politicians whose names are more familiar to the man in the street. And he is, with the exception of Delius, the only British composer with a high reputation on the Continent; yet at home he is politely disregarded by the older and patronized by the younger generation of musicians. That he has had to wait till his seventieth year to receive anything like widespread appreciation in his own country is a curious sidelight on English musical history, and it is all the more odd when one remembers that in his earlier days he scored two direct successes with the *Enigma Variations* and *Gerontius*: the former rapidly establishing itself as a favourite, both here and abroad, and the latter sharing with *Elijah* and *The Messiah* the distinction of being the most frequently performed oratorio in England. Yet the fact remains that we have had to wait till within the last ten years for signs of a real understanding of the significance of the works of Elgar's maturity, and even now there are too many who regard him simply as the composer of *Gerontius* and *Land of Hope and Glory*.

It may be said that when a composer arouses great interest with his early compositions and subsequently fails to attract attention, we are justified in assuming that the quality of his work has deteriorated in some way, and that he has outlived his earlier inspiration. But this explanation will not square with the facts as far as Elgar is concerned. *Gerontius*, far from marking the close of

Elgar's creative genius, was the herald not only of two more oratorios but of a succession of symphonic masterpieces which more than justified the high hopes raised by his earlier achievements. Yet none of these later works repeated the success of their fore-runners. And perhaps if we look more closely into the matter we shall be forced to admit that it was owing chiefly to the fact that Richter had sponsored the *Enigma* and Richard Strauss had publicly blessed *Gerontius* that the British public were made vaguely aware that we had at long last produced a really great composer. Richter had conducted the *Enigma*, and Richter was known to conduct nothing of which he had not a high opinion. And *Gerontius*, which was something of a failure on its first production over here, was given shortly afterwards at a music festival at Düsseldorf, at which Richard Strauss was a leading figure, and Strauss, with a generosity that did equal credit to his heart and head, toasted Elgar at a banquet at which he spoke of the pleasure he had in raising his glass to 'the first Progressivist in English music.' The phrase caused some fluttering in the academic dovecotes over here, where Elgar was by no means *personâ grata*, originality of any sort being held suspect at our schools and colleges in those days, but it had the effect of stirring up the torpid imagination of the average musician and amateur, who felt that Strauss, while he might be the stormy petrel of musical Europe, was nevertheless someone to be reckoned with, and whose utterances commanded respect. Accordingly these two works, having been blessed by German authority, became part of the general repertory, and as a result of frequent performance their intrinsic merit and beauty were recognised by the public at large and afterwards by professional musicians. But after this, public appreciation waned. *The Apostles*, lacking the Straussian benediction, failed to attract as *Gerontius* had done; the first Symphony had a good send-off, but was gradually shelved; Richter left England, and though some of our conductors laboured hard for Elgar they were unable to extract him from the *niche* prepared for him by the public. The indifference of audiences at that time to Elgar's work was most painfully shown at a concert given by Sir Landon Ronald at Queen's Hall not long before the War. The programme was entirely devoted to Elgar; the new Symphonic poem *Falstaff* was receiving its first London performance, and the second Symphony (still something of a novelty) and the *Enigma* completed the scheme. None present will easily forget the desolate scene. Here we had a programme conducted by a musician who had prominently identified himself with Elgar's music; a brand-new work from our greatest composer; a first-rate orchestra, and—to mark the occasion—an array of empty benches! (The music critic of *The Daily Telegraph* commented caustically on the absence of students and representatives of our academies and schools of music.) Those of us who counted ourselves staunch Elgarites began to wonder if Elgar was to be regarded for an indefinite period by the English audiences as merely one of our respectable 'festival' composers, who turned out with monotonous regularity works which received one Cathedral performance and were then left to drift into obscurity.

The War years were lean ones for British music, but Elgar summed up all that was worthiest in our pride and noblest in our grief in his setting of Binyon's *For the Fallen*; a work so poignant in expression that it seemed almost too painful to listen to during those times of agonized grief and suspense. Here was a masterpiece summing up the spirit of the time as greatly and memorably as did the orations of Pericles and the epigrams of Simonides. Elgar showed that he was the fittest Laureate of our 'proud thanksgiving'—the one musician who could best express patriotism without vainglory and sorrow without self-pity.

Then came the peace, and with it high hopes of a real musical renaissance in England. Elgar was still disregarded; he was held in suspicion by the younger men as representing the German tradition in music which had too long held our English music in Teutonic fetters. Vaughan Williams was the hero of the hour; the healthy influence of folk-song was to free us from our pseudo-Germanic past, and English music would arise Phoenix-like from the ashes of its discreditable immediate ancestors by reviving the glories of a past age. Folk-tunes became all the rage; young composers diligently flattened their sevenths and modalised their tunes; parties of enthusiasts went back to the land, where they implored the rustics to warble songs their mothers taught them, which effusions were carefully noted down to be worked up into English Suites, English Rhapsodies, and English dance tunes. Nor was it surprising that with such a spirit of enthusiasm in the air new geniuses were discovered every month, and it became difficult to keep pace with the young men who were turning out masterpieces almost before they had finished cutting their musical teeth. Song-writing in particular became a sort of fever; contemporary poets were ransacked wholesale to provide material for this lyrical outburst, which had at least the merit of being far removed from the too facile drawing-room songs of an earlier day. It was inevitable that the movement should lend itself to a good deal of foolishness, but it must be remembered that there was behind it a real conviction that we were on the eve of a musical revolution; England seemed about to take her place among the nations of Europe with a national idiom and a new tradition. It was, in fact, a healthy reaction against the foreign-musician worship that had gone on too long, but it overlooked the truth that you cannot create a ready-made renaissance by a form of folk-tune serum; and these young people likewise overlooked the work of Elgar, who had contrived to write music as 'English' as any of the newer generation without the factitious aid of folk-song and its inevitable accompanying mannerisms.

Ten years have passed, and already many of the names that were like trumpet-blasts in those days of hope and optimism have ceased to arouse enthusiasm or even interest. The young men of whom so much was expected just after the War have signally failed to live up to their bolstered reputations. And if anything were needed to confirm one's belief that Elgar still towers above all other English composers (Delius excepted), it is the season of Promenades that has just concluded. For at these concerts, in addition to examples of most of the prominent composers of the British school, we have had an opportunity of hearing some of Elgar's greatest compositions—the two Symphonies, the two Concertos, *Falstaff* and the *Enigma Variations*—besides lesser works, and it is scarcely an exaggeration to say that Elgar has shown himself like some 'sea-shouldering whale' among the little dolphins and porpoises who have floundered uncomfortably in his immense wake. And what is the most gratifying thing to record is that the general public seems at long last to have recognised him for what he is. After some of the Symphonic Depressions of our younger men his music comes like a health-giving tonic, which has been thankfully swallowed by audiences sick of the acidities of too many Bright Young People. It is becoming more and more evident that he, who has never worried about 'nationalism,' is the most *national* of all our composers. His music could have been written only by an Englishman, and that is one reason why English audiences should understand him best. Many of his movements might be labelled *Allegro Democratica-mente*, so redolent are they of all that is most essentially English—jovial humour and unaffected sincerity. He writes for no clique; he has gathered round him no solemn band of devotees whose mission in life is to explain the 'master' to the world. Instead, he has preferred to write largely for the man in the street, who is after all the ultimate bestower of immortality on the artist.

And he has consistently refrained from the extravagances of modernism, the narrowness of 'schools,' and the self-conscious poses of the 'advanced set' in music.

The Musical Times,
1st January 1931

Elgar: 'The First of the New'
by Hans Keller

Elgar was the first of the new. Since Purcell, England had not produced a composer for the European common market. Against—much against—the background of academicians who were destined to remain dilettanti, there emerged a self-taught amateur destined to become a master.

At the time of Elgar's birth Brahms was 24, Dvořák was 16, and Wagner 44. When he died, Vaughan Williams was 62, Walton was 32, Britten was 20 and Schoenberg 60. Elgar's musical fathers were far away; many, almost all of them were of the Austro-German tradition, with Brahms, rather than Wagner, as the most powerful influence; and none of them English.

In a penetrating article in the current issue of *Music and Letters* Donald Mitchell goes so far as to submit 'that to find Elgar today specifically English in flavour is to expose oneself as the victim of a type of collective hallucination.' Elgar's early success on the Continent, and with Continentals, was indeed striking. It needed a Continental—Hans Richter—to introduce the *Enigma Variations, The Dream of Gerontius* and the first Symphony (dedicated to him) to English audiences; and Düsseldorf heard *Gerontius* before London.

So wide are Elgar's Continental sources that they have not yet been fully explored. Tovey, a really independent researcher, has drawn attention to very curious relations between Saint-Saëns' third fiddle concerto and Elgar's work in this *genre*, even though the two 'are almost at opposite poles of artistic outlook'; but it is amusing that hitherto nobody has mentioned Dvořák, for the simple reason, I think, that Elgar didn't mention him among his idols. True, Dvořák's influence is intermittent, but when it comes I find it glaring. Where a composer's melodic and harmonic characteristics recur simultaneously in another's music, I refuse to believe in coincidence.

The second subject of the Elgar Violin Concerto is a case in point, 'grandioso' and all. Incidentally, the work is in the unusual string-concerto key of B Minor, like the just-mentioned Saint-Saëns piece and Dvořák's 'Cello Concerto. When we arrive at the slow movement the influence can even be pinned down quite precisely; not unnaturally, the model for this particular solo phrase is to be found in the parallel movement of Dvorák's own Violin Concerto. The top line is Dvorák, the lower is Elgar:

Psychologically, it is not at all surprising that Elgar should have evinced such sympathy for someone we might call Brahms's creative brother-in-law. But however much Elgar liked the Continent and the Continent used to like Elgar, things would seem to have changed a little nowadays; and it has variously been asked why it is that Elgar is unexportable. For me, this is a complicated question: I consider it partly wrong and partly right.

Wrong part first. Twice in the course of writing the present article I took time off and twiddled about with the wireless. A busman's holiday was the result: first I picked up Elgar's 'Cello Concerto, then the *Enigma*, both from the Continent and neither played on a centenary occasion. Part of the English belief in Elgar's insularity is in fact a group delusion: there are far more Elgar performances on the Continent than the English think. Our musical community still suffers from the hangover of having been regarded as 'the land without music' by the authoritative Austro-German group, which ruled Elgar's creativity and his audiences' receptivity alike.

However, a delusion is all the more potent for having *some* foundation in fact, and the fact is that Elgar is distinctly less popular on the Continent than he would be if Mr. Mitchell's submission were altogether true. To be sure, Mr. Mitchell got hold of the right end of the stick, but the question remains whether the stick had not still better be held somewhere nearer the middle.

Admittedly, Elgar had no English tradition of 'art music' to work upon, but there was an English influence which he could not escape, though it manifested itself so subtly and unobtrusively that it has not so far been analysed and defined—the influence of folk song. That the second subject of the *Introduction and Allegro* was inspired by a group of Welsh singers is an established fact, but the principal subject is far more profoundly, though far less obviously, folkish in character:

Take the folkish black keys of the piano, the so-called pentatonic scale. Transpose it to G, and you have the material of this phrase. The reason why the various folk scales are not easily detectable in Elgar's music is that he all but submerges them in his European, diatonic idiom; the above-cited five-note scale, for instance, is immediately contradicted by a C in the bar ensuing; at the same time, it still remains more easily recognisable than many folkish elements in Elgar's more pronouncedly Continental style. And the reason why Mr. Mitchell does not spontaneously hear this specific English flavour which, however faint on the surface, permeates virtually all Elgarian music, is that he was born and bred in England and thus subjected to the same early folkloristic influences as Elgar himself: they do not strike him as something to write home from home about, as long as they are sufficiently concealed by a central-European harmonic idiom.

In the central-European tradition itself, on the other hand, you have to search—significantly enough—as far as Dvořák if you want to find, say, occasional pentatonicism, and a much more superimposed variety than Elgar's at that. The average Continental musician automatically reacts against any constant folkish flavour; we must not forget that Elgar's early success on the Continent was chiefly with the musical *élite,* from Strauss downwards, which is always concerned more with the matter than with the manner.

We thus arrive at the paradoxical conclusion that the conservative Elgar's manner is still a little too new for the broad Continental public. 'New' is indeed the word: this consistent naturalisation of undiatonic modes into a diatonic framework was something unprecedented, and has become a precedent. Britten, above all, whether he likes it or not, owes a great deal to Elgar's unnoticed revolution, which Walton, Elgar's more obvious successor, has not much further exploited; whereas the far more self-consciously national Vaughan Williams has taken the opposite course of naturalising diatonicism into his archaic, modal frame of mind.

Right across these diverse developments, the stunning effect of the Schoenbergian revolution has made itself felt, and the Continent is far too busy assimilating the changes thus wrought in its own musical tradition to appreciate the full significance of Elgar's conservative progressiveness. But it may well be that, presently, Continental audiences will come to understand Elgar's innovations *via* Britten, just as a twelve-noting pupil of mine has come to understand Wagner *via* Schoenberg.

Music and Musicians,
June 1957

Some Thoughts on Elgar
by Donald Mitchell

It is a commonplace that Elgar's reputation has suffered a certain decline. His music, to put it crudely, is a little out of fashion. I doubt whether we shall ever again experience the musical atmosphere—perhaps social or cultural would be the better word—in which public enthusiasm for his music will call for performances that stagger one in their sheer numerical extravagance. (I have in mind the reception of the first Symphony: in England alone, 'nearly one hundred performances in its first year'.[1])

Demand, at this pitch, is unlikely to recur. On the other hand, Elgar remains widely played and widely cherished—hence my cautious choice of adjectives above, 'certain' and 'little'. He may, to a degree, be out of fashion, but he is not out of favour. In the not very long roll of great English composers he continues to wear his greatness without discomfort, without serious challenge. The 'fashion' that has, in a sense, contributed to Elgar's unfashionableness has been this very assumption of his significant calibre, an assumption more in the nature of passive tribute than the result of active acquaintance with the manifestation of his greatness that resides in his music. There is a real danger, I think (at least in my generation), of simply taking Elgar for granted—a polite expression for what elsewhere might be termed indifference or neglect. If I have a wish for this centenary year, it is that we should be prodded into a genuine recognition, rather than a mere admission, of Elgar's genius.

I have no immodest wish to indulge in autobiography on such an occasion, but a personal event may illustrate how fashion and a hardened habit of mind may combine to Elgar's disadvantage. I was invited, recently, to participate in a series of broadcasts (for consumption in a Commonwealth country) entitled *Twentieth-Century Masterpieces*. Each contributor was asked to offer three works by different composers. It did not take me more than a moment's thought to jot down my three composers' names (the

---

[1] Diana M. McVeagh, *Elgar* (Dent, London, 1955), p. 50.

works are of no importance here): Mahler, Stravinsky and Britten. The trinity, I well realize, represents not only personal inclination but fashion—we are all children of our time—besides, of course, what I hope is a measure of good judgment. It was not until long after, when reading through the complete list of chosen 'masterpieces', with its inevitable omissions, that I noted that Elgar was absent; and it was then that I suddenly—and guiltily—realized that I might have promoted Elgar as a candidate had the thought occurred to me—but it hadn't. Since I am a warm-hearted admirer of Elgar's music and since the programmes themselves were liberally conceived—there was none of that inverted parochialism about them that concentrates solely on progressive continental masters, and a work, to qualify, only required to be composed after 1900—I am obliged to attribute my forgetfulness not just to fashion but to that slack taking-for-granted turn of mind that can effectively bury a composer while ostensibly keeping his memory green.

Looked at from the 'masterpiece' point of view, it would seem to me that almost any one of Elgar's major works written between 1900 and 1919—*Gerontius*, either of the two Symphonies, *Falstaff*, the violin or 'cello Concerto (the *Enigma Variations* just miss the chronological boat)—would have deserved a place amid master-pieces composed after 1900. 'Twentieth-century masterpiece', however, implies something other than simply written *after* 1900, and here, perhaps, we uncover some excuse for not immediately shouting 'Elgar!' in a twentieth-century context.

If we examine the careers of three of Elgar's leading European contemporaries, Strauss, Mahler and Reger, all of them born long before the turn of the century and creatively active—substantially so—after it, we find that in relation to them, or to their works rather, 'twentieth-century' takes on another colour: their music, in fact, has coloured, in a very real sense, the century. The transition from Reger to Hindemith, for instance, is an obvious one, while Mahler's influence is evident not only in the younger generation of his day—Berg, Schoenberg—but in the younger generation of our own—Copland, Britten, Shosta-kovich. The question of masterpieces apart, there is no denying the fact that both Reger and Mahler (Strauss, perhaps, to a lesser degree) not only anticipated certain prominent trends in twentieth-century music proper but actually assisted in the formation of our twentieth-century musical language.

The same can scarcely be said of Elgar, neither from a European angle nor from an English one. His successors here, in so far as he has had any, have been minor creative figures who have cultivated only very minor aspects of his genius—its secondary characteristics, not its breadth or depth (for example, the whimsicality of the *Serenade for Strings,* not the heroic poetry of the symphonies or the human insight of *Falstaff*). The two composers of weight who have reacted to Elgar are Bliss and Walton, both of whom, oddly enough, set out as innovators rather than traditionalists, and both of whom, far from being born out of Elgar, have, as it were, regressed *into* him: their Elgarian characteristics represent a dilution of their once specifically 'modern' tensions. In either case, Elgar's influence has entered the scene as a portent of relaxation.

We cannot, of course, measure Elgar's stature by the failings of others; and there is no rule that obliges the great composer to contain within him the seeds that flower in a succeeding generation. None the less, the remoteness, for our century, of Elgar's idiom, does stress his singular isolation as a composer. That he had no hand in forming the musical language of our own day, if no justification for our tendency to pass him by, memorial-wise, with hat raised, is one more factor that conditions a prevalent neglectful attitude: our present does not forcibly remind us of what Elgar has contributed to our past.

No sooner does one make a generalization than a qualification is entailed, and qualifications are legion when discussing a composer as enigmatic as Elgar. In two respects, without doubt, he foreshadowed a future that *is* our present. His sheer competence—his technical brio (so much part of his musical character!)—set a precedent in the orchestral sphere whose value we can begin to appreciate today: the impact may be a distant one, but Elgar's well-nigh singlehanded rescue of English music and the English musician from a slough of provincialism and insipid eclecticism echoes on in the highly professional accomplishments of the younger school of English composers. Then again his patent cosmopolitanism—once more a postponed influence—while reflecting his own time (more of this below) no less anticipates the widespread cosmopolitanism that is the distinguishing feature of present-day English music—a postponed influence, because the nationalist revival intervened. (It had to intervene, historically speaking, otherwise we should have had no national tradition from which, as now, to diverge and evolve.) It was the eclectic Holst's misfortune to peddle a cosmopolitanism when it was a suspect practice. It was Elgar's misfortune, too, in so far as his style could provide the basis for no

national school, a style, in addition, that was to be partly
discredited by the twentieth century's revulsion from a typically
nineteenth-century mode of utterance.

Small wonder that from this complex historical situation
Elgar's reputation did not emerge altogether unimpaired. Nor,
for that matter, did the reputations of his European colleagues,
all of whom, especially, perhaps, Mahler and Strauss, found
themselves with a foot in either century; but Mahler, in his late
symphonies, Strauss intermittently (only at his best) and even
Reger in his middle period succeeded, if I may change the
metaphor mid-stream, in making themselves bi-lingual—at
home, as it were, in either century—something that Elgar was
never able to do. (It is valid, I think, to stick to comparisons with
Austro-German contemporaries: no stretch of the imagination
can relate Elgar to the new French school headed by Debussy.
The influence of the Wagnerian Franck is, of course, altogether
another story.)

I do not drag in Mahler, Strauss or Reger to disparage Elgar:
indeed, if driven, I would place Elgar as a composer greater than
two of these eminent contemporaries, judging him, moreover, as
a European rather than an English artist. But a point of substance
rests in, say, Mahler's capacity not only to accommodate himself
to the twentieth century but to advance its cause. (Elgar's two
Symphonies, as it happens, coincide chronologically with
Mahler's last three and *Das Lied von der Erde*.) It may well be asked:
What is demonstrated by exposing the obvious enough differences between Mahler's style and Elgar's? (I choose Mahler,
rather than Strauss, because of the mutual symphonic link.) The
answer falls into two main parts that might be entitled
'Convention' and 'Tradition', both of which I believe, throw
light on the nature of Elgar's achievement and the physiognomy
of his art, while 'Convention', in addition, raises the question of
how English, idiomatically speaking, Elgar was.

Let me take this last point first. Elgar's success in Germany,
Strauss's famous praise, Hans Richter's well-known judgment of
the first Symphony (Richter, at this very time, had been
dislodged by Mahler from the Vienna Opera: it is curious how
the strands of musical history intertwine)—these eminently
European appraisals confirm what was, in fact, the case: that
Elgar's convention was thoroughly post-Wagnerian in character, English, in any stylistic sense, not at all.

It has, I must confess, always astonished me that Elgar has been
so strenuously claimed as a representative English figure; he has

never struck me as such, and were I, in a state of aural innocence, confronted with, say, the middle pair of movements from either of his symphonies and asked to guess the composer's country of origin, England, I fancy, would be the last place that I should light upon. I should recognize, I hope, the impress of a most powerful and original personality, evident in no end of unique mannerisms (Elgarian could be defined in a dictionary of music by the use of music examples alone), but I doubt whether the Englishness of it would have offered me a clue sufficiently pronounced to solve the question correctly. Is there not something of a paradox here? That the composer who became a spokesman, in music, for a whole national era, was intimately bound up with a convention so wholeheartedly foreign? The paradox is all the more striking when one remembers how suspicious was the succeeding national school, prompted by Dr. Vaughan Williams in word and deed, of continental influences.

Elgar, as we know, aided and abetted by some tiresome friends, did everything possible to play, in life, the part of the Kiplingesque Englishman rather than the artist. The stiff upper lip only rarely quivered, and when it did—as in the extraordinary *folies de doute* that pursued him in connection with the Peyton Professorship—we catch a glimpse of a nervous, feminine, even neurotic sensibility that intermittently breaks out in the music. More so than with most great composers, Elgar the man and musician walked different paths. Perhaps his disinclination to expose his nerves, except under violent creative pressure, may be accounted an English characteristic—certainly this reticence marks him off from his European contemporaries. It also, to a degree, circumscribed the range of his feelings, and thus limited his expressiveness—some regions of feeling were taboo—and the potential versatility of his talent. But that emotional frigidity which is, perhaps, part of the English make-up, inherent or inculcated, was no part of Elgar's musical personality, as distinct from the face he wore in public. He was as frankly emotional as any late nineteenth-century composer in the great romantic tradition. His 'vulgarity', in part an asset, I might add, speaks for itself as a manifestation of emotional liberation, though, as I shall attempt to show, Elgar was not in some respects liberated enough.

But if, as I believe, Elgar's English character is partly mythical, it is also partly musical, not, to be sure, in the character of his invention, but in its identification with a climate of national belief: there was, indeed, a two-way identification, not only

Elgar's convinced committal to what we may generally term 'imperial' topics (the *Coronation Ode, Crown of India, Spirit of England* and the rest)—to this extent he was English of his period through and through—but the public's immediate and enthusiastic adoption of the music (Elgar in his pomp and circumstance guise) as the perfect vehicle for the mass expression of current national sentiment. Thus his not in any sense peculiarly English style was endowed with a fervent Englishness, an assertive patriotism, through what was, basically, the chance association of an eminently serviceable and sympathetic idiom with a dynamic social force. There was nothing, of course, essentially English in the power-sentiments of Edwardian imperialism, colonialism, etc.; any group, given a like historical context, would have expressed its power complex in similar terms and, at the same time, laid claim to those terms' uniqueness—hence their 'superiority', which, in turn, confirms and promotes the group's self-confidence. Unfortunately, however, most group-behaviour is depressingly identical. Imagine (?) Germany as a nineteenth-century England. Would not Strauss have served as Elgar's twin, in more senses than one?

It is Elgar's occasional music that has dated—inevitably so, since the kind of social ideals with which it became inextricably involved have little validity for our own day. I believe, none the less, that the best of his occasional pieces will survive as more than mere historical documents, though the reason for their survival— the quality of their invention and strength of character (the best *Pomp and Circumstance* marches, for example, are profoundly Elgarian, very much of a piece, despite their simplicity, with his major music)—hinders rather than facilitates a genuine re-valuation of his status: in hearing (rightly) a precise relation between his major and minor works, we incorporate, to his detriment, the period feelings aroused by the latter into our response to the former. Thus Elgar's most important and complex works, however remote their social connotations, are coloured by—damaged by—a pre-determined attitude of mind on the part of the listener. We tend to hear—and condemn as 'dated'—trends in his music that, by the standards of the convention within which he created, are wholly unexceptionable: it is the extra-musical significance they have been obliged to bear—their social symbolism—that obscures the issue, that prevents us from hearing the music, as it were, straight; and at the root of this confusion lies the muddling relation between his committed (minor) and non-committed (major) art, with our extra-musical response to the one infecting our approach to the other.

A similar act of transference results in our hearing an explicit voice of England embedded not only in the occasional music but in the symphonies and concertos. *Falstaff*, perhaps, is a special case. But though I would not deny the penetration of Elgar's portrait, its manner of execution is cosmopolitan, or, more exactly, Straussian (more brilliant and original in its parts than a Strauss symphonic poem, I think, but as a big structure less successful than Strauss's best). If penetration of dramatic character were the test of national spirit, would not Verdi's *Falstaff* be the most English of operas? There is not space here to pursue further the beguiling problem of Elgar's Englishness. It is my view that to find Elgar to-day specifically English in flavour is to expose oneself as the victim of a type of collective hallucination, an achievement, incidentally, that has had its consequences abroad. After all, Elgar has not always been considered a local genius: witness his early European successes, successes that preceded his popularity at home. Now, he is 'not for export'. Our conviction that he is a home-grown product has not only hoodwinked ourselves but those elsewhere, whose familiarity with this convention eased their early recognition of his outstanding talent.

I hope that my commentary on the very singularity of Elgar's reputation as an English composer will in itself have emphasized the cosmopolitanism of his convention—that despite what he called his 'peremptorily' English name, his idiom evolved from a tradition that he summed up himself in letters dating from his visit to Leipzig in 1883: 'I heard no end of stuff. Schumann principally and Wagner no end. They have a good opera in Leipzig and we went many times'; or, '... I got pretty well dosed with Schumann (my ideal!), Brahms, Rubinstein and Wagner, so had no cause to complain'.

The derivation of a composer's convention is, of course, altogether of less importance than an analysis of what he makes of it. Elgar, there is no doubt, succeeded to a very intense degree in expressing his personality in music that is demonstrably his and his alone. On the other hand, his use of his chosen language, while minutely moulded to the contours of his personality, is not markedly original. (The distinction between originality of style and idiosyncrasy of idiom is a fine one, but I think it can be made.) But not only personal factors shape a composer's style, as important—perhaps overridingly important—as these are: for instance, Elgar's emotional inhibitions, which, one day, must be subjected to full-scale examination. There are also historical considerations to be taken into account which, in his case, significantly conditioned the style.

Since Elgar's basic convention, his vocabulary, had so much in common with that of his European contemporaries, there is much to be gained by a brief comparison of his work with theirs. The introduction of Strauss and Mahler clarifies the picture, illuminates Elgar's characteristics—and, I think, in isolating them, does something to explain why he wrote the kind of music he did. While his idiosyncrasies have been both recognized and analysed, the influence of his historical environment and the nature of the pressures exerted by personal factors have not. A complete understanding of his musical character, however, depends upon some understanding of the formative agents involved in the make-up of his personality.

Let us see where Elgar differs from Mahler or Strauss and attempt to nail down the reasons for the differences. For a start, Elgar's European colleagues were not only idiosyncratic in idiom but also original—original, that is, in the sense (my sense, when I use the word in this article) that each anticipated, practised and furthered the evolution of established twentieth-century procedures of composition: Strauss's and Mahler's inspired harmonic adventures, for instance, or Mahler's late contrapuntal style, a consequence of his tonal emancipation. Has anyone remarked upon the absence of counterpoint in Elgar's music, except on a few set occasions, in the *Introduction and Allegro* or *Gerontius* and particularly *Falstaff*? It was a general feature of music at the turn of the century: counterpoint (Reger!) came in as tonality went out, the logic of parts prevailed as progressions lost their structural functions. That Elgar's music did not develop a genuinely linear contrapuntal character is symptomatic of his relatively low rate of harmonic tension: counterpoint, as it were, was not forced upon him by tonal disintegration. His greatest gift, on the other hand, his rich flow of melody, was promoted by—depended upon—his harmonic stability.

The temptation to pursue stylistic contrasts is acute, but I must resist it. I do not believe it would be difficult to demonstrate with a wealth of convincing detail that, say, Mahler's ninth Symphony (1908-10) was, in tendence, progressive, whereas Elgar's second (1910-11) was conservative, despite, let me repeat, a shared basic vocabulary. (I must stress that neither 'progressive' nor 'conservative' is intended as a value-judgment.) But I am assuming here the validity of that contention, so far as style alone is concerned; and it is my purpose not to show the how but the why.

Personal factors, of course, play a part. Extensions of style meet the expressive challenge of new feelings; new sounds symbolize the uncovering of hitherto untapped sources of inspiration. There were many new sounds in Strauss, generated by such exploratory pieces as *Elektra* or *Salome*, many in Mahler, in his symphonies, which often present contents not previously encountered in music. It is important, too, to remember that it is often just when a new nerve is exposed that the composer is charged with vulgarity. But every revelation of this kind provokes a like shocked resistance, not only in the field of music; and what is vulgar for one generation is accepted by succeeding generations as a valid enlargement of feeling or knowledge, though doubtless they ride 'vulgar' hobby-horses of their own.

Elgar's conservative personality — self-imposed, as I believe it was in part — did not mean that he felt less deeply, but rather that the range of his feelings was inhibited: he did not plunge into those new regions of feeling that might have forced his style to widen its scope. That there were uncharacteristic elements in Elgar that he sternly suppressed I have no doubt: the volcanic eruption in the second Symphony's scherzo-rondo has always suggested to me a side to Elgar's character the very opposite of his habitually affirmative self. What he wrote of his first Symphony — 'a *massive* hope in the future' — holds true of much of his assertive music, but here and there, fleetingly, when the hope breaks down, one glimpses a massive if deeply buried anxiety. (I sense it again in that oddly sinister tableau, *The Wagon Passes,* from the *Nursery Suite.*) It is difficult to speculate in this context, but it is my guess that had Elgar liberated himself from a host of protective emotional prohibitions and permitted his tensions to rise to the surface, he might well have responded with some out-of-character music that would have crossed the threshold of the new century in style, not chronology alone. As it was, Elgar lavished a maximum of unleashed feeling only in his most *nobilmente* mood; while his choice of occasion for a total liberation from restraint is revealing, the concentration of feeling released with such violence was all too often disproportionate and damagingly tasteless in effect. Elgar's feelings, in short, were sometimes bigger than the occasion demanded, either in the explicitly occasional music or in the implied drama of the symphonies (*e.g.* the *grandioso* conclusion of the first Symphony's finale). Hence Elgar's vulgarity is of a kind less functional than

Mahler's or Strauss's (when on form); the searching, profoundly motivated feelings were there, but they became almost obsessively diverted into a narrow channel of '*massive* hope': protested so insistently, the security of that hope strikes one as perhaps more slenderly based than the affirmations would have us believe ('over-compensation', the psychologist might call it). Had Elgar's straining after nobility drained off less of his emotional energies, we might have heard more of the note of 'heroic melancholy' that impressed W. B. Yeats in the incidental music to *Grania and Diarmid,* and more, perhaps, of a pessimism that the emphatic optimism, one may think, seeks to conceal. But there can be no doubt that in one field — Elgar in his English *musical* context — the aggressively assertive character of his personality, its vulgarity in fact, aided him in the establishment of his unique voice.

It was, indeed, Elgar's vulgarity, the boldness and flashiness of his genius, that enabled him to break with the good taste of Parry, Stanford and the rest. Elgar, instead of revering the European classics and at the same time fearing them, instead of turning out page after page of tasteful but, in a final analysis, anonymous music, grasped the nettle with both hands: he accepted the late romantic convention, threw taste to the winds and succeeded in writing great music in established symphonic forms (he was no formal innovator) as full-blooded and pulsing with life as comparable gestures from Germany and Austria. It was a phenomenal achievement, the size of which must compel our continuing admiration. In a handful of big works Elgar challenged and, in some substantial respects, measured up to the accomplishments of Europe's great tradition. The size of his genius, of course, has something to do with the size of his achievement, but it is safe to say that his success would have been endangered had he not swept awe and taste aside and flourished without shame his, to put it rudely, creative 'guts'. Parry and Stanford — whose objectives, in the long run, were not so very different from Elgar's — were paralysed, bled white, by their fastidiousness. Elgar's 'vulgarity' saved him from their fate and facilitated his confident approach to his monumental task. We are indebted to it. Miss McVeagh states the matter concisely: 'Had he been more fastidious, he might well have been less great.'[2]

Most of what I have written above, including my commentary

---

[2] *Op. cit.,* p. 186.

on Elgar's Englishness, has centred upon convention, its derivation and the personal forces that went to mould it. I wrote earlier that tradition, too, must be taken into account. Part of the phenomenon of Elgar rests in the very absence of a native tradition from which he might have evolved (hence his dependence on a European convention): the tradition-less character of his achievement only emphasises its singularity. The fact, moreover, that he did not emerge from a tradition increases our understanding of the make-up of his convention, especially its relative orthodoxy when compared with Mahler's or Strauss's. For it was not only personal factors that conditioned the latter composers' expansions of their convention, any more than it was personal factors alone that inhibited the development of Elgar's. History, too, exerts influential pressures. Mahler and Strauss lived at the end, the tail-end, of a great tradition: they inherited, in part, an exhausted convention. To develop new trends, new forms, new sounds, was an obligation: they had, in a very pressing sense, to originate, and originate hard, if they were to survive as independent voices. Elgar, on the other hand, was encumbered by no tradition. He could handle his more conventional convention with all the enthusiasm of an early starter; the convention simply had not aged for him as it had for his contemporaries in Europe. The oddity of his English situation spared him the necessity of composing, as it were, with history at his elbow. Free of the burden of a tradition, he was able, as an outsider — he owes England this much, at least — to employ a convention that had grown old elsewhere (and thus new!), at an earlier stage in its development; and the power and, indeed, originality of his musical personality charged his — from history's point of view — conventionalities with a conviction and spontaneity that will ride out any fluctuations in fashion.

What is generally accepted as an evil — the composer without a tradition — proved not to be so in Elgar's case; it is only in his chamber music that the absence of tradition is felt as a loss. A composer, I think, needs to be born out of an active chamber-musical tradition if, for example, he is to write a successful string quartet. Chamber music is a craft that has to be lived over a long period: it cannot be learned, as can orchestral technique, of which Elgar, of course, was a virtuoso master. It is a pity that downright amateurishness of texture mars his string Quartet and piano Quintet (the violin Sonata is both more inspired and accomplished); a double pity because, along with the magnificent 'cello Concerto, this group of chamber works — the classical challenge it represents is typical of Elgar's spirit — is the nearest we have to a late period. These works flounder badly, I fear, but they are deserving of study for their intermittent inspirations and their hints at the stylistic direction in which Elgar's art might have travelled had it not come to an abrupt stop. Whatever inhibition it was that here stifled Elgar's fertility, it cost us twenty years or so of potential music-making from a great English composer who, none the less, belongs in every best sense of the word to Europe: in that — his! — achievement should rest our pride.

Music & Letters,
April 1957

Elgar as Conductor
by Stephen Lloyd

When in February 1911, at the unanimous wish of the self-governing London Symphony Orchestra, Elgar was invited to become their principal conductor, it was a signal honour. In the first year of the orchestra's existence (1904-5) Elgar's had been one amongst several eminent names to appear as their conductor: Colonne, Cowen, Nikisch, Stanford and Steinbach. In 1911 it was no less a figure than Hans Richter whom he was succeeding. While Elgar's tenure of office was to last one season only, his appointment set the seal on a rare affiliation between composer and orchestra, a bond that was to last a life-time. Almost to the end Elgar made frequent conducting appearances, often with the LSO, and although he could not be ranked with the best of conductors, he was, especially in his own works, nonetheless remarkably successful. Among those privileged to have heard him conduct, it is a generally held view that performances of his own works under his direction, if sometimes lacking precision in the technical sense, have rarely been surpassed for releasing the very spirit of the work. No-one knew better than he the elusive secrets to their interpretation, those subtle inflections and the right placing (or eschewal of) emphasis. If he was not, judged by professional standards, a first-rate conductor, what deficiencies he may have had in that department were more than compensated in other ways. After a performance of *The Kingdom* at the 1907 Leeds Festival, the *Manchester Guardian* critic wrote:

> Like most eminent composers, Sir Edward Elgar is not the best of conductors. His beat is not sufficiently decided for that: it has not the necessary clearness, the precision which enables the orchestral player to know his whereabouts. Yet I have never heard a performance conducted by him which in any way lacked interest and even refinement. The fact is, he supplies the want of more practical qualities with qualities of a different order. He is not the conductor who can help the orchestra out of a scrape, should they ever fall into one, but when once the players have mastered the technicalities of the music he can bring them to follow his intentions like the best of conductors, for, if one may say so, he looks the music;

his gesture has a wonderfully inspiring influence on the orchestra and on the chorus; it acts on them like a charm. He has the spirit, if not the art, of the conductor.

Like many a sensitive artist Elgar was highly strung. He was often restless and, especially in public, nervous. These characteristics exhibited themselves in varying degrees in his general manner and speech, 'in the quick, jerky movements of his hands and in a little mannerism he had of blinking rapidly'.[1] In 1904 the journalist and biographer R.J. Buckley described Elgar's talk as 'presto scherzando' and remarked also on his 'nervous sensibility'.[2] Sir Adrian Boult has had occasion to remember Elgar's voice as being 'pleasant and rather quiet' but 'when he was telling a story or speaking of something that interested him particularly, it all came out in rather a rush, the words tumbled over one another'.[3] W.H. Reed, a close friend and for many years the leader of the London Symphony Orchestra, knew Elgar's changing moods and similarly observed his often excited manner, how he would be 'bubbling over with excitement' when explaining something of interest.[4] This enormous vitality and his 'quick nervous response to life at its most salient and most energetic', wrote Ernest Newman, 'had a curious way of betraying itself in his gestures: the spiritual thrill had to find expression in physical movement. I never stood or sat by him when he was listening to music — especially his own — that soared upward on the wings of its own ecstacy without finding him gripping my arm convulsively. He could rarely listen to fine-souled music without tears coming into his eyes . . . .'[5]

It is hardly surprising that Elgar should bring such characteristics to the conductor's desk or that his temperament and personal idiosyncrasies should have an important bearing on his ability as a conductor to communicate his wishes. On the rostrum his nervousness, allied to a fundamental shyness, was probably a contributory factor to his stiff and jerky beat. Bernard Shore, violist in the LSO and later in the BBC Symphony Orchestra, found Elgar 'somewhat stiff in all his movements' and while he never considered him 'an inspiring conductor' he nevertheless added that 'the orchestra somehow never seemed to want much

---

[1]   Diana McVeagh *Edward Elgar - his life and music* (Dent 1955) p.88
[2]   *Sir Edward Elgar* (Bodley Head 1905) p.42
[3]   BBC Radio talk
[4]   Elgar as I knew him (Gollancz 1936) p.57
[5]   *Elgar - some aspects of the man in his music* in the *Sunday Times* October 25 1933

more from him, but just gave that extra ounce of energy and feeling which only the great conductors ever succeed in drawing from the players'.[6] Shore was of the opinion that in later life Elgar 'conducted some things extremely well, though he was perhaps never quite first-rate. His command of the stick increased with his years, and though he did not overcome a certain woodenness and failed to accompany his concertos well, his *Variations* and particularly *Falstaff* and the 2nd Symphony were admirable under his direction . . . . He obtained fine performances of his own works, since what he had principally to do was to give a clear rhythmic beat, every detail being accounted for in the score. His stick was fairly clear, but curiously unimaginative in its movements. It was his face and certain expressive gestures of his left hand that would sometimes lighten up a page . . . . His manners and quiet dignity, the quick, nervous gestures of his expressive hands, the twinkle in his eye when he cracked some old chestnut we were supposed never to have heard before; above all the sheer sight of the grand old man, looking the picture of a beloved country squire — this always charmed the players, and they were conscious of contact with a great man . . . . Never was he seen to lose patience, and certainly never his dignity . . . . One can still hear that vibrating, deep voice explaining at rehearsal some point in the music while he restlessly turned back the corners of the score . . . .'[7]

With orchestras like the LSO with whom he could easily establish a rapport any problems were minimised. The composer William Alwyn, as LSO flautist, first played under Elgar in the 1927 Three Choirs Festival at Hereford and has warm memories of him conducting in his last years:

He was a splendid interpreter of his own music, his beat was admirably clear and his performances essentially musical and refined; nothing was exaggerated and his own careful markings in his scores were followed meticulously to obtain plastic but admirably controlled interpretations. Elgar could have been a great conductor in his own right.[8]

Sometimes when conducting an orchestra to which he was not so accustomed he was less successful. Eric Coates, who played in

---

6 *Edward Elgar 1857-1934* in *The Gramophone* June 1957
7 *The Orchestra Speaks* (Longmans 1938) p.134 and *Sixteen Symphonies* (Longmans 1949) pp.260-1
8 Notes accompanying *Dream of Gerontius* recording Decca SET 525-6

the old Royal Philharmonic Orchestra and the Queen's Hall Orchestra until giving up the viola in 1919, did not find Elgar very satisfactory as a conductor in those earlier years. In his autobiographical *Suite in Four Movements* he wrote:

> I think the most uncertain of all the composers I played under was Sir Edward Elgar (whom I was to meet in later years and for whom I have always felt an affection), for his highly strung nature, added to a habit he sometimes had of starting to conduct a work before the orchestra was ready, was unnerving. How well I remember the night at Queen's Hall when he was conducting a performance of his overture *In the South;* he raised the stick without warning and executed a terrific down-beat, which was responded to by the first desk of the violas only (that being myself and my colleague), the remainder of the orchestra joining in on the second bar![9]

It certainly seems that in the days before Elgar had come to the fore as a composer, his conducting skills were forged through a tough apprenticeship. Rosa Burley, in her sometimes bitter but otherwise revealing portrait of Elgar, has described his difficulties as conductor of the amateur Worcestershire Philharmonic Society:

> For years he had never cut a very successful or distinguished figure on the platform. As a conductor he had been very nervous, fidgety and in consequence ill-tempered. ('Why must he be so fierce?' members would ask.) . . . Things were undoubtedly difficult for him. He felt that he deserved something much better than the members could give him, especially when in cold weather the drive into Worcester had numbed the players' fingers and the rehearsals were in an unheated room. But it is also true that, being anything but a born teacher, he could not make the best of the talent that was available. His wide vague beat would sometimes baffle the best of us and in matters of interpretation he seemed incapable of explaining exactly what he wanted. Again and again he would stand shading his eyes with one hand (a very characteristic position) and would exclaim angrily 'No, no, that was all wrong'.[10]

With his own works before the turn of the century, having to direct their first performances himself, matters — perhaps understandably — did not always run smoothly. Havergal Brian remembered the first performance of *King Olaf* at Hanley in 1896:

---

[9]   (Heinemann 1953) p.147
[10] *Edward Elgar - the record of a friendship* by Rosa Burley and Frank C. Carruthers (Barrie and Jenkins 1972) pp.161, 108

The unknown Elgar walked on to conduct his work in a light woolly suit and was obviously fidgety and nervous.. When [Edward] Lloyd sang 'And King Olaf heard the cry', something went wrong — subsequently Hess [the leader of the orchestra] saw that Elgar was losing his grip. Hess jumped to his feet and straightened the thing out by his presence and his bow. He saved *King Olaf*. Elgar admitted to me years afterwards: "But for Willy Hess, what a fiasco that performance would have been!"[11]

When it was the turn of *Caractacus*, at the 1898 Leeds Festival, E.A. Baughan wrote in *The Musical Standard:* 'It is a pity, I think, that *Caractacus* is not to be conducted by a professional conductor at Leeds, for Mr Elgar is not a good conductor at all, and during the rehearsals it has been evident that he cannot make the men under his command understand to the full precisely the effect he desires to obtain . . . .' But in time Elgar was to emerge as a composer-conductor of distinction.

In an address he gave in 1904, Elgar singled out Richter as the greatest conductor in England. Those qualities he particularly admired in Richter — absolute dignity in gesticulation, no exuberance of gesture — he lived up to in his own conducting. 'That is what conductors should aim at,' he was reported as saying, 'the absolute purity of a rendering without any . . . humbug.' Richter, he went on, conducted 'an orchestra of artists, and consequently he had only to give them a lead, explain a piece to them, and they followed him . . . .'[12] But things were not generally so ideal, and over a year later, with characteristic outspokenness, he commented that the orchestral players 'turned out of our institutions . . . lack fire; they have to be whipped to enthusiasm in many cases'.[13] It was enthusiasm that he himself infused into orchestras. Reed has recorded how 'having roused the orchestra to the necessary enthusiasm, he would beam on them with a seraphic smile of satisfaction, though this gradually faded and changed to dismay as he realised that the furore he had provoked was too loud by far for any merely mortal choir, singer, or solo instrument to be heard through; so he had — with a fleeting touch of irritability — to hush the orchestra down,

[11] *Havergal Brian - the man and his music* by Reginald Nettel (Dennis Dobson 1976) p.13

[12] *The Musical Standard* July 30 1904 p.70 quoted in Percy Young *A Future for English Music* (Dobson 1968) pp.115-6

[13] *English Executants* Birmingham University lecture November 29 1905; Percy Young op.cit. p.133

and restrain the ardour he himself had aroused, in order to give the vocalist a chance.'[14] This injection of enthusiasm was all done without any loss of dignity, and with no exuberant gestures. As Reed put it, 'no need to flog the orchestra with superhuman gestures and wild efforts to rouse them. They had only to look on his face, and they gave him everything that they had, to the last ounce . . . . He allowed the band to play; he obtained fire, passion, serenity, and, above all, spirituality, often when his expressive hands hardly moved.'[15]

Whatever Elgar's shortcomings as a conductor may have been, he possessed one rare quality with which his very presence on the rostrum was often sufficient to guarantee success — a powerful personality. Few who performed under Elgar's baton failed to sense this. For many it was like coming under a spell. The face and hands became the chief instruments of communication: they told the players all they needed to know. Despite Baughan's strictures, Reed felt these qualities the first time he played under Elgar, during a rehearsal of *Caractacus* in 1898 prior to its first performance. Forty years later he recounted the experience. There he was confronted with . . .

> . . . a very distinguished-looking English country gentleman, tall, with a large and somewhat aggressive moustache, a prominent but shapely nose and rather deep-set but piercing eyes. It was his eyes perhaps that gave the clue to his real personality: they sparkled with humour, or became grave or gay, bright or misty as each mood in the music revealed itself. His hands, too, gave another clue: they were never still even when he was not conducting; they moved restlessly, turning up the corners of the pages of the score or giving some indication by a gesture of what he wanted or how he wished a passage to be played; but they were always eloquent, always saying something and giving an inkling of the extreme sensitiveness of his mind and character. He looked upstanding, had an almost military bearing and was quite unlike the accepted idea of a musical genius. The orchestra, it is almost needless to say, adored him. From that day to his death every orchestral player privileged to play under his baton or to take part in his works bore him an unquenchable affection. He was practical to a degree, he wasted no time making unnecessary speeches and when he did speak it was always to the point, with few words used to convey his meaning. He obtained all he wanted from his executants by the movements of his delicate and well-shaped hands, by his eyes, which expressed the whole gamut of

---

[14]   op.cit. pp.142-3
[15]   ibid. pp.161, 160

emotions, and by his whole facial expression, which lit up in an amazing manner when he got the response he desired and when his music throbbed and seethed as he intended that it should. The author was completely overcome by this experience and though he saw him again and again and repeatedly played under his baton in later works he has that first vision indelibly impressed upon his consciousness.[16]

Another musician to be struck forcibly by Elgar's magnetic personality was Alan Kirby, the renowned conductor of the Croydon Philharmonic Choir with whom he established a strong Elgar tradition with his performances of the oratorios. Kirby first met Elgar in 1909 when taking part in a performance of *The Kingdom* under the composer's direction. He wrote of that occasion: 'I shall never forget Elgar's striking personality, nor the spiritual atmosphere he engendered. His works never sound quite the same as when he conducted them. The impact of that performance is something I shall always remember.'[17]

In May 1933 Elgar came to Croydon to conduct *The Apostles*. A member of the Croydon Philharmonic Choir remembered that 'he wasn't an easy conductor: his beat was very difficult to follow, but I should think with the orchestra we'd hardly been half an hour with him before he cast a spell over us which we cannot forget'.[18] Burley has written that 'a very distinguished musician who does not admire *Gerontius* joined the choir which was performing the work under Edward's own direction and confessed that, while the conducting was technically inefficient, he was completely swept away by Edward's personal magnetism'.[19]

This was not something that performers alone felt. After a Three Choirs Festival performance in 1931 the *Birmingham Post* critic wrote: 'Sir Edward Elgar conducted *The Dream of Gerontius* himself last night and again astonished us by the magic power of his personality . . . . To listen to the sound of his own music under him is to feel that all the performers are controlled by a great mind from the moment he raises his baton'.[20] Sir Ivor Atkins, the

---

[16]   *Elgar* (Dent 1939) pp.50-1
[17]   Alan J. Kirby *The Apostles and the Kingdom* in *Edward Elgar Centenary Sketches* (Novello 1957) p.25
[18]   BBC Radio feature May 23 1964 marking the Golden Jubilee of the Croydon Philharmonic Society
[19]   op.cit. p.163
[20]   *Birmingham Post* 10.9.31 quoted in Watkins Shaw *The Three Choirs Festival* (Baylis & Sons 1954)

Worcester Cathedral organist and close friend of Elgar, sensed this aura that clung to the composer's performances: 'There can be no question that Elgar was at his greatest as a conductor when he was conducting his own orchestral works,' he has written. 'The deep sympathy which existed between him and the players was one reason for this. They knew him as their master — as one whose magic gave them an outlet for their greatest powers — as a very magician in his handling of orchestral effect. But it was more than that. He brought to the conductor's desk an atmosphere of inspiration. Every man knew that he was facing a great mind.'[21]

Especially in later years many orchestral players had a particular reverence for Elgar, a feeling born of mutual respect. He treated them as equals, regarding himself as 'one of them' as indeed in a sense he was. During his years as a struggling composer he had supplemented his meagre income from teaching by either playing in, leading or conducting the orchestras of the many choral societies around Worcester. He had played among the first violins in Stockley's orchestra in Birmingham for about seven years, and when every three years the Three Choirs Festival came in rotation to Worcester he was from 1878 to 1893 to be found in the Festival orchestra, even playing under other composer-conductors like Barnet, Dvořák and Parry. His dedication of *Cockaigne* 'To my many friends the members of British orchestras' was no vain gesture. In *'First Flute'*, commenting on how Elgar's deep love of London musicians was returned by them, the flautist Gerald Jackson recalled his remarks addressed to the orchestra at a gramophone recording session: 'You know, I love you all, and there is nothing I wouldn't do for any of you.' Jackson continued: 'This atmosphere of devotion was mutual, and a seasoned old tuba player, Ben Ash, once told me that he found it very hard to play for Elgar, so lost was he in admiration for the man.'[22]

Elgar himself could sometimes become lost — immersed in his own music, and the Croydon *Apostles* provides a fine example. 'Although because of his infirmity he had to sit down to conduct,' Alan Kirby has written, 'the rehearsal seemed to put him in good spirits. At the performance Elgar became more and more lost in the music. A slow smile came over his face, and he almost stopped conducting: his spirit seemed to have taken wings. Had it not been for the usual alertness of Billy Reed, who was leading the

[21] Communicated by E. Wulstan Atkins in a letter to the author 16.8.78
[22] (Dent 1968) p.59

orchestra, and who literally kept the performance together until Elgar came out of his dream, there might have been complete breakdown. When Elgar left the rostrum it was obvious that he was greatly moved.'[23]

There was one feature of Elgar's conducting style which, while at times it might have been regarded as a fault, may well otherwise paradoxically have proved an asset. What the contralto Astra Desmond called Elgar's 'very curious jerky beat' was possibly largely responsible for imparting that essential ingredient to Elgarian performance — nervous energy, a quality that critics have frequently commented on. In a broadcast interview Astra Desmond, a distinguished Angel in *Gerontius* performances, said that much as she loved singing for Elgar she did not always find him an easy person to work with. She had to be very much on her toes, as she put it, because of that jerky beat which she nonetheless felt suited the music admirably. 'These people who smooth over all the ritenutos . . . don't really get the essence of Elgar . . . . What he liked to do is he'd do an *accelerando* up to a point and then *a tempo* at once, not *accelerando* and gently back. He'd do an *allargando,* but that *allargando* only went up to a certain point; it must be *a tempo* after it. You mustn't just drift into a slower tempo, you must go back to your original tempo which gives a nervous energy to a great deal of the writing.' Astra Desmond also recalled Elgar's delight in holding her on a high note and how he would glance down at her 'with a wicked look' and keep her there.[3] Sir Steuart Wilson, a noted Gerontius, also broadcast some impressions of performing under Elgar and commented that as a conductor he 'was not the easiest in the world to follow. The thing I remember most was the kind of feeling that you caught up from his mysterious way of conducting. Technically, he was a bad conductor, but, emotionally, he managed to make everybody give the best performance of their lives.'[24] Horace Fellowes, who led the orchestra under Elgar on several occasions, was also much impressed by the way 'he seemed to get every ounce out of the players'.[25]

The economy of movement in Elgar's beat brought its problems, as *The Times* critic pointed out after a performance of *The Kingdom* given by the Royal Choral Society in the Royal Albert Hall in March 1929:

---

[23] op.cit. p.26
[24] *Elgar Society Newsletter* September 1978 p.10
[25] Letter to the author 22.2.75

Such defects as were noticeable in Saturday's performance were due to the size of the ensemble, and the distance of some of the singers from the conductor and from each other. Sir Edward Elgar was not always conscious of the executive difficulties of the organisation, and there were places where only those possessing a first-class certificate for eyesight could be expected to follow him accurately.

But, as Astra Desmond suggested, this strange beat had its compensations. After a 1927 *Gerontius* given by the same forces, the *Musical Times* critic remarked on the advantages (in a review that brings to mind Eric Coates's *In the South* experience):

Elgar may have faults as a conductor, and the attack on the National Anthem made us fear that these should not be forgotten during the oratorio. The baton descended just a trifle too quickly for all the performers to realise and respond to the signal, and in consequence that attack was anything but unanimous.... As soon as the oratorio started, however, it became evident that the very quick, sharp gesture of Sir Edward would be an asset, for it kept the singers on the alert, and the performance had a vitality and freshness unobtainable by other means.

During the Elgar Centenary Basil Maine contributed an article to *Radio Times* entitled 'Passing on the Secret of Elgar'. 'If we can, we must pass on the secret,' he wrote. 'That is easily said. An age of cut-throat speeding is as harmful to the sensibility of a conductor or an interpreting soloist as to all other sensibilities. During the past few years I have heard Elgar readings so insensitive as to hint that the secret could easily be lost.' He cited passages from *The Music Makers* and *The Kingdom:* 'At such speechless moments, we feel we are holding the trembling secret in our hands. No-one who has not been aware of these intimations could possibly be an interpreter of Elgar.'[26] Ernest Newman knew one of the secrets (if it may so be called) of Elgarian interpretation. In his *Sunday Times* 'The World of Music' column he wrote:

It is more true of [Elgar] than of most composers, perhaps, that the key to his music is to be found only by those who, being by nature one with him, already possess it. Without for a moment disparaging his interpreters, one or two of whom have shown admirable insight into his mind, it remains true that the best conductor of Elgar's works was generally Elgar himself. He alone knew that his music needed no emphasis, for all the emphasis required is implicit in the sounds

---

[26] May 31 1957

themselves. The emotional exaggeration with which he has been sometimes charged was never in the music itself, but only in some of the interpreters of it. More than once he protested to me that all his music required was to be left alone to say what it had to say in its own way: the expression was *in* the music, and it was not merely unnecessary but harmful for the conductor to add to it an expression of his own . . . . It is because of this excess zeal on the part of some of his interpreters, not because of anything in the music itself or in the constitution of the composer's mind, that Elgar's music is too often credited with a 'vulgarity' that is completely alien to it.[5]

In his own conducting Elgar was master of the understatement. This seeming reticence in his 'unfussy' approach to his own music is borne out in a review of an all-Elgar concert he conducted with the LSO on April 26 1926:

It is indeed a privilege thus to have great music interpreted by its author when it so happens that he is incomparably its best interpreter. Sir Edward has a drastic way of hacking at his music. All sorts of things which other conductors carefully foster, he seems to leave to take their chance. He cuts a way through in a fashion both nervous and decisive.

And again after he had conducted his Second Symphony at the Proms in October 1931:

It is good to have the authority of his own tempi, his own rubato, and above all his own blend of outward dignity and inward charm. But as he allows the score for the most part to play itself the listener gets less help in following the complex train of thoughts than he would from a conductor who makes the points for him. This is particularly noticeable in those mosaic sections in which the themes are developed — these passages seem to require more elucidation from the conductor. On the other hand when the music is by nature simple the composer's unemphatic treatment brings out its peculiar Elgarian beauty, which is easily destroyed by heavy handling.

In Elgar's scores there are many temptations to linger, as Bernard Shaw, writing to the composer after attending with Landon Ronald the *Falstaff* recording sessions, knew only too well. 'It is mistaken kindness to invite [Ronald], because he knows your scores by heart, and suffers agonies in his longing to conduct them himself. He wants to make more of every passage than you do. A composer always strikes an adorer as being callous. Same thing on the stage. Producers always want to overdo titbits.'[27] It was this emotional restraint, his refusal to

[27] *Letters of Edward Elgar and other writings* edited by Percy Young (Bles 1956) p.333

'sign-post the way', that in Elgar's own performances allowed the works to speak for themselves. This might seem to imply a cold indifference to the beauties in the scores. That this was not so is amply demonstrated in his gramophone recordings. What they further show is a keen sense of overall structure, a feeling for architectural proportions.

It has been said that, fine though they are, Elgar's recordings pale in comparison with his live performances. With the large-scale works apparently no two Elgar performances were identical for they would vary according to his mood, the atmosphere of the building, and the forces involved. The critic Ferruccio Bonavia, who for ten years played violin in Richter's Hallé Orchestra from the 1902-3 season onwards, wrote that 'in the last ten years of his life Elgar, conducting *Gerontius* at the Three Choirs Festivals, surprised the listener by readings which differed essentially from his own former interpretations, more liberal, more delicate, giving the phrase fuller scope and time to reveal its tonal quality.. .. One specially memorable performance of *Gerontius* was given three years before his death, when his tempi became distinctly slower and the leisurely pace brought out the charm of gracious detail with new and enchanting effect.'[28]

As might be expected, things did not always go well. There were difficulties, moments of irritation, flashes of temperament, even a loss of interest. There was the well-known occasion during a performance of *The Kingdom* when Agnes Nicholls' splendid singing of 'The Sun goeth down' seemed to revive Elgar's flagging interest and so saved a performance that had been going from bad to worse. Samuel Bor, violinist and a founder member of the BBC Symphony Orchestra, once spoke in a broadcast talk of Elgar's difficulty in getting the Second Symphony started and how with a final despairing stab of his baton the work eventually got under way.

But the fault could not always be laid at the conductor's door. W. H. Reed remembered Elgar's face — 'a picture of horror' — at the rehearsal for the 1902 Worcester *Dream of Gerontius* when the drummer made an unwarranted second entry a bar after Gerontius had come before the glance of God.[29] While Bernard Shore found Elgar extremely easy to work with and the moments of trouble few, he instanced an isolated occasion in *Falstaff* when

---

[28] *Penguin Music Magazine* reviews and *Elgar* in *Lives of the Great Composers* (Penguin 1935)

[29] *Elgar* p.68

the side-drum player, having been behind the beat at the rehearsal, was caught out again in the actual performance at the moment of Falstaff's death. 'A spasm of anger' crossed Elgar's face; he stopped conducting and left the orchestra to struggle to the end.[6] But these occasions, that tend to receive the anecdotal spotlight, were few. More than often instead of anger, according to Reed, Elgar's face would be suffused with joy elsewhere in *Falstaff* when the side-drum did his little tap by himself.[30] 'How his eyes roved from one instrument to another! How they lit up when one of his pet phrases or passages arrived!'[31] Throughout his conducting life Elgar was called upon to conduct a variety of choirs and orchestras of varying excellence and his irritation could understandably be aroused when at a final rehearsal he found himself faced with a choir that had been insufficiently prepared. He rightly expected much from his performers and the strength of his personality was usually enough to coax the best out of them. Herbert Sumsion, who as Cathedral organist was responsible for the Gloucester Festivals from 1928 onwards, sensed Elgar's attitude in his dealings with those under his baton: 'He expected the chorus to be on the same musical level as the orchestra, and he did not consider it his responsibility to give them all their entries or in any way to spoon-feed them. His concern was fundamentally with the music rather than the performers.'[32]

Works other than his own formed a substantial part of Elgar's 1911-12 LSO concerts as their Principal Conductor and of the provincial tours he took them on in 1905, 1909, 1915 and 1916 (the otherwise excellent Reed would seem to be at fault in crediting Elgar with 1912 as well, for Nikisch was their conductor for that tour). In March 1922 he also stood in for an indisposed Landon Ronald for part of a tour with the Royal Albert Hall Orchestra. Besides the many smaller works, the symphonies which appeared in his programmes included Brahms' Third (eight times on the 1905 tour, once in 1911 and 1913),[33] Schumann's Second (1905 and 1912), Mozart's 40th (as a guest conductor in Italy in 1911, and 1912), Beethoven's Fifth (1922

---

[30] *Elgar as I knew him* p.161
[31] ibid. p.160
[32] *Random Reminiscences* in *Two hundred and fifty years of the Three Choirs Festival* (Three Choirs Festival Association 1977) p.49
[33] In *Elgar* p.119 Reed states that this Brahms symphony was played on the 1916 tour, but concert reviews do not seem to suggest this to have been the case

tour) and Seventh (1911), Dvořák's *New World* (1915 tour), César
Franck's (1912), and Tchaikovsky's Fourth (1911). There were
some impressive readings by all accounts. After Brahms' Third in
Manchester Adolph Brodsky, one time leader of the Hallé as well
as his own quartet and a friend of Brahms, came round 'weeping
saying oh if Brahms cd. have heard yr. rendering'.[34] The
concertos went less well for there was not always the necessary
unanimity between soloist and orchestra. On a rarer and grander
scale Elgar gave Berlioz's *Te Deum* in February 1915 with the
Hallé in Bradford, securing a performance 'which was not
lacking in a certain splendour and gravity'. A scheduled LSO
performance in 1912 of Strauss's *Also Sprach Zarathustra* was
unfortunately changed at a later date and so what might have
proved an interesting reading was never heard. However, Elgar's
stature as a conductor was sufficiently recognised for him to be
accorded the honour of sharing the conducting at the 1913 Leeds
Festival with Arthur Nikisch and Hugh Allen. He was allocated
two concerts on the opening day: in the morning Beethoven
Leonora No 3, Gerontius, Parry's *Ode to Music,* Brahms' *Alto Rhapsody*
and Third Symphony; and in the evening a taxing programme
which included the first performance of *Falstaff* as well as works
by Bantock, Boito and Verdi. (When by 10.45pm the concert had
not run its full course, it was abruptly terminated and Mozart's G
minor symphony dropped.)

But it was of course as a composer that Elgar was primarily
celebrated, and his own works figured prominently in his concert
tours, bringing them within hearing of a much wider audience
outside the musical capital. His regular guest appearances
around the country were devoted to his own works and by the
mid-twenties it was only these that he conducted, either sharing
in a concert or directing an all-Elgar programme. While Elgar's
popularity can be said to have waned later in his life, this was
made all the more apparent by the extraordinary heights it had
reached in earlier years. In the autumn of 1909, within a year of
the First Symphony's production, Henry Wood had put the work
down for three Prom performances while three orchestras were
independently touring the country with the new symphony:
Beecham with his own orchestra, Richter with the Hallé, and
Elgar with the LSO.

---

[34] Diary entry of Lady Elgar's, November 15 1905, quoted in Percy Young's *A
Future for English Music* p.111

Richter and Elgar had been the symphony's first exponents and the proximity of their performances inevitably brought comparisons which testified most favourably to Elgar's excellence as a conductor of his own music. After their initial performances the *Monthly Musical Record* critic commented: 'Dr Richter's readings have not been surpassed for breadth and dignity of conception, but the composer himself, by sweeping the performance along, and imparting to it a warmth of expression that had been wanting previously, made the points where the music seemed to make little advance far less evident than when a more deliberate and straightforward manner was adopted. The first movement, in particular, had more intensity, and so, too, had the adagio, which was found to contain a warmth of feeling unsuspected before.' By the end of the year, when frequent performances had made the work more familiar to audiences and critics alike, the *Musical Times* critic also drew comparisons between Richter and Elgar: 'Each reading has its qualities: one was characterised by greater breadth and force, the other rather by perfection of detail . . . .' And of Elgar's reading: 'Points are made, shadows and lights are specially and often very delicately contrasted, and the whole work seems to be more organic than when other conductors direct it.' Looking back seven years later, the same journal laid bare one important difference: 'Richter always emphasised its architectonic character — the big climaxes had wonderful majesty — but his temperament lacked that quick, nervous, rhythmical spring which is always in evidence when the composer is at the desk, and which makes a theme such as that in D minor (immediately following the opening one, *Nobilmente*) like a flaming sword . . . .'

Elgar's last conducting appearances were a memorable Prom performance in August 1933 of the Second Symphony ('rather more frank and expansive than Sir Edward's readings of his own work sometimes are . . . the full beauty of its eloquence was poured out without effort, mellow, benign, serene . . .'), and the following month at the Hereford Three Choirs Festival (*Gerontius, The Kingdom,* and the viola transcription of the 'Cello Concerto). It was an appropriate valediction, in a cathedral setting which seemed a natural home for his music, and with the London Symphony Orchestra which each year had supported him at the meetings of the Three Choirs. But in December 1932 there had been a fine summation of his career when the BBC honoured Elgar's seventy-five years with three concerts which amounted to an Elgar Festival, Adrian Boult assisting the elderly composer by

sharing the conducting load. Bernard Shore vividly described
the occasion:

> So, on that . . . morning rehearsal, as the beloved Squire came once
> more amongst his tenants, there was a roar of applause as we stood up
> and gave him one of the receptions of his life. Hale and hearty at 75,
> only his white hair and a rather curious impression of hunched
> shoulders gave much indication of his age, as he climbed on to the
> rostrum and faced us in his typically nervous manner . . . . After a few
> halting remarks in his attractively nervous vibrating voice which
> revealed his pleasure at coming amongst very old friends again, he at
> once got down to business as if he hated fuss. His peculiarly
> expressionless stick tapped the stand almost irritably and then began
> that unforgettable journey through all his major works . . . .[6]

Index

Acworth, H.A., 15, 21
Apostles, The, 57, 88-9, 104, 121-3, 132, 139, 164, 166, 172, 194, 208, 236-44, 271, 297, 298
Atkins, Sir Ivor, 32, 65, 68, 168-9, 297
Atkins, Wulstan, 71, 75, 298
Auld Lang Syne, 52-9, 71-2, 76-7, 79-81, 86

Bach, C.P.E., 37, 142
Bach, J.S., 36, 74, 81-3, 85-6, 89-90, 93, 98, 112, 164, 241, 258, 263, 267
Banner of St George, 35, 44, 150, 184
Bantock, Granville, 187, 193, 197, 198, 250, 304
Baughan, E.A., 19, 91, 133, 192-3, 236-44, 295-6
Bax, Sir Arnold, 105, 147
Bayreuth, 106, 110
Beecham, Sir Thomas, 192-4, 198, 232, 304
Beethoven, 27, 37, 57, 67, 72-4, 107, 141, 147, 154, 175, 177, 204, 206, 245-7, 258, 267, 269, 303-4
Bennett, William, 91, 96-9
Berlioz, 22, 99, 107, 109, 130, 159, 160, 203, 265, 304
Birmingham Music Festival, 35, 48, 91, 93-4, 96, 98, 106-7, 109-10, 123, 150, 166, 183
Black Knight, The, 11-13, 33, 44, 64, 111, 121, 150
Blackwood, Algernon, 233-5
Bliss, Sir Arthur, 281
Boughton, Rutland, 145, 250

Boult, Sir Adrian, 175, 292, 305
Brahms, 92-3, 98, 108, 123, 139, 163, 175, 177, 192, 194, 204-6, 241, 247, 275-6, 285, 303-4
Brewer, Herbert, 187, 257
Brian, Havergal, 134
Britten, Benjamin, 275, 277-8, 280
Broadheath, 36, 116, 173
Broadhurst, Edgar, 82
Buck, Dr. C.W., 69, 73-4
Buckley, R.J., 78, 111-14, 142, 292
Burley, Rosa, 86, 294, 297
Busoni, 143
Buths, Julius, 103, 123, 191, 197
Butt, Clara, 150

Calm Sea and Prosperous Voyage, 65
Cambridge, University of, 115, 183, 185, 268
Caractacus, 19-25, 35-6, 44, 75-6, 115, 150, 166, 192, 231, 242, 244, 268, 295
Cherubini, 37, 118
Chopin, 86, 127, 144
Choral Symphony, 18, 20
Coates, Eric, 293, 300
Cockaigne, 123, 138, 155, 194, 243, 246, 261, 266, 298
Coleridge-Taylor, 92, 98, 206
Corelli, 38-9
Coronation Ode, 123, 242, 284
Cosi fan tutte, 72, 82
Costa, Sir Michael, 106
Coward, Henry, 109
Cowen, Sir Frederic, 30, 106, 178, 291

307

Covent Garden, 104, 109, 115, 120-1, 128, 198, 206, 246
Crown of India, 171, 284
Crystal Palace, 45, 117, 121

Davies, Walford, 88
Debussy, 245-6, 264, 266, 282
Defoe, Daniel, 136
Delius, 189-99, 262, 267, 273
Dent, Prof E.J., 267
Dickens, Charles, 196
Dorabella, 50, 61, 64, 66, 72, 75-6, 78, 82, 85-6, 91, 100
Dragonetti, 36
Dream Children, 232
Dunhill, Thomas, 82, 181, 183
Düsseldorf, 103, 123-4, 138, 185, 191-2, 271, 275
Dvořák, 18, 30, 93, 98, 265, 275-7, 298, 304

Edwards, F.G., 35, 178
Elgar, Alice, 50, 62, 74, 88, 103, 145, 183, 186-7, 230
Elgar, Carice, 69, 74-5, 85, 88, 210, 216, 224
Elgar, Frank, 37
Elgar, Lucy, 26, 69
Elgar, Society, 82, 147
Elgar W.H., 36-9, 42
Elijah, 29, 34, 41, 46, 93, 98, 150, 270

Falstaff, 155, 172, 198, 217, 221, 231, 265, 271, 273, 280-1, 285-6, 293, 301-4
Fiske, Dr. Roger, 76-81, 83
Fitton, Isobel, 62
Flanders, Moll, 136
For the Fallen, 272
Fox Strangways, A.H., 54, 56, 72, 80-1
Franck, Cesar, 205, 282, 304
Free Trade Hall, 128, 131
Froissart, 11, 32-3, 44, 155, 166, 168, 243
Fuller-Maitland, J.A., 182

Gaisberg, Fred, 195, 197, 199
Glastonbury Music Drama Festival, 145
God Save the King, 71, 86
Goddard, Scott, 184
Godfrey, Sir Dan, 145
Goossens, Eugene, 108
Gordon, General, 48
Gorton, Canon, 88
Greene, Plunket, 102, 184-5, 187
Greening, Ann, 36
Griffiths, Troyte, 64, 66, 71, 77
Groves, Dictionary, 96-7, 118, 150-1, 178

Hallé, 108-9, 302, 304
Handel, 27, 38, 100, 102, 164, 175-7, 213, 241, 246, 248, 263
Hanley, 14, 43, 104, 121, 124, 151
Hardy, Thomas, 234
Haydn, 114, 117, 142, 177
Haym, Hans, 192
Heap, Swinnerton, 91, 96, 98, 101, 105, 121
Hiawatha, 92-3, 98
Holst, Gustav, 234, 281
Home, Sweet Home, 86
Hull, Sir Percy, 66, 75
Hurd, Michael, 86
Hussey, Dyneley, 58, 80, 182

Imperial March, 44, 123
In Smyrna, 88
In the South, 56, 67-8, 121, 154, 231, 242, 294, 300
Introduction and Allegro for Strings, 169, 198, 259, 276, 286
Iolanthe, 72

Jacobson, Maurice, 89
Jaeger, A.J., 62-3, 66-7, 73, 78-9, 84-5, 88-9, 103, 105, 178-81, 184, 192
Joachim, 107

Kelly, Michael, 143
Kennedy, Michael, 79, 86-7, 188

Khayyam, Omar, 128
King Edward VII, 151
King Olaf, 14-18, 35, 43-4, 48, 63, 112, 121, 124, 166, 206, 242-4, 268, 294-5
Kingdom, The, 88-9, 104, 164, 166, 175-7, 263, 291, 297, 299, 300, 302
Kozeluch, 142

Leeds Festival, 19-20, 23, 291, 304
Legge, Robin, 158
Leicester, Hubert, 27
Leipzig, 43, 116, 190, 208, 285
Leitmotiv, 17, 46, 216, 224, 238
Light of Life, 14, 33, 44, 111-14, 121, 242-3
Liszt, 258, 262
Littleton House School, 37, 116
Lloyd, Edward, 25, 102, 295
London Symphony Orchestra, 34, 69, 291-3, 301, 304-5
Lower Rhine Festival, 123, 192
Luther, Martin, 87
Lux Christi, (see *Light of Life*)
Lygon, Lady, 65

Mackenzie, Sir Alexander, 30, 178, 193
Mahler, 194, 200-2, 280, 282, 286-9
Maine, Basil, 82, 85, 97-8, 178, 230, 300
Malvern Hills, 21, 35, 76, 174
Manns, Sir August, 117
Marl Bank, 170, 197, 199, 219
Mass in B minor, 72, 81
Masterlinck, 61, 83, 232
McVeagh, Diana, 70, 78, 86, 181, 279, 288
Mendelssohn, 11, 23, 46, 57, 65, 100, 113, 150, 247
Menuhin, Yehudi, 56, 175, 195
Messiah, The, 27, 29, 34, 93, 98, 109, 113, 164, 175-7, 238, 270
Mitchell, Donald, 275-7, 279-90

Moore, Dr. Jerrold Northrop, 26-34, 178
Morris, R.O., 182
Mozart, 29, 37, 39, 81, 118, 142-3, 177, 207, 232, 248, 267, 303
Music Makers, The, 53, 61, 63, 67, 69, 78, 139, 172, 194, 231, 260-1, 300
Musical League, 193
Musical Standard, The, 19, 91, 95, 192-3, 295
Musical Times, The, 35, 49, 66, 81, 96, 104, 193, 300, 305

Nevinson, Basil, 62
Newman, Cardinal, 48, 97, 99, 104, 124, 135-6, 138, 234
Newman, Ernest, 50, 61, 68, 71, 75, 132-4, 154-7, 181, 193, 199, 292, 300
Nietzsche, 189
Nimrod, 57, 67, 72-4, 88, 103
Norbury, Florence, 69
Norbury, Winifred, 65-6, 80
North Staffordshire Festival, 14, 33, 104, 121
Nursery Suite, 167, 169, 199, 287

Odyssey, The, 115
Orr, C.W., 194, 270-4

Pachmann, 144
Paderewski, 143
Parry, 19, 47, 92-3, 98, 118, 158, 178-88, 248, 267-8, 288, 298, 304
Pathetique Sonata, 57, 72
Patmore, Coventry, 176-7
Piers the Plowman, 35, 115
Pollitzer, Adolph, 40, 45, 117, 120, 190
Pomp and Circumstance, 123, 171, 205, 208, 242, 261, 266, 270, 284
Pope, Michael, 147, 180
Priestley, J.B., 235

Promenade Concerts, 104, 120-1, 301, 304
Purcell, 175, 249

Queen's Hall, 96, 128, 144, 158-61, 163, 169, 175, 189, 203, 271, 294

Rachmaninoff, 161
Reed, W.H., 34, 68-70, 87, 187, 209, 213, 216, 219, 292, 295-6, 298, 302-3
Reeve, Francis, 88
Reger, 280, 282, 286
Richter, Hans, 85, 91, 93-4, 96-7, 99, 101, 105-10, 121, 150, 180, 268, 271, 275, 282, 291, 295, 302, 304-5
Rimsky-Korsakov, 163, 232
Ring, The, 109, 113
Riseley, George, 92
Roberts, Alice, (see also Elgar, Alice), 30-1, 43, 166, 191
Ronald, Landon, 152, 271, 301, 303
Rosen, Jelka, 191
Royal Albert Hall, 106
Royal College of Music, 76
Rule, Brittania!, 86

St. George's R.C. Church, Worcester, 37, 43, 116-17, 165
St. James's Hall, 189
St. Matthew Passion, 74, 93, 98
St. Paul, 76, 84, 88-9, 177
Saint-Saëns, 172, 265, 275
Salut d'Armour, 31, 147, 205
Sammons, Albert, 175
Scenes from the Bavarian Highlands, 44, 231
Schobert, 142-3
Schönberg, 247, 267, 277-8, 280
Schubert, 177, 258, 266-8
Schumann, 13, 63, 143, 247, 285, 303

Schuster, Frank, 68, 89, 180, 187, 192
Schuster, Leo, 186-7, 254-5
Scriabin, 246-7, 258
Sea Pictures, 44, 61, 150, 161
Serenade for Strings, 155, 281
Severn Suite, 167
Shakespeare, 135, 205, 211, 248, 265
Shaw, G.B., 168-9, 175, 209, 245-50, 268, 301
Shepherd's Song, 229
Shore, Bernard, 292-3, 302, 306
Sibelius, 195
Smyth, Ethel, 260
Spirit of England, The, 67, 69, 155, 164, 284
Stainer, Sir John, 29
Stanford, Sir C.V., 19, 57-8, 92, 106-8, 158, 178-88, 268, 288, 291
Stockley, William, 42, 91, 96, 98-9, 101, 120, 166, 298
Strauss, Richard, 22, 108, 128, 134, 151, 160, 192, 203-8, 210, 213, 218, 271, 277, 280, 282, 284-9, 301
Stravinsky, 245-6, 280
Sullivan, 94, 106, 120-1, 173
Symphony No. 1, 105, 109, 171, 188, 194, 206, 271, 275, 279, 287, 304
Symphony No. 2, 161, 169, 293, 301-2, 305
Symphony No. 3, 106, 172, 175, 220

Ta-ra-ra-boom-de-ay, 86
Tchaikovsky, 47, 127-8, 205-6, 232, 304
Te Deum, 44
Terry, Sir Richard, 96-7, 150-3
Three Choirs Festival, 11, 26-34, 36, 41, 193, 257, 293, 298, 302, 305
Toscanini, 163

below.   Endplate for 2nd Edition

Tovey, Sir Donald, 275
Trefusis, Lady (see Lygon, Lady)
Turner, W.J. 159, 175-7, 260

Vaughan Williams, 175, 263-9, 272, 275, 277, 283
Verdi, 171, 205, 229, 262, 304
Violin Concerto, 56, 166, 175, 194-5, 206, 251-7, 275
Violincello Concerto, 161, 203, 259, 261, 276, 289
Virelai, 168

Wagner, 13, 22, 46, 106, 113, 119, 130, 141, 154, 163, 175, 177, 192, 218, 222, 238, 242, 247-8, 262-3, 265, 267-8, 275, 278, 285
Walton, Sir William, 75, 275, 277, 281
Wand of Youth, 75, 172, 231

Weber, 107
Well-tempered Klavier, 112
Wesley, S.S., 28, 267
Westminster Cathedral, 104, 151
Westrup, Sir Jack, 60-75, 77-81, 83-4
Whately, Archbishop, 122
Wolf, Hugo, 130
Wolsterholme, William, 41
Wood, Sir Henry, 186, 193-4, 304
Worcester Cathedral 113, 121, 124, 201, 298
Worcester Glee Club, 38, 120
Worcester Philharmonic Society, 38, 45
Worthington, Julia, 66

Young, Dr. Percy M. 60, 65-6, 68-9, 75, 83, 89, 186, 195, 301

R.I.P.

St. Wulstan's,

Little Malvern. Worcs.

G.G.H.